Applied Psychometrics Using SPSS and AMOS

Applied Psychometrics Using SPSS and AMOS

W. Holmes Finch
Ball State University

Jason C. Immekus
University of Louisville

Brian F. French
Washington State University

IAP
INFORMATION AGE PUBLISHING, INC.
Charlotte, NC • www.infoagepub.com

Library of Congress Cataloging-in-Publication Data

A CIP record for this book is available from the Library of Congress
http://www.loc.gov

ISBN: 978-1-68123-526-4 (Paperback)
978-1-68123-527-1 (Hardcover)
978-1-68123-528-8 (ebook)

Printed in the United States of America

Contents

Preface

This book was developed to provide a "one-stop" resource for many common analyses that an applied researcher might complete when working with various instruments to measure educational and psychological traits. We have developed examples, collected our favorite examples and resources, and provided explanations of analyses in one easily digestible text. Many of the analyses presented assist in providing the recommended evidence to support the inferences drawn from scores from such instruments. That is, the results from applying these techniques assist providing score reliability and validity evidence.

Through our years as graduate students and the first segment of our academic lives, we have explored the use of various programs for scale development and the study of the psychometric properties of the scores to provide such evidence. We have had the experience, as I am sure many of you have had, of turning to multiple books for instructions and examples to complete analyses in the scale development and validation process. For those readers just beginning on the psychometric ride, you too will soon experience this. By no means will this book stop the need for multiple sources, in fact, that is always encouraged. However, this book should allow the reader to use this as a main guide and supplement to experience analyses described in major text books. Our examples are intended to be clear and concise with SPSS examples that can be easily adapted to fit many situations, as the reader learns and uses various techniques.

Applied Psychometrics Using SPSS and AMOS, pages ix–x

The anticipated audience for this book includes researchers, practitioners, and graduate students searching for a guide to perform common psychometric analyses on various types of assessment data. We assume a basic level of statistical knowledge but review concepts throughout. We envision that this text will (a) patiently wait on some office shelves begging to be handed to a student as a resource, (b) have a permanent home on desks where it continually rises to the top of the stacks for daily use of the applied researcher, (c) be happily carried in bags to and from work and class by the graduate student learning techniques, (d) be listed proudly as a reference text on syllabi, and finally (e) as an occasional drink coaster while deep thoughts are pondered about how to solve measurement problems. We hope that through such uses, particularly the latter, that we have provided some insight and assistance to the user in appropriately applying the techniques and concepts discussed.

We cover major topics such as item analysis, score reliability and validity, generalizability theory, differential item functioning, equating, and so on. Under each topic we present foundational ideas and give examples of how to apply these ideas immediately in ones work. Chapter 7, for instance, contains information on differential item functioning (DIF). We discuss DIF, its importance in the score validation process, and provide three techniques using SPSS to detect DIF, including how to handle clustered data in such analyses. The caveat is we do not provide a detailed discussion of each topic but rather the essence of each topic and several resources for additional reading. Again, we remind you that this is just one resource to promote your psychometric knowledge and practice.

We do assume the user has some basic knowledge and skill level in operating SPSS. At the same time, we do attempt to present material in a very understandable language avoiding or explaining jargon as we go. You may find the occasional joke thrown in from time to time to spice it up. But remember we are researchers, not comedians, even though students and family seem to laugh often at us for the things we think about!

We do ask that if you have feedback, efficiency techniques, improvements, or just plain find mistakes to please notify us. We welcome user feedback and will incorporate this into a revision, if demanded by the reader!

So with that, let us get started on our SPSS adventure in applying psychometric techniques. In the words of Dr. Seuss, "Take it slowly. This book is dangerous."

Enjoy.

—W. Holmes Finch, Brian F. French,
and Jason C. Immekus,

1

Introduction to Psychometric Concepts

Measurement Basics

Measurement is a mainstay of educational and psychological practice. Teachers and schools measure student performance through tests, psychologists measure client mood through scales such as the Beck Depression Inventory, and colleges and universities use measurements of scholastic aptitude in making admissions decisions. In all of these cases, obtained scores on the measurements plays a critical role in decision making about individuals and groups. Therefore, these scores must be well understood and carefully studied to ensure that they provide the best information possible. Over the last roughly 100 years, a subspecialty combining statistics and educational psychology has developed in order to study such measures. This field, known as psychometrics, focuses on the development, and vetting of educational and psychological assessments using a wide variety of tools. Together, these tools represent a wide array of statistical analyses that can provide the researcher with a great deal of information regarding the performance of a particular measure. We will cover many of these tools together in this book, focusing on how the SPSS software system can be used to obtain information about individual items as well as the scale as a whole.

Applied Psychometrics Using SPSS and AMOS, pages 1–13

In the course of reading this book, you will become familiar with methods for analyzing data involving an entire scale (i.e., the collection of items), as well as the individual items themselves. In addition, you will learn about differences and similarities in studying both dichotomous items, which have two possible outcomes, and polytomous items, which have more than two potential outcomes. We will discuss methods for understanding performance of an instrument at the scale level, including assessment of reliability and validity. We will also learn about item analysis, which will provide information regarding the difficulty of individual items (i.e., how likely an individual is to endorse the item), as well as its ability to differentiate among examinees with different standings on the measured trait, known as discrimination. Throughout the text we will refer to the individuals completing the items as examinees, for convenience sake. Similarly, we may refer to the instruments as tests, though in fact they may not always be tests in the sense that we often think about them. It is important to note that virtually all of the topics that we study together in this text are equally applicable to traditional tests of achievement or aptitude, as well as to affective assessments of mood, and other non-cognitive constructs. Finally, throughout the text we will discuss the notion of the latent trait being measured. This simply refers to the thing that we believe our instrument is assessing, be that intelligence, depression, or political outlook. The score obtained from the instrument will typically serve as the manifest indication of this unobserved, or latent variable. Prior to getting into the nuts and bolts of how to analyze data using SPSS, let us first discuss the two primary paradigms that underlie nearly all of these analyses, classical test theory and item response theory.

Classical Test Theory

In many ways, classical test theory (CTT) serves as the basis for much of what we think of as psychometrics and measurement. Developed over the last 100 years or so, it underlies the notion of instrument reliability, and much of validity assessment. In addition, although the form of the CTT model differs substantially from that of the later developed item response theory (IRT) model, which we will discuss shortly, they share many of the same basic concepts. At its heart, CTT is simply a way to link an observed score on an instrument to the unobserved entity that we are hopefully measuring. Thus, for example, if we give a class of 5th graders a math exam, we rely on individual scores to tell us how much math the students know. Ideally we would directly assess this knowledge, but for reasons that will soon become clear, this isn't possible. However, if our test is well designed, the score should be a reasonably accurate and reliable estimate of that knowledge.

In this section, we will discuss the ideas underlying CTT, and their implications for educational and psychological measurement.

The basic equation in CTT is simply $X = T + E$, where X is the observed score on the measure for some individual, T is the individual's true score on the construct of interest, and E is random error. Put into words, this equation states that the observed score an individual receives on a test is a function of their true knowledge of the subject (assuming we're discussing some type of cognitive or achievement measure) and a set of other factors that are random in nature. In a general sense, we can think of T as a stable characteristic inherent to the individual that would remain unchanged over repeated administrations of the instrument, if that could be done so that after each test examinees forgot that they had taken it (Haertel, 2006). Error, on the other hand, is generally conceptualized as ephemeral and unstable factors influencing examinee performance on the measure. One way to consider error is by classifying it into four distinct types or categories, including (a) natural variation in an individual's performance due to factors specific to them on the day of testing (e.g., fatigue, hunger, mood); (b) environmental factors present during test administration (e.g., room temperature, ambient noise); (c) scoring variation (e.g., ratings by evaluators); and (d) test items selected (Feldt & Brennan, 1989).

The random nature of error leads to a number of interesting properties of the CTT model. First of all, if a particular examinee could be given the test repeatedly over a very large number of times, and each time forget that (s)he had taken it, the mean of the errors across those test administrations would be 0 (i.e., the population mean, $\mu_E = 0$). Furthermore, the random nature of error leads to the conclusion that it is completely uncorrelated with T. In other words, if we had a group of students taking our test a large number of times, and calculated Pearson's r between the true score and error, it would come out to be 0 (i.e., $r_{T,E} = 0$). In addition, if we had multiple forms of the same exam, the errors across those forms would also be uncorrelated, again because their errors are random. Thus, $r_{E1,E2} = 0$.

While these results are interesting in and of themselves, they lead to a relationship that is key in CTT. In general, whenever we have one variable that is the composite of two other variables, like $X = T + E$, we express the variance of the composite as $\sigma_X^2 = \sigma_T^2 + \sigma_E^2 + 2\text{cov}(T,E)$. Given that we know T and E are uncorrelated, we also know that the covariance between them (cov) is also 0. Therefore, we can rewrite the composite variance of X as $\sigma_X^2 = \sigma_T^2 + \sigma_E^2$. This relationship is central to the idea of test reliability, which we discuss in some detail in Chapter 3. For the moment, we can simply define the concept of reliability as the ratio of variance in T to the variance in X, or

$$\rho_{xx} = \frac{\sigma_T^2}{\sigma_T^2 + \sigma_E^2}. \tag{1.1}$$

In Chapter 3, we will discuss in detail how to estimate reliability for a scale using a set of data.

Often in practice, consumers of test information are interested in learning something about the likely value of an examinee's true score on the trait being measured. Though T can never be known exactly, using some of the basic elements of CTT it is possible to construct a confidence interval within which we have a certain level of confidence (e.g., 95%) that T exists. In order to construct such an interval, we first need to understand the standard error of measurement (SEM). Theoretically, if we could give the same individual a measure many times, and each time they would forget they had taken the measure, we would obtain a distribution for X. With such a distribution, we could then calculate the standard deviation, and if there were multiple such examinees who each had taken the test many times, then we could get standard deviations (σ_{Ei}^2) for each of them as well. For a given examinee, this standard deviation would be a reflection of the variability in his/her scores. Given that we assume T is stable for an individual, these standard deviations would actually reflect the error variation for each individual. If we were to average these standard deviations across all of the individual examinees in a given sample, we would obtain the SEM. In other words,

$$\text{SEM} = \frac{\Sigma_{i=1}^{N} \sigma_{Ei}^2}{N}. \tag{1.2}$$

Of course, in practice we will not be able to have individual examinees take a test many times while forgetting that they've done so before, so consequently we will not have access to σ_{Ei}^2. However, using a bit of algebra, it is possible to obtain a method for estimating SEM that is based on easily obtained statistics such as a reliability estimate (ρ_{XX}) and the standard deviation of the observed test scores (σ_X). In this formulation,

$$= \sigma\sqrt{1 - \rho_{XX}}. \tag{1.3}$$

As we will see in Chapter 3, the SEM can be used to construct a confidence interval around T for examinees in the sample.

Prior to completing our discussion of CTT, it is important to consider the issue of parallel forms of a measure. The idea of parallel forms is important in CTT, particularly with regard to the estimation of reliability. Multiple forms of an instrument are said to be strictly parallel when they are developed using identical test specifications, produce the same distributions of X (same mean and standard deviation), have equal covariances between any pairs of forms, and covary equally with other measures. In addition, individual examinees will have the same value for T for strictly parallel forms. Finally, given the random nature of E, the covariance between error terms for two strictly parallel forms will be 0. We will revisit the concept of parallel forms in Chapter 3, when we discuss the estimation of scale reliability.

Item Response Theory

Another approach to thinking about psychometrics and measurement comes in the form of a series of statistical models known collectively as item response theory (IRT) (van der Linden & Hambleton, 1997; Yen & Fitzpatrick, 2006). Whereas the focus of CTT is typically (though by no means exclusively) at the scale level with issues such as reliability and validity, the focus of IRT is at the item level. Indeed, the set of models that make up the suite of IRT tools all have in common a focus on the relationship among characteristics of the items, the examinees and the probability of the examinee providing a particular response to the item (e.g., correct or incorrect). As we will see, IRT models are available for both dichotomous and polytomous item responses. In this section, we will first focus on models for dichotomous data, such as is common for items scored as correct/incorrect, and then on models for polytomous data that might be seen with rating scales and graded responses.

Dichotomous Items

Probably the single most common family of models in IRT is based in the logistic framework. For dichotomous items there are three such models that are commonly used, each differing from the others in terms of how much information they contain about the items. The simplest such model, which is known as the 1-parameter logistic (1PL) model, will serve as our general (and hopefully gentle) introduction to IRT. The 1PL model can be expressed mathematically as:

$$P(x_j = 1 | \theta_i, a, b_j) = \frac{e^{a(\theta_i - b_j)}}{1 + e^{a(\theta_i - b_j)}} \tag{1.4}$$

where x_j is the response to item j, where we code correct as 1 and incorrect as 0. The variable θ_i is the value of the latent trait being measured by the test (e.g., reading aptitude) for examinee i. The 1PL model also contains two item parameter values: a_j, item discrimination; and b_j, item difficulty. For this model it is assumed that a_j is constant across items, while b_j is allowed to vary across items. In terms of their meaning, we can view b_j as an indicator of how likely an individual with low proficiency is to answer the item correctly, when discussing proficiency exams. It is important to note that item difficulty and examinee level on the latent trait are on the same scale, which is centered at 0 and theoretically ranges from $-\infty$ to ∞, though in practice it typically lies between –3 and 3 (de Ayala, 2009). An item with a lower difficulty is relatively easier than those with higher difficulty values, such that examinees with lower levels of θ_i are more likely to answer it correctly. Item discrimination, a_j, reflects how well the item can differentiate among those with greater or lesser amounts of θ_i, with larger values indicating greater such discriminatory power.

For the 1PL model, all items are assumed to have equal values for item discrimination, which is what differentiates it from other IRT models as we will see. In some cases, researchers want to assume that the value of $a_j = 1$, thus defining a special case of the 1PL known as the Rasch model. Therefore, we can think of the Rasch model as a special case of the 1PL. However, it should be noted that in the broader measurement community the two models carry with them very different implications for practice. We will not discuss the issues surrounding the Rasch model further in this book, but do encourage the interested reader to investigate them. Interesting and brief summaries can be found in Embretson and Reise (2000) and de Ayala (2009), among others.

The item characteristic curve (ICC) is a common tool used in examining the qualities of individual items. It relates the latent trait being measured (on the *X* axis), with the probability of a correct response (in the case of dichotomous items) based on the particular model selected on the *Y* axis. As an example, consider two items based on the 1PL model where $b_1 = -0.4$, $b_2 = 0.7$, and $a = 1.2$. The ICC's for these two items appear in Figure 1.1. We can see that while the shape of the items is the same, Item 2 is shifted to the right of Item 1, because it has a higher difficulty parameter value. In addition, we could use the ICC to determine the probability of a correct response for an individual with a given value of θ by drawing a straight line up from the *X* axis until it reaches the curve, at which point we would draw a second line from that point on the curve to the *Y* axis to obtain the probability of a correct item response.

When we cannot assume that item discrimination values are equal across the items, we can use the 2-parameter logistic (2PL) model, which has very similar form to the 1PL:

$$P(x_j = 1|\theta_i, a_j, b_j) = \frac{e^{a_j(\theta_i - b_j)}}{1 + e^{a_j(\theta_i - b_j)}}. \tag{1.5}$$

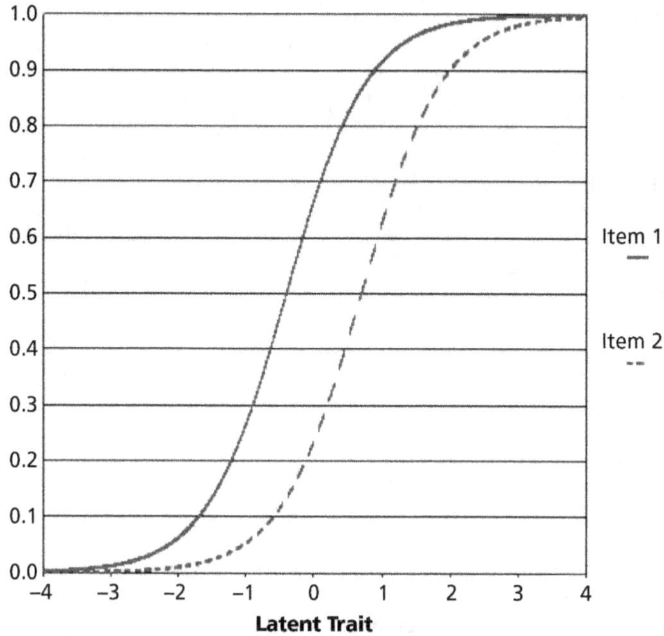

Figure 1.1 Item characteristic curves for two hypothetic items based on 1PL Model.

The difference is that now a_j is specific to item j. By allowing item discrimination to vary, it is possible to identify those items that are best able to differentiate among individuals based on the level of the latent trait being measured, with higher values indicating an item that is more discriminating. The ICC's for a pair of 2PL items with item parameters $a_1 = 1.2$, $b_1 = -0.4$, $a_2 = 0.8$, and $b_2 = 0.7$, respectively, appear in Figure 1.2. As with the 1PL model, the more difficult item (2) is shifted to the right of the easier item (1). In addition, the higher discrimination value of Item 1 is reflected in its steeper ICC as compared to that of Item 2.

A third variation on the logistic framework for dichotomous items is the 3-parameter logistic model (3PL), which incorporates the probability that an examinee will provide a correct item response simply due to chance, perhaps by guessing. The 3PL model is expressed as

$$P(x_j = 1 | \theta_i, a_j, b_j) = c_j + (1 - c_j)\frac{e^{a_j(\theta_i - b_j)}}{1 + e^{a_j(\theta_i - b_j)}}, \tag{1.6}$$

where c_j is the pseudo-chance (or pseudo-guessing) parameter, representing the probability of a correct response for an examinee whose value of θ_i

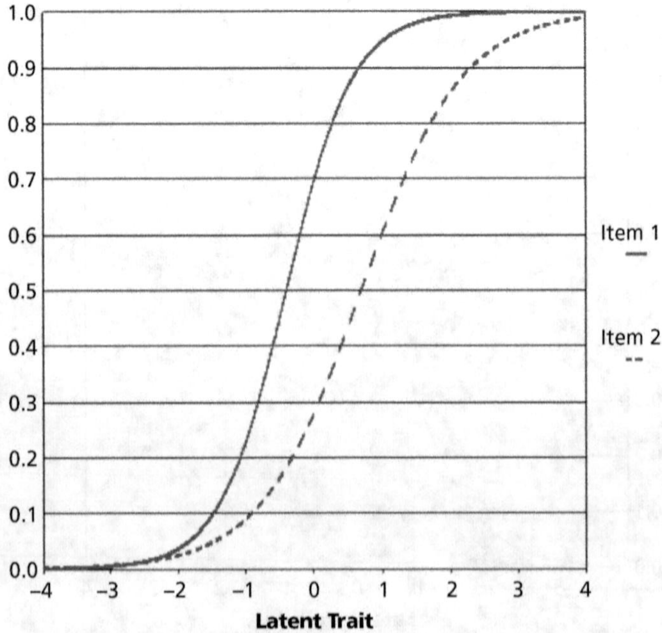

Figure 1.2 Item characteristic curves for two hypothetic items based on 2PL Model.

approaches –∞. As an example, imagine a multiple choice test item with five options to select from. An individual with an extremely low value of θ_i would also have an extremely low probability of answering the item correctly, based on their knowledge of the subject being tested. However, for a multiple choice type item, there is the possibility that such an examinee could randomly select the correct answer. This possibility is captured in the item parameter c_j. It is important to note that c_j is referred to as a pseudo-chance or pseudo-guessing parameter (rather than simply the guessing parameter) because it reflects not merely the probability of totally random selection of the correct answer, but also differences in how well the options in a multiple choice exam might be worded (making them relatively more or less attractive), and the propensities of different examinees to guess and guess well. Figure 1.3 includes ICC's for two 3PL items, which have identical difficulty and discrimination parameter values to those in the 2PL example, and where $c_1 = 0.2$, while $c_2 = 0.1$. The difference between these ICC's and those in Figure 1.2 is the lower asymptote for each item. Whereas in the 2PL case, the probability of a correct response converges to 0 as θ_i approaches –∞, for the 3PL models, the probability of a correct response converges to the value of c.

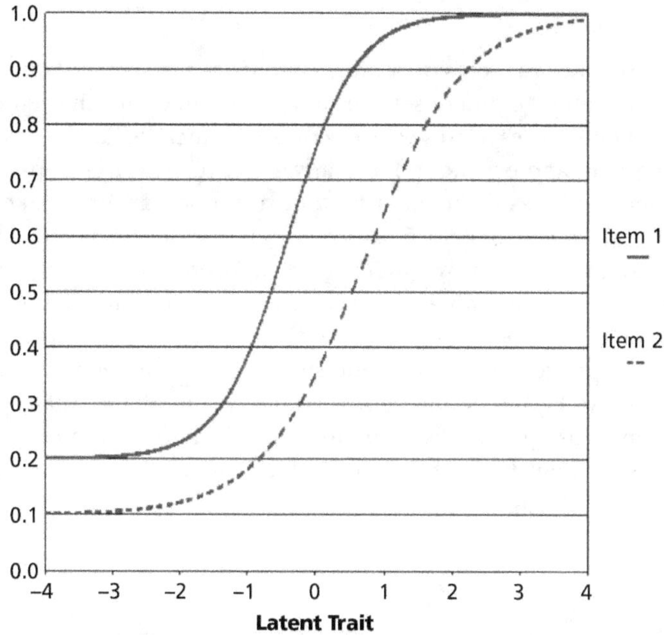

Figure 1.3 Item characteristic curves for two hypothetic items based on 3PL Model.

There are three common assumptions that underlie these logistic models. The first of these, unidimensionality, is that only a single latent trait is being measured by a set of items. Thus, a test designed to measure reading fluency in young children should only measure the construct of reading fluency, and not other, additional constructs. A second, related assumption is that of local independence, which states that responses to any pair of items should be completely uncorrelated if we hold θ_i constant. Another way to view this assumption is that the only factor that should influence an examinee's item response is her/his proficiency on the trait being measured. The third assumption underlying IRT models is that the model form is correct for the data being analyzed. In other words, if we select the 2PL model for a set of item responses, we are assuming that this functional form is correct, such that the probability of a correct response increases concomitantly with increases in θ_i, that items have different values of a_j, and that there is no possibility of obtaining a correct answer due to chance.

Polytomous Items

In many contexts, items on an instrument are not scored dichotomously, but rather can take one of several values. Examples in achievement testing include graded responses where scores may include categories such as poor, fair, good, and excellent. For many affective measures in psychology, such as personality assessments, the item responses are on a Likert Scale taking the values 1, 2, 3, 4, or 5, for example. In all of these cases, the IRT models described previously would not be appropriate for modeling item responses because they only account for dichotomous outcomes. A number of more general models have been developed, however, which do accommodate such polytomous items. One such model, the generalized partial credit model (GPCM), is analogous to the 2PL model in that it models item responses using item discrimination and location parameters, and an individual's propensity on the measured latent trait (Muraki, 1992). The GPCM takes the form:

$$P(X_{jk} | \theta_i, a_j, b_{jk}) = \frac{e^{\sum_{h=1}^{kj} a_j(\theta_i - b_{jh})}}{\sum_{c=1}^{m_j} e^{\sum_{h=1}^{c} a_j(\theta_i - b_{jh})}}, \tag{1.7}$$

where θ_i and a_j are the latent trait and discrimination parameters, as defined previously. The parameter b_{jh} is a threshold that reflects the level of the latent trait necessary for an individual to go to item response h from response $h - 1$. The value of m_j represents the number of categories (e.g., 5) possible for item j. As an aside, this suggests that the items can have different numbers of categories. If we assume that the values of $a_j = 1$ for all items, then we have the partial credit model, which is simply the Rasch version of the GPCM.

As an example of how the GPCM works, imagine for a specific item that we have four categories (0, 1, 2, 3) from which an individual can endorse. Further, assume that for Item 1, the threshold values are –1, 0, and 1. This would mean that individual respondents with θ_i values below –1 are most likely to provide an answer of 1 to the item. Similarly, those with $-1 \leq \theta_i < 0$ have the highest probability of yielding a response of 2, while those with $0 \leq \theta_i < 1$ have the highest probability of a 3 response. Finally, individuals with $\theta_i \geq 1$ have the greatest probability of producing a value of 3 on the item. The ICC for this item appears below in Figure 1.4. While for dichotomous items there was only one curve linking θ_i and the item response probabilities, for polytomous items there are separate curves associated with each of the response options. Using these curves, we can discern the probability that an individual with a given level of the latent trait will produce a

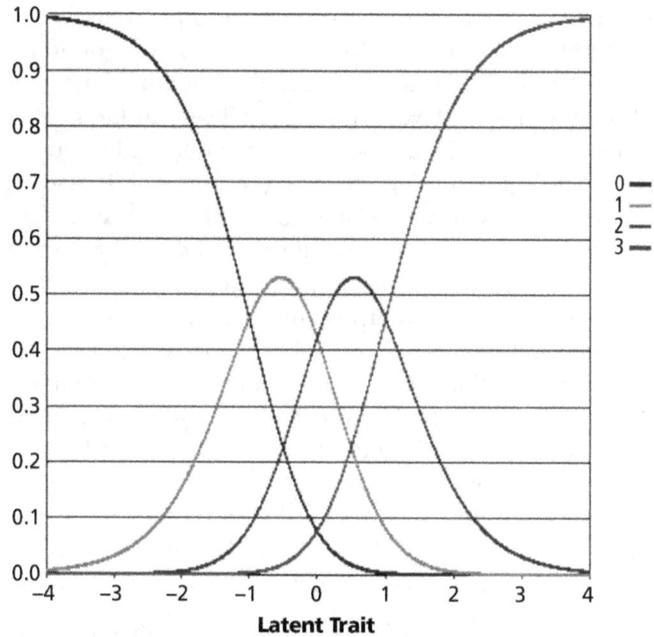

Figure 1.4 ICC for item based on Graded Partial Credit Model.

particular response to the item. For example, respondents with $\theta_i < -2$ are most likely to respond with a 0, while those with $\theta_i = -0.5$ will most likely respond with a 1. It is also clear from viewing these curves that individuals with, for example, high values of θ_i could still provide a response of 0 or 1, but the probability for such is quite low.

An alternative to the GPCM for polytomous data is the graded response model (GRM) developed by Samejima (1969). Whereas the GPCM compares the likelihood of an individual responding in two adjacent categories (h versus $h-1$), the GRM focuses on the probability of responding in category h or higher versus categories less than h. In other words, rather than focusing as the GPCM on a series of dichotomous choices between adjacent categories, the GRM instead compares the probability of one category or higher versus all lower categories. The GRM is expressed as

$$P(X_{jk} \text{ or higher}) = \frac{e^{a_j(\theta_i - b_{X_j})}}{1+e^{a_j(\theta_i - b_{X_j})}}. \quad (1.8)$$

Once again, a_j and θ_i are as defined previously. In this case, b_{X_j} is the boundary point between a value on the item of h or higher, versus all responses below h.

To illustrate the GRM, let's consider the example described above for the GPCM. We have an item with four possible response options to select from, with thresholds of –1, 0, and 1. The meaning of these threshold values is slightly different in the GRM than for the GPCM. In the latter case, the first threshold marked the border between a response of 1 versus 2, whereas for the GRM it marks the border between a response of 0 versus 1, 2, or 3. Thus, a respondent with a θ_i value of 0.5 is more likely to produce a response of 3 or 4 versus 1 or 2. In order to obtain probabilities for a specific item response, we would use the following equation: $P_{ix}(\theta) = P_{ix}(\theta) - P_{ix+1}(\theta)$. Therefore, to obtain the probability of an individual providing a response of 2, we would simply calculate $P_{i2}(\theta) = P_{i2}(\theta) - P_{i3}(\theta)$. Figure 1.5 contains an ICC for the GRM of this item. Its general form is very similar to that of the GPCM, with a separate curve for each response option. However, notice that the curves are shifted somewhat on the *X* axis, and the maximum probabilities associated with specific item responses are somewhat lower for the GRM. For example, while the maximum probability of producing a response of 2 is approximately 0.52 in the GPCM, it is only 0.4 for the GRM. This difference in probabilities is reflective of the different model forms.

In addition to the GPCM and GRM, a third general approach for dealing with ordinal item responses is the rating scale model (RSM). While

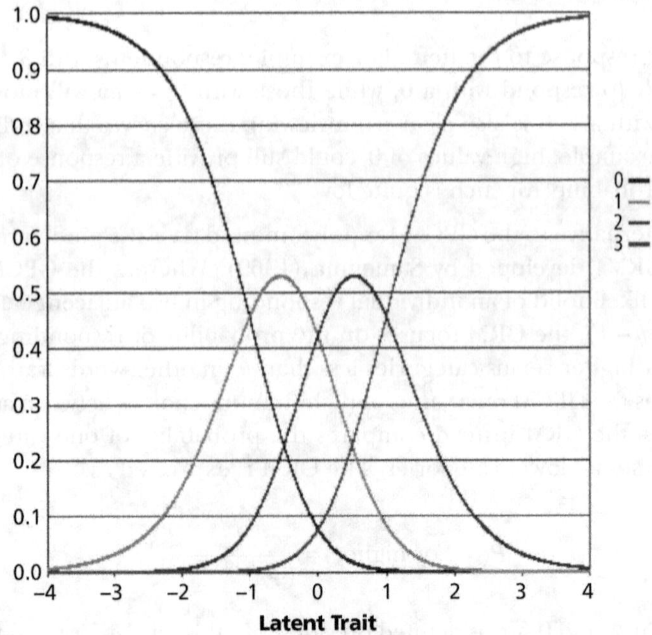

Figure 1.5 ICC for item based on Graded Response Model.

conceptually similar to both the GPCM and GRM, the RSM has somewhat different properties, which can be highlighted by looking at the model formulation:

$$P(X_j|\theta_i,\delta_j,\tau)=\frac{e^{-\Sigma_{h=0}^{x_j}\tau_h+x_j(\theta_i-\delta_j)}}{\Sigma_{h=0}^{m_j}e^{-\Sigma_{h=0}^{x_j}\tau_h+x_j(\theta_i-\delta_j)}}. \tag{1.9}$$

In this model, τ_h represents the threshold for item response h, and is on the scale of the latent variable being measured. Thus, for an ordinal item with 1, 2, 3, 4, and 5 as response options, there would be 4 thresholds (number of categories minus 1), where τ_1 separates a response of 1 from 2, τ_2 separates 2 from 3, τ_3 separates 3 from 4, and τ_4 separates 4 from 5. The value x_j corresponds to the number of parameters that an individual has passed, based on their value on the latent trait being measured. The δ_j parameter indicates an item's location, or central point, on the latent trait, around which the thresholds gather. To see how the RSM works, let's consider an item that has 5 response options, where $\delta_j = 0.5$, and the thresholds are as follows: $\tau_1 = -0.6$, $\tau_2 = -0.1$, $\tau_3 = 0.7$, and $\tau_4 = 1.2$. An individual completing the instrument who has $\theta_i = 0.54$ would pass thresholds 1 and 2, but not 3, leading them to provide a response of 3 on the item. Now that we are familiar with CTT and IRT models, let us move to item analysis in Chapter 2 with these ideas in mind. We also want you to be aware that many of our datasets and code are available to download at the website for this book (https://labs.wsu.edu/psychometric/resources/).

2

Item Analysis

Introduction

This chapter introduces statistical procedures to conduct item analyses based on classical test theory (CTT). These analyses typically serve as a first step in the investigation of the psychometric properties of scale scores. Analyses described in this chapter provide ways to estimate the difficulty and discrimination of dichotomously (e.g., correct/incorrect) and polytomously (e.g., Disagree, Neutral, Agree) scored questionnaire and test items. Understanding the characteristics of scale items is a necessary step for deciding which items will remain, be revised, or excluded from the final version of an educational or psychological measure (e.g., motivation, mathematics achievement).

Classical Test Theory Item Difficulty

CTT Item Difficulty for Dichotomous Items

Item difficulty is an index of how examinees answered an item. For dichotomously scored items, CTT defines item difficulty as the proportion of persons who obtained a correct item response (i.e., proportion passing), or

Applied Psychometrics Using SPSS and AMOS, pages 15–46

the proportion of those agreeing with items measuring agreement to a statement. In this case, item difficulty can range from 0.00 to 1.00, with values approaching 0.00 indicating more difficult items and those close to 1.00 considered somewhat easier items. Within applied testing contexts, it has been argued that values between 0.30 and 0.70, with a mean of 0.50, provide the most useful information about examinees' knowledge or skill level (Allen & Yen, 1979), if the purpose of the test is to produce a normal distribution of score estimates of ability levels. For criterion assessments, a more restricted range is generally desired with a mean difficulty value of 0.80.

SPSS provides two approaches for estimating CTT item difficulty. The first approach involves calculating the item means, which represents the proportion of examinees obtaining a correct response. The following example estimates the CTT item difficulty of a 20-item measure based on the responses of 2,000 examinees, using the ex2.sav data. To conduct this analysis, in the menu bar, select **Analyze**, followed by **Descriptive Statistics** and then **Descriptives**. We will then obtain the SPSS dialogue box shown in Figure 2.1.

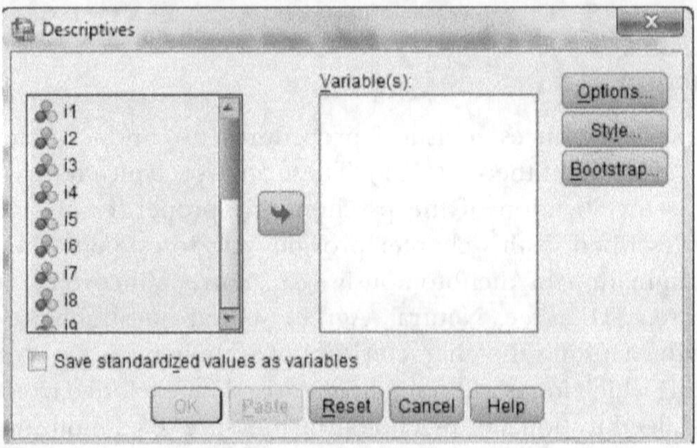

Figure 2.1 SPSS Descriptives dialogue box without items assigned to Variable(s) window.

As shown in Figure 2.1, the items in the dataset appear in the left-hand side of the dialogue box. To estimate item difficulty, we simply highlight the items and click the arrow pointing to the Variable(s) window. Figure 2.2 shows what the dialogue box would look like.

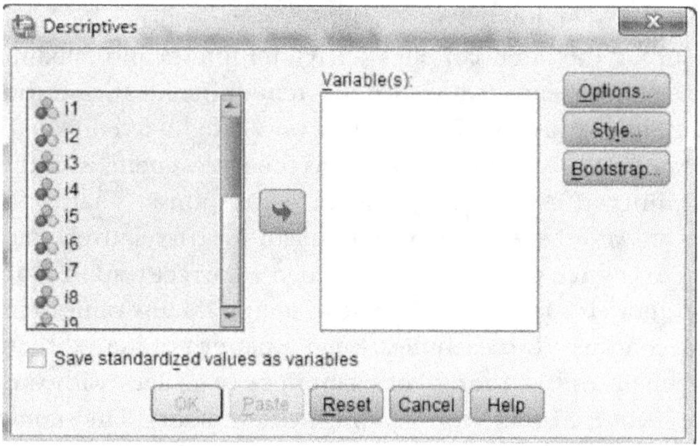

Figure 2.2 Descriptives dialogue with variables assigned to Variable(s) window.

By default, SPSS will provide us with the following information for each selected item: Minimum, maximum, standard deviation, and the mean. If we don't want to change any of these values, we would simply click **OK** to obtain the output reported in Figure 2.3.

Descriptive Statistics					
	N	Minimum	Maximum	Mean	Std. Deviation
i1	2000	0	1	.91	.290
i2	2000	0	1	.61	.489
i3	2000	0	1	.51	.500
i4	2000	0	1	.32	.466
i5	2000	0	1	.36	.479
i6	2000	0	1	.67	.469
i7	2000	0	1	.59	.492
i8	2000	0	1	.51	.500
i9	2000	0	1	.79	.405
i10	2000	0	1	.81	.392
i11	2000	0	1	.54	.499
i12	2000	0	1	.48	.500
i13	2000	0	1	.21	.405
i14	2000	0	1	.84	.369
i15	2000	0	1	.78	.412
i16	2000	0	1	.59	.492
i17	2000	0	1	.59	.492
i18	2000	0	1	.36	.479
i19	2000	0	1	.36	.480
i20	2000	0	1	.35	.476
Valid *N* (listwise)	2000				

Figure 2.3 SPSS Descriptive Statistics output window.

The output in Figure 2.3 includes descriptive statistics for each of the 20 items, including the item, sample size (*N*), minimum and maximum values for each item, the means (which are the item difficulties), and the standard deviations (Std. Deviation). The analyses were conducted on 20 items based on 2000 examinees. As shown, Item 1 was the easiest item, with the majority of the examinees (0.91) obtaining a correct response. That is, 91% of the examinees answered the item correctly. In contrast, a relatively small proportion of the examinee group (0.21) obtained a correct response on Item 13. In general, there is a fairly broad range of item difficulty values across the 20 items, between these two extremes. Such a pattern of item difficulty values is desired when testing a range of examinees (e.g., age) with varied standing on the measured trait (e.g., reading achievement). The standard deviation column shows that the examinee distribution was most varied when an item's proportion correct approximates 0.50 (Crocker & Algina, 1986). Finally, the Minimum column indicates that the lowest item score was 0 (incorrect), whereas the Maximum column reports that the highest item score was 1 (correct) across the item set. This last information is quite useful when we first screen the items, as a way of detecting miskeyed entries. If the minimum and maximum values for each item were not 0 and 1, respectively, we would know that there were one or more typos when the data were entered.

Referring to Figure 2.4, if we wish to change the statistics that are displayed in the output, we would simply click on the **Options** button in the dialogue box.

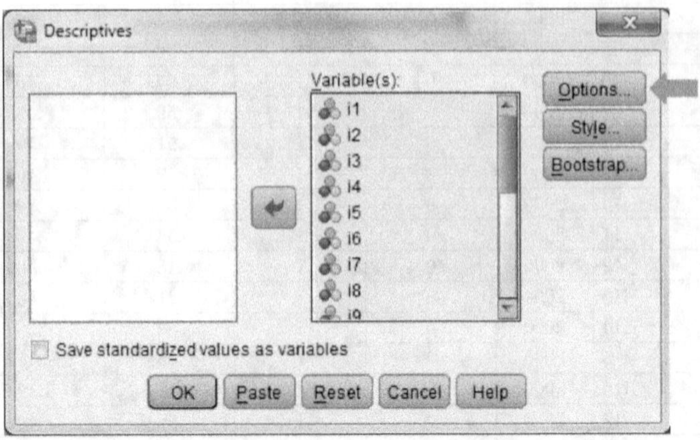

Figure 2.4 Using the **Options** button for selecting which descriptive statistics to display.

Clicking on **Options** yields the following window:

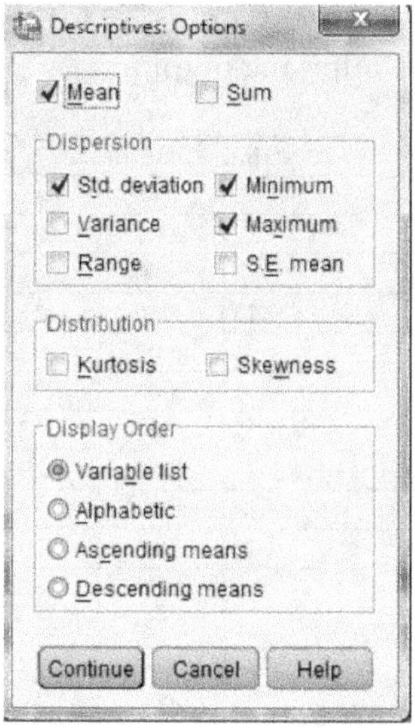

Figure 2.5 Options window for descriptive statistics.

We can see that the SPSS default statistics of **Mean**, **Std. Deviation**, **Minimum**, and **Maximum** were all selected. If we only wanted to display the mean, we would simply unclick the boxes for the other statistics, so that the window appears as follows:

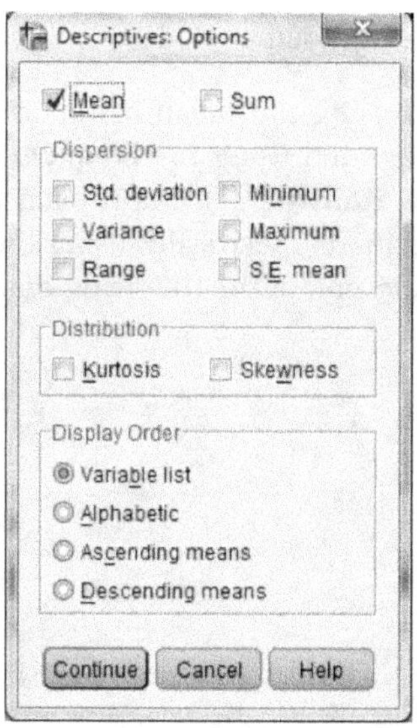

Figure 2.6 Options window for descriptive statistics with only the Mean selected.

By clicking **Continue** in the options box, and then **OK** in the Descriptives box, we would obtain the following output.

Descriptive Statistics		
	N	Mean
i1	2000	.91
i2	2000	.61
i3	2000	.51
i4	2000	.32
i5	2000	.36
i6	2000	.67
i7	2000	.59
i8	2000	.51
i9	2000	.79
i10	2000	.81
i11	2000	.54
i12	2000	.48
i13	2000	.21
i14	2000	.84
i15	2000	.78
i16	2000	.59
i17	2000	.59
i18	2000	.36
i19	2000	.36
i20	2000	.35
Valid *N* (listwise)	2000	

Figure 2.7 Descriptive Statistics output window.

As an alternative to using the mean of dichotomous items, difficulty estimates can also be obtained using the **Frequencies** menu option under **Analyze** and **Descriptive Statistics**. This approach produces frequency tables for all variables specified. Specifically, using the previously mentioned menu sequence, we would obtain the following dialogue box:

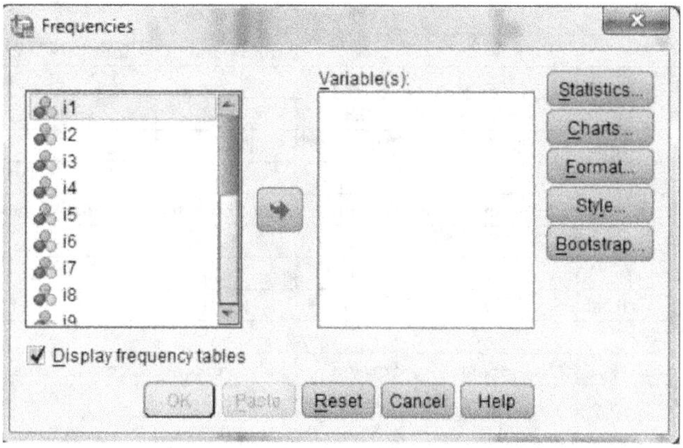

Figure 2.8 Frequencies dialogue box with no items selected.

As with the previous dialogue box examples, our first step is to move the desired items from the left hand box to the Variable(s) box on the right, using the arrow button in the middle.

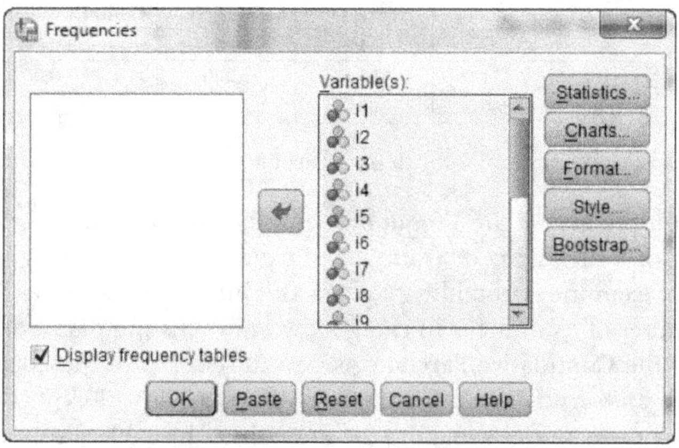

Figure 2.9 Frequencies dialogue box with all items selected.

We will want to leave the **Display frequency tables** box checked so that the tables will appear in the output. We can click **OK**, and obtain the following individual tables for each item. In order to save space, only tables for the first 5 items appear below.

i1					
		Frequency	Percent	Valid Percent	Cumulative Percent
Valid	0	185	9.3	9.3	9.3
	1	1815	90.8	90.8	100.0
	Total	2000	100.0	100.0	

i2					
		Frequency	Percent	Valid Percent	Cumulative Percent
Valid	0	789	39.5	39.5	39.5
	1	1211	60.6	60.6	100.0
	Total	2000	100.0	100.0	

i3					
		Frequency	Percent	Valid Percent	Cumulative Percent
Valid	0	989	49.5	49.5	49.5
	1	1011	50.6	50.6	100.0
	Total	2000	100.0	100.0	

i4					
		Frequency	Percent	Valid Percent	Cumulative Percent
Valid	0	1362	68.1	68.1	68.1
	1	638	31.9	31.9	100.0
	Total	2000	100.0	100.0	

i5					
		Frequency	Percent	Valid Percent	Cumulative Percent
Valid	0	1289	64.5	64.5	64.5
	1	711	35.6	35.6	100.0
	Total	2000	100.0	100.0	

Figure 2.10 Frequency tables for Items 1 through 5.

The output shows the Frequency (number of examinees in the given item category) and Percent (number of examinees in category/total sample size) of examinees obtaining correct and incorrect responses, Valid percent (number of examinees in category with no missing data/total sample size), and the Cumulative Percent. As we can see, 185 of the 2000 examinees (9.3%) answered Item 1 incorrectly, whereas 1815 (90.7%) provided a correct response, thereby making the item difficulty 0.908. Proportions can be obtained by dividing the values in the Percent column by 100.

The **SPSS Frequencies** menu selection offers two additional options that might be useful for the researcher examining item difficulties. First, it is possible to obtain the means (and other descriptive statistics) of the item responses through the **Statistics** button in the frequencies dialogue box.

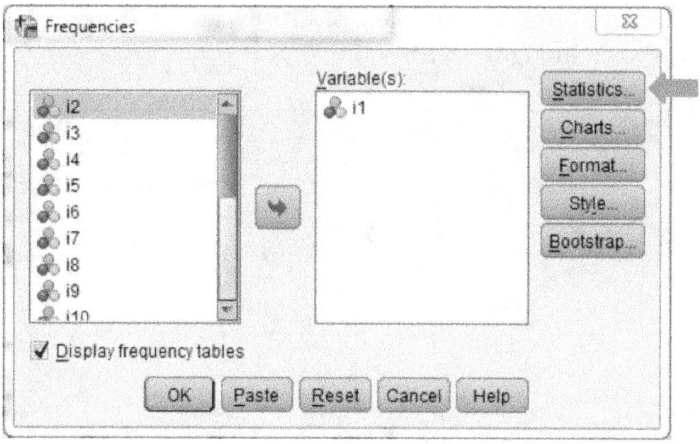

Figure 2.11 Frequencies dialogue box with Item 1 selected, and highlighting the **Statistics** button.

Doing so opens the dialogue box shown in Figure 2.12.

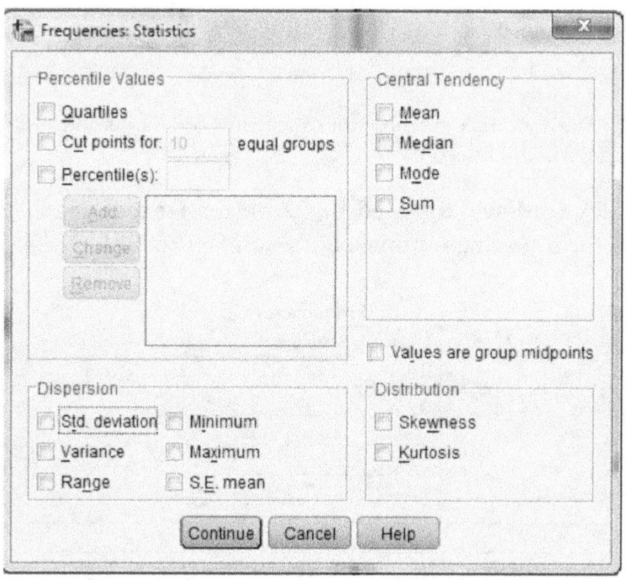

Figure 2.12 Statistics dialogue box under Frequencies menu option.

The user is presented with a number of options in terms of statistics that can be produced for each variable. In this case, we would like to obtain the mean (item difficulty), and the standard deviation, and therefore will click the boxes next to them. For the sake of brevity, we will only present results for Item 1, shown in Figure 2.13.

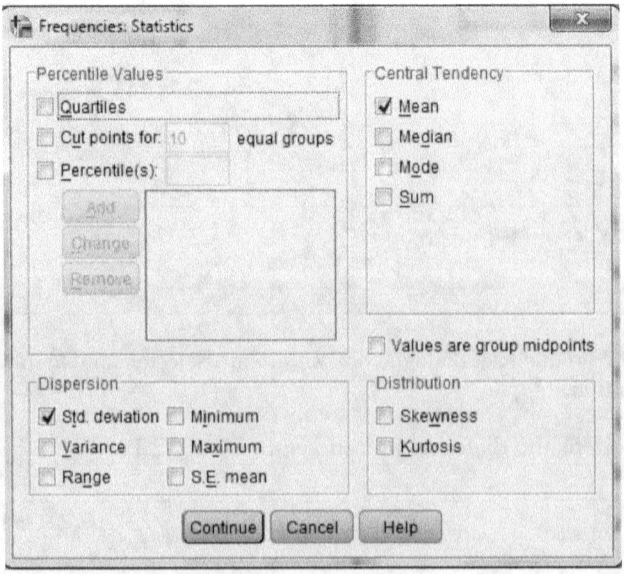

Figure 2.13 Statistics dialogue box under Frequencies menu option with mean and standard deviation selected.

We then click **Continue**, followed by **OK** on the **Frequencies** dialogue box, and obtain the following output reported in Figure 2.14.

Frequencies

Statistics

i1		
N	Valid	2000
	Missing	0
Mean		.91
Std. Deviation		.290

i1					
		Frequency	Percent	Valid Percent	Cumulative Percent
Valid	0	185	9.3	9.3	9.3
	1	1815	90.8	90.8	100.0
	Total	2000	100.0	100.0	

Figure 2.14 Mean, Standard Deviation, and Frequency table for Item 1.

As shown, this mean matches that obtained using the **Descriptives** command, and is an estimate of the CTT item difficulty.

In addition to the mean (and other descriptive statistics), it is also possible to obtain graphs representing the distribution of item responses. For the dichotomous items this will perhaps not be so interesting, but for the polytomous items to be discussed below, such graphs might prove to be quite helpful for characterizing the item response patterns. Figure 2.15 shows how to obtain such graphs by again using the menu sequence to pull up the **Frequencies** dialogue box.

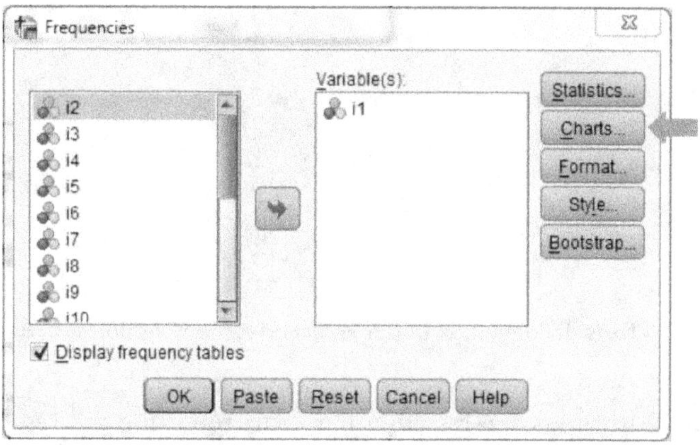

Figure 2.15 **Frequencies** dialogue box with Item 1 selected, and highlighting the **Charts** button.

When we click on this button, the dialogue shown in Figure 2.16 appears.

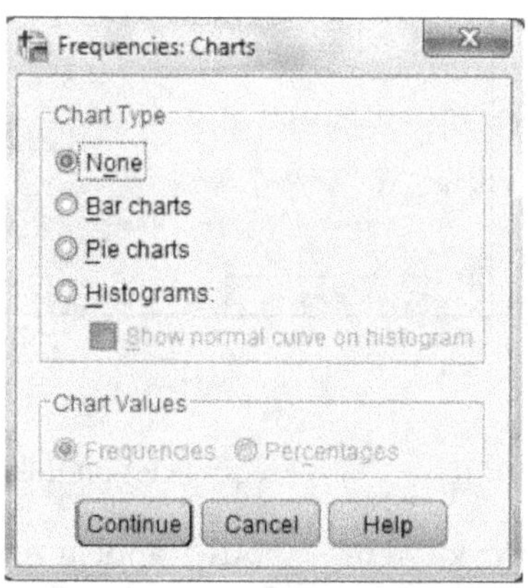

Figure 2.16 **Charts** dialogue box under **Frequencies** menu option.

As shown, we have three choices in terms of the graph type. As an example, we will select the **Bar charts**, by clicking on the radio button next to that option, as demonstrated in Figure 2.17.

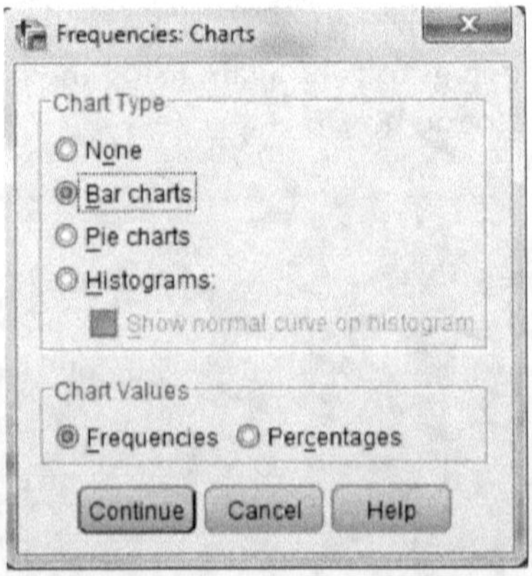

Figure 2.17 **Charts** dialogue box under **Frequencies** menu option with **Bar charts** selected.

Figure 2.18 shows the resulting bar chart reporting the response frequencies for Item 1.

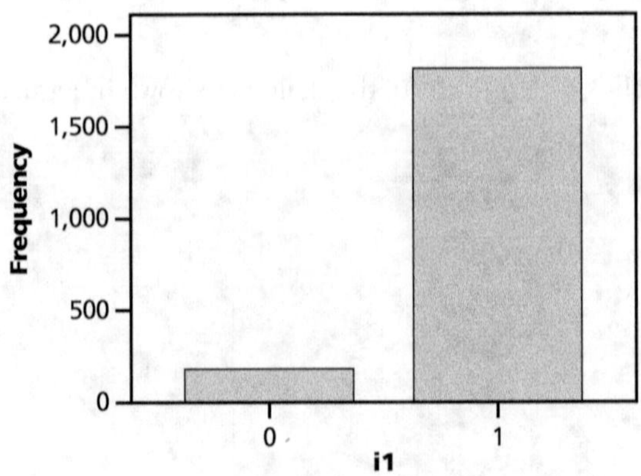

Figure 2.18 Bar chart for Item 1 with Frequencies on the *y*-axis.

By default the frequency of item responses appears on the *y*-axis, with item responses appearing on the *x*-axis. By selecting **Percentages** under **Chart Values** (see Figure 2.17), we can place the percentages on the *y*-axis, shown in Figure 2.19.

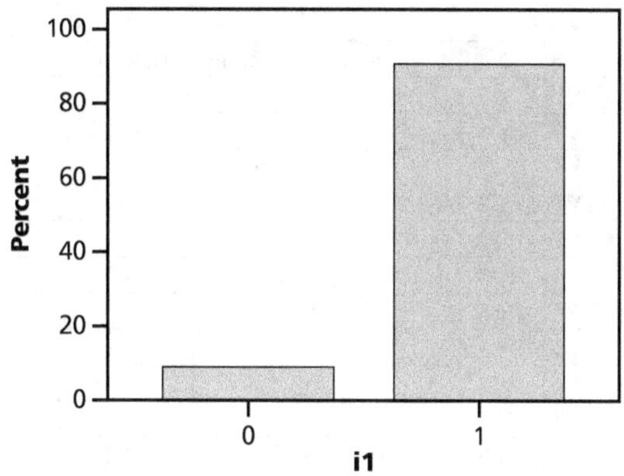

Figure 2.19 Bar chart for Item 1 with Percentages on the *y*-axis.

CTT Item Difficulty for Polytomous Items

Because item difficulty within CTT is defined as the average performance of the examinee group on a particular item, means obtained through the **Descriptive Statistics** menu sequence described above can be used to estimate the item difficulty for polytomously scored items. The following example involves a scale consisting of 20 polytomous items that are scored on a 5 point Likert Scale, measuring the extent to which respondents disagree/agree (e.g., 1 = *Strongly Disagree,* 2 = *Disagree,* 3 = *Neutral,* 4 = *Agree,* 5 = *Strongly Agree*) with a series of survey statements. The instrument was administered to 1,533 respondents, and the resulting data are contained in a file called `poly1.sav`.

In order to obtain the means for the items, we can use the same sequence of menu options that appears in Figures 2.1 and 2.2. The resulting output appears in Figure 2.20.

Descriptive Statistics					
	N	Minimum	Maximum	Mean	Std. Deviation
V1	1533	1	5	4.12	.550
V2	1533	1	5	3.75	.686
V3	1533	2	5	4.00	.573
V4	1533	1	5	3.99	.608
V5	1533	1	5	4.00	.579
V6	1533	1	5	4.06	.545
V7	1533	1	5	3.95	.665
V8	1533	1	5	3.89	.636
V9	1533	1	5	3.90	.622
V10	1533	1	5	3.80	.678
V11	1533	1	5	3.94	.616
V12	1533	2	5	4.06	.586
V13	1533	1	5	3.94	.675
V14	1533	1	5	3.80	.743
V15	1533	2	5	4.04	.593
V16	1533	1	5	3.79	.741
V17	1533	2	5	3.86	.696
V18	1533	1	5	3.60	.776
V19	1533	1	5	4.01	.603
V20	1533	1	5	3.85	.695
Valid *N* (listwise)	1533				

Figure 2.20 Descriptive Statistics output window.

The previous output shows that overall, respondents generally agreed with each scale item. That is, all items had a mean value above 3.5. Item descriptive statistics also suggest that respondents were most varied in their responses to Items 18 (SD = .776), 14 (SD = 0.743), and 16 (SD = 0.741). Furthermore, the range of observed item responses was between *Strongly Disagree* (1) and *Strongly Agree* (5). Note that a few items (i.e., 3, 12, 15, 17) had a restriction of range. That is, no one selected option 1.

To gain insights into the distribution of all responses to each item, the **Frequencies** menu sequence outlined above can be used to obtain the frequency of responses to each option for each item. Such output will help the researcher understand not only the relative difficulty of each item, but also the distribution of responses. For brevity, Figure 2.21 provides the output only for Item 1.

V1					
		Frequency	Percent	Valid Percent	Cumulative Percent
Valid	1	1	.1	.1	.1
	2	9	.6	.6	.7
	3	120	7.8	7.8	8.5
	4	1084	70.7	70.7	79.2
	5	319	20.8	20.8	100.0
	Total	1533	100.0	100.0	

Figure 2.21 Frequency of responses to Item 1.

Results in Figure 2.21 show that the majority of individuals in the sample responded to the item with a 4, and that 91.5% gave either a 4 or a 5, indicating high agreement with the item. Only 10 individuals, or 0.7% indicated that they disagreed or strongly disagreed with the item. We can also examine the bar chart for the responses to this (or any of the other) item using the command sequence in Figures 2.15 through 2.17. In this case, we elected to place the Percent on the *y*-axis (Figure 2.22).

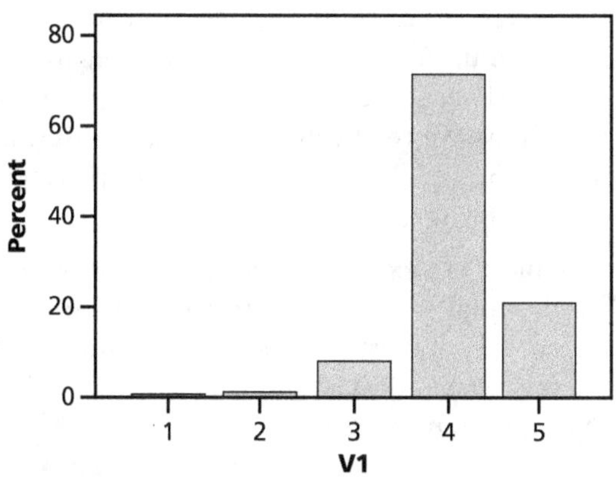

Figure 2.22 Bar chart for Polytomous Item 1 with Percentages on the *y*-axis.

Classical Test Theory Item Discrimination

Item discrimination refers to the degree to which an item functions to differentiate respondents with relatively higher levels of the trait being measured by the scale from those with lower trait levels. Therefore, understanding the items' discriminatory power is critical to developing a useful measure. The underlying notion of item discrimination is that a larger proportion of high scoring (high total score) persons should respond correctly or more highly endorse the item in comparison to persons with lower total scores on the scale. There are several ways to estimate item discrimination and we discuss a few here including the extreme groups calculation method, biserial and point biserial correlations, and Cronbach's coefficient alpha. We do not show how to calculate the biserial correlation in SPSS because it was not an option at the time of this printing. This section provides the SPSS steps to calculate item discrimination using several methods. A detailed discussion of coefficient alpha will appear in Chapter 3, including more discussion on item discrimination.

Extreme Groups Calculation Method

The extreme groups calculation method, or the *index of discrimination* (Crocker & Algina, 1986), is used with dichotomously scored items. It is calculated as the difference between the proportion of the highest scoring (upper) and lowest scoring (lower) groups of examinees obtaining a correct item response. Estimation thus requires first establishing the upper and lower examinee groups, typically based on the total test score. Discrimination values can range from –1.00 to 1.00, with positive values indicating items that favor the upper scoring group and negative values showing items that favored the lower scoring group. Items are considered to be performing well when they have relatively large positive discrimination values, meaning a larger portion of the high scoring group responded correctly compared to the low scoring group.

In order to calculate the extreme groups discrimination index, we first need to calculate the total score on the instrument. We'll go back to the 20 dichotomous item test that was discussed earlier in this chapter. To calculate the total score, we would use the **Transform** and **Compute Variable** menu options, shown in Figure 2.23.

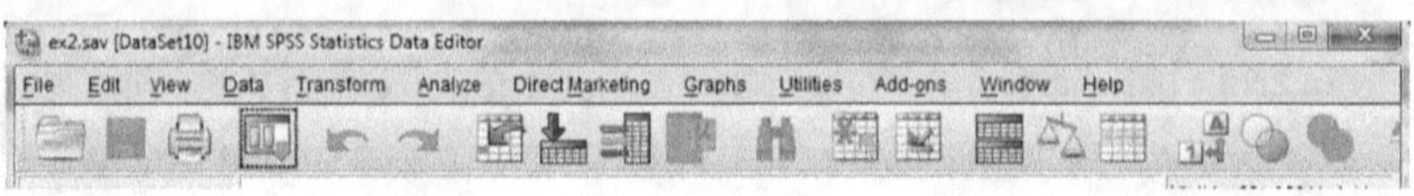

Figure 2.23 SPSS menu bar.

The dialogue box shown in Figure 2.24 will subsequently appear.

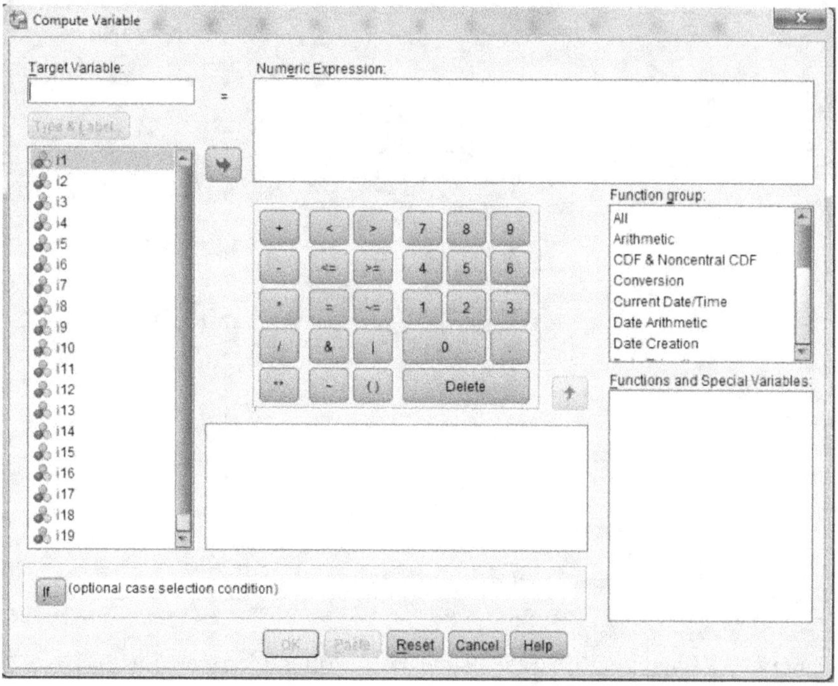

Figure 2.24 Compute Variable dialogue box.

In the **Target Variable** slot, we assign a name for the new variable that will appear in our dataset. In this example, we call the new variable "score." Next, in the numeric expression box, we will sum the items using the statements provided in Figure 2.25. When we are done, the window will look as follows.

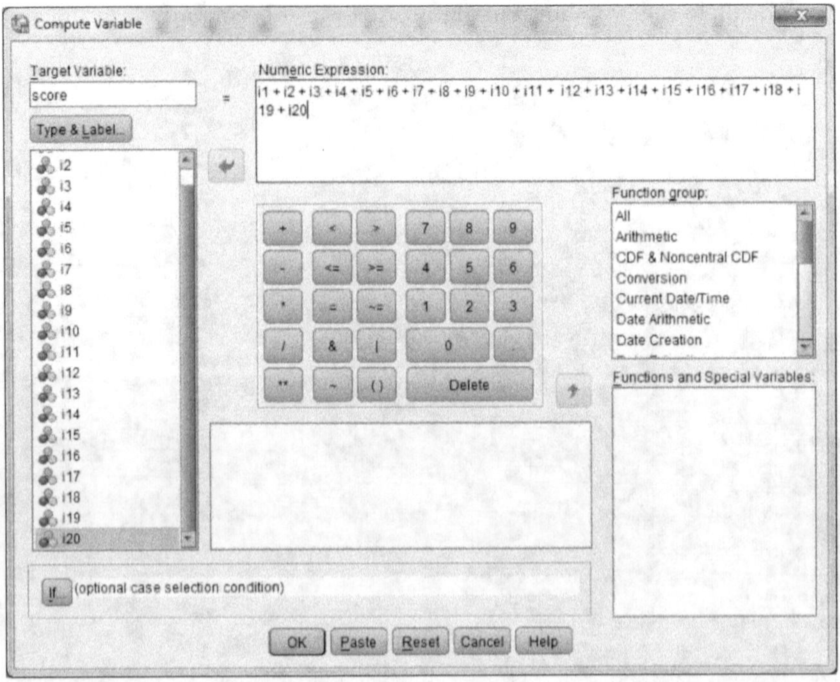

Figure 2.25 Compute Variable dialogue box for computing score variable.

When we click **OK**, a new column containing the score will be added at the end of our data set.

In order to calculate the extreme groups discrimination values for each item, we will need to identify the upper and lower scoring groups. In this case, we will use the top 25% and the bottom 25% of examinees, based on the total test score. First, we need to identify the 25th and 75th percentile values. We can do this going through **Analyze ► Descriptive Statistics ► Explore** menu sequence, which yields the dialogue box in Figure 2.26.

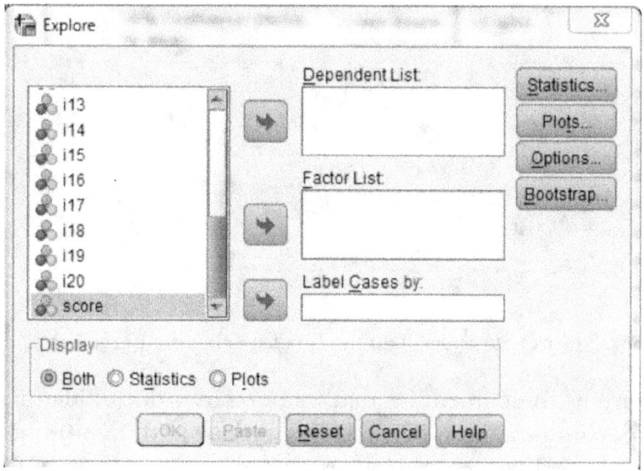

Figure 2.26 Explore dialogue box.

As shown in Figure 2.27, we will need to move the score variable to the Dependent List window.

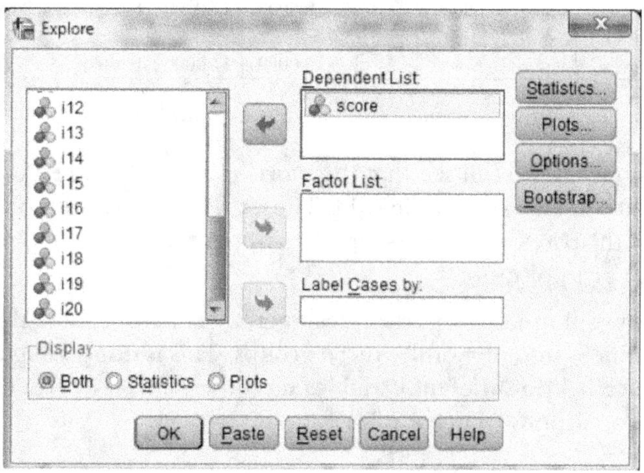

Figure 2.27 Explore dialogue box for the score variable.

We then click **Statistics** and get the window shown in Figure 2.28, in which we will click **Percentiles**.

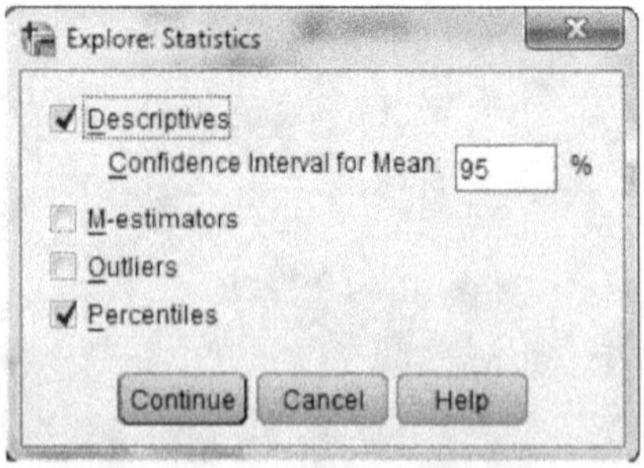

Figure 2.28 Explore: Statistics dialogue box for selecting percentiles.

This will give us the percentiles that we need in order to identify the 25th and 75th percentile values. By clicking **Continue** and then **OK** in the previous window, we obtain the output reported in Figure 2.29. Of particular interest to us in the current example is the following table.

Percentiles								
		Percentiles						
		5	10	25	50	75	90	95
Weighted Average (Definition 1)	score	5.0000	6.0000	9.0000	11.0000	14.0000	16.0000	18.0000
Tukey's Hinges	score			9.0000	11.0000	14.0000		

Figure 2.29 Percentiles output from the explore command.

From this output, we can see that the score at the 25th percentile is 9, and the score at the 75th percentile is 14. Thus, the bottom 25% group consists of those with scores of 9 or less, and the upper 25% group includes those with scores of 14 or more.

We now will use these percentiles to create a new variable that categorizes examinees into one of the three groups. This is done using the **Transform ► Recode Into Different Variables** menu sequence, in order to obtain the following window (Figure 2.30).

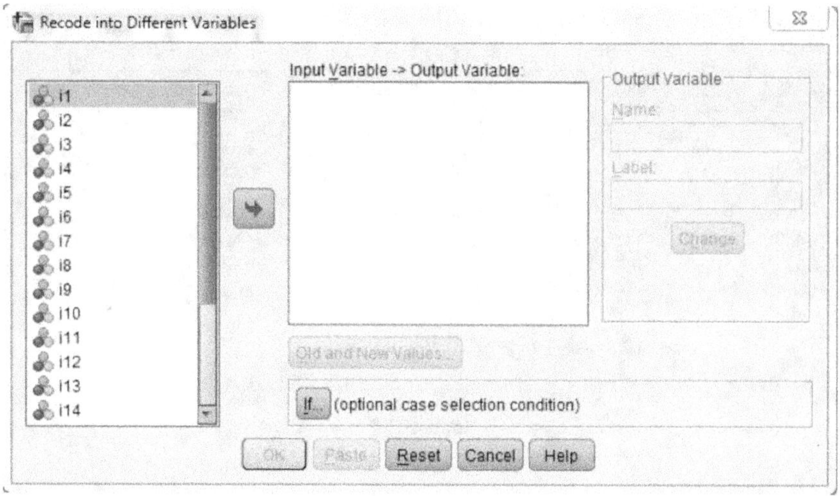

Figure 2.30 Recode Into Different Variables dialogue box.

We can then recode the variable score into a variable consisting of 3 separate groups, those with scores of 9 or below, those with scores between 10 and 13, and those with scores of 14 or more. First, as shown in Figure 2.31, we move the score variable into the Numeric Variable -> Output Variable box, and provide the name of the new variable, along with any variable label that we would like.

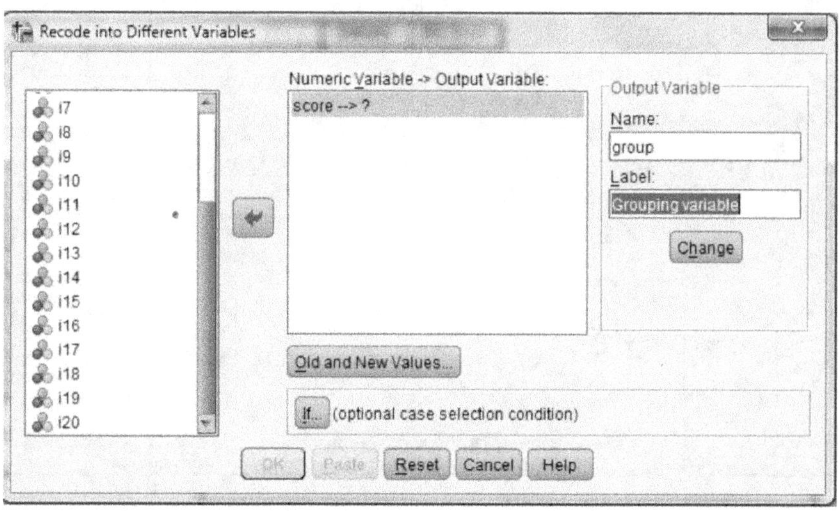

Figure 2.31 Recode Into Different Variables dialogue box for score.

By clicking the **Change** button, we will then obtain the window in Figure 2.32.

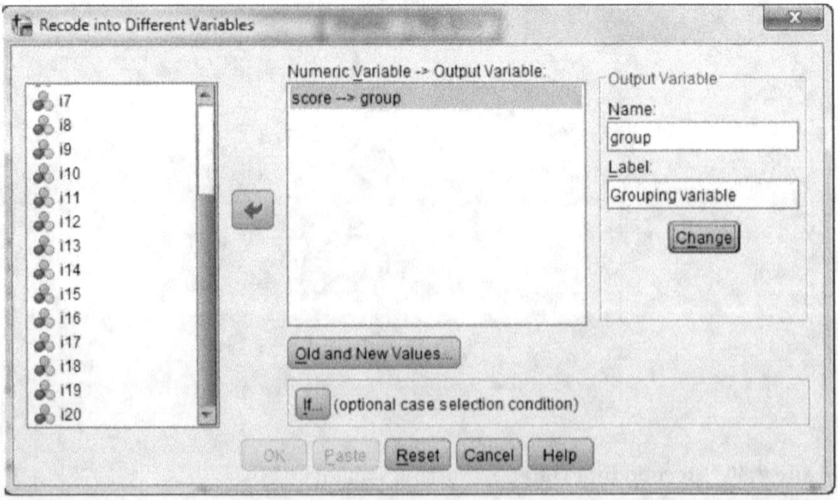

Figure 2.32 Recode Into Different Variables dialogue box for score with group variable.

Next, we click the **Old** and **New Values** button, which yields the window shown in Figure 2.33.

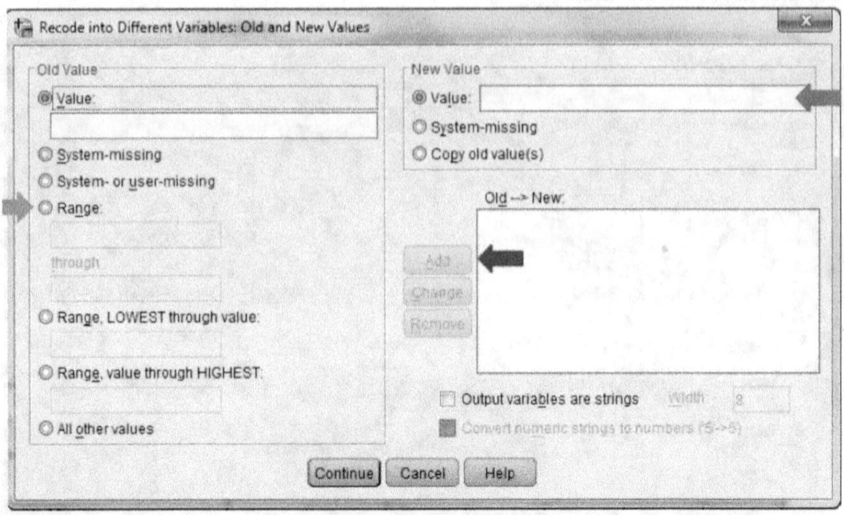

Figure 2.33 Recode Into Different Variables: Old and New Values dialogue box.

In this window, we will want to indicate which values on the score correspond to the grouping category. For instance, we will label the lowest 25% group with a 1. To do this, we will click the button next to **Range, LOWEST through value**. In the box associated with this button, we will put the 25th percentile value of 9. In the upper right hand corner of the box (identified by the red arrow) we will put the group identifier value of 1. We will then click the **Add** button (Indicated by the blue button) next to the Old –> New box in order to create the recoded variable. The window in Figure 2.34 will then appear.

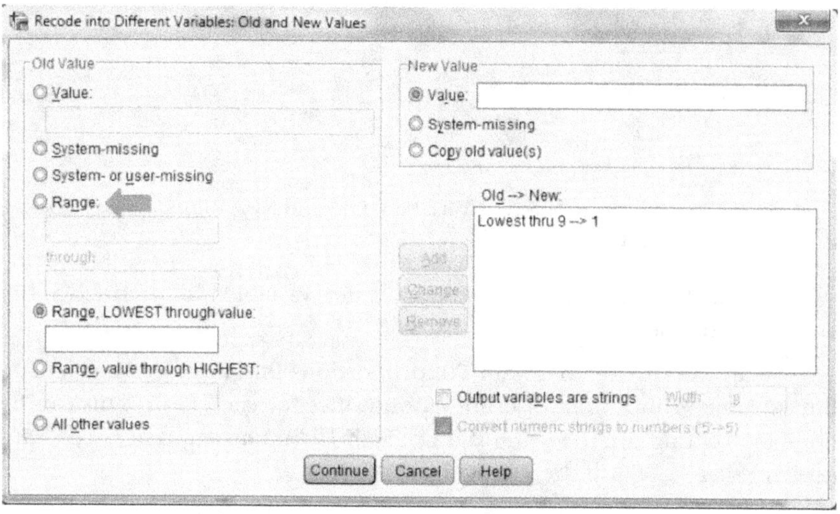

Figure 2.34 Recode Into Different Variables: Old and New Values dialogue box featuring the Range button.

We will repeat this sequence by clicking the button next to **Range**, placing 10 and 13 in the accompanying boxes, typing a **2** in the **Value** box, under New Value, and clicking **Add**. Finally, we will follow the same sequence for the upper group by clicking on the **Range, value through HIGHEST** button, typing **14** in the accompanying box, putting **3** in the box next to Value under New Value, and clicking **Add**. The window in Figure 2.35 should then appear as follows.

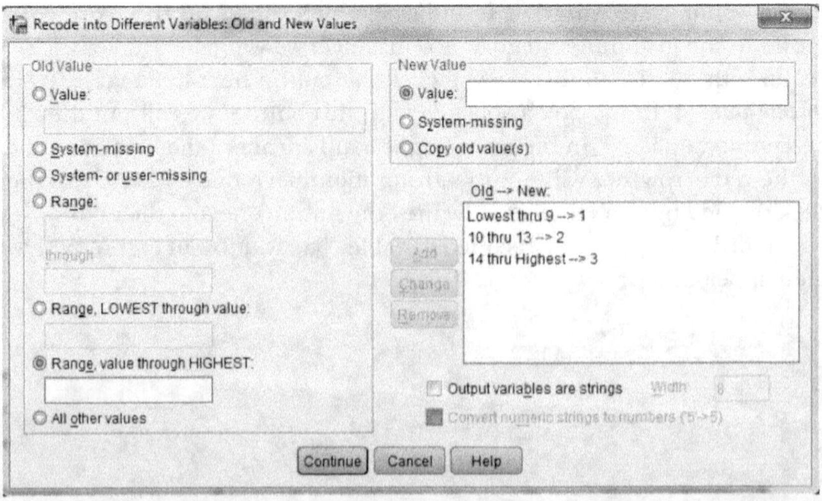

Figure 2.35 Recode Into Different Variables: Old and New Values dialogue box with all group categories included.

When we click **Continue**, followed by **OK**, a new variable will be added at the end of the dataset.

We are now ready to obtain the proportions that we need to calculate the extreme groups item discrimination values for each item. This can be done by splitting the file using **Data ► Split File** menu sequence. The window in Figure 2.36 will then appear.

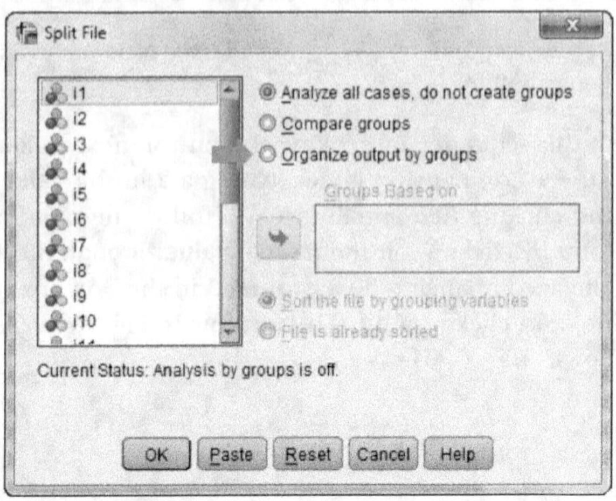

Figure 2.36 Split File dialogue box

We will then click on the **Organize output by groups** button, and place the grouping variable in the Groups Based on window, as shown in Figure 2.37.

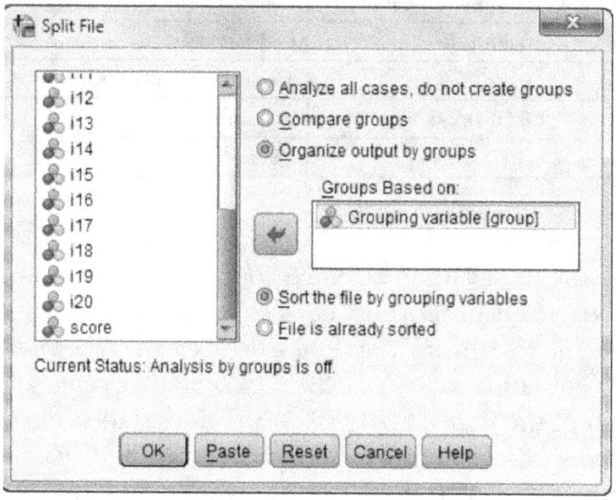

Figure 2.37 Split File dialogue box with Grouping Variable selected.

We then click **OK**, after which we will rerun the analysis described in Figures 2.6 and 2.7. The resulting output in Figure 2.38 will appear.

Descriptives								
Grouping variable = 1.00			Grouping variable = 2.00			Grouping variable = 3.00		
Descriptive Statistics			**Descriptive Statistics**			**Descriptive Statistics**		
	N	Mean		*N*	Mean		*N*	Mean
i1	677	.76	i1	804	.97	i1	519	1.00
i2	677	.38	i2	804	.64	i2	519	.86
i3	677	.22	i3	804	.53	i3	519	.83
i4	677	.21	i4	804	.29	i4	519	.51
i5	677	.20	i5	804	.27	i5	519	.69
i6	677	.39	i6	804	.75	i6	519	.93
i7	677	.31	i7	804	.64	i7	519	.89
i8	677	.25	i8	804	.52	i8	519	.85
i9	677	.62	i9	804	.85	i9	519	.94
i10	677	.59	i10	804	.89	i10	519	.98
i11	677	.37	i11	804	.52	i11	519	.78
i12	677	.27	i12	804	.45	i12	519	.78
i13	677	.11	i13	804	.16	i13	519	.40
i14	677	.68	i14	804	.88	i14	519	.98
i15	677	.55	i15	804	.86	i15	519	.97
i16	677	.36	i16	804	.62	i16	519	.85
i17	677	.37	i17	804	.61	i17	519	.84
i18	677	.21	i18	804	.34	i18	519	.57
i19	677	.17	i19	804	.32	i19	519	.67
i20	677	.18	i20	804	.32	i20	519	.62
Valid *N* (listwise)	677		Valid *N* (listwise)	804		Valid *N* (listwise)	519	

Figure 2.38 Proportion of correct responses for items, organized by group.

TABLE 2.1 Ebel's (1965) Guidelines for Interpreting Extreme Groups Item Discrimination Values

Item Discrimination Values	Label
0.40–1.00	Satisfactory
0.30–0.39	Minimal to no revision
0.20–0.29	Revision necessary
-1.00–0.19	Delete

The item discrimination values will then need to be calculated by hand. For example, for Item 1 the extreme groups item discrimination value is the difference in the proportion correct for Group 3 (the high group) and Group 1 (the low group), or 1.00 – 0.76 = 0.24. Likewise, for Item 17, the item discrimination is 0.84 – 0.37 = 0.47. Similar calculation would be made for each of the items. Ebel (1965) provides statistical criterion levels to identify items' discriminatory power based on their discrimination values. These values and corresponding labels appear in Table 2.1. One final note here is that the user will need to remember to turn off the split file command when she is done obtaining the proportions by group, otherwise all subsequent analyses will be divided by groups, creating quite a lot of unwanted output.

Biserial/Point Biserial Correlations

In addition to the extreme groups discrimination method described above, an alternative approach for estimating item discrimination is the correlation between the item and a measure of the level on the construct of interest. Typically, the total score on the instrument (e.g., number correct in the dichotomous case) is used to estimate this trait (Crocker & Algina, 1986). Two commonly used methods for estimating the relationship between a dichotomous variable, such as an item response, and a continuous variable are the biserial and point-biserial correlations. Conceptually, the two correlations differ in that the biserial is calculated under the assumption that there is a normally distributed latent variable underlying each item response, while the point-biserial treats the item response as a true dichotomy with no such latent continuous variable. Thus, the biserial correlation estimates the relationship between the underlying latent variable and total scale score, while the point-biserial correlation is simply the standard product-moment value between the score and the dichotomous item. It should be noted that when this total score includes the target item, the resulting correlation will be positively biased. For this reason, it is recommended that the score be calculated so as to exclude the target item (Crocker & Algina, 1986). Unfortunately, SPSS does not calculate the biserial correlation with ease. Thus, we focus on the point-biserial for this example. This is also the one used by most practitioners and should lead to the same conclusion about the items.

The point-biserial correlation for dichotomous items, as well as other item level statistics, can be obtained using the **Analyze ► Scale ► Reliability** menu sequence. Figure 2.39 displays the Reliability Analysis dialogue box, discussed in more detail in Chapter 3. As shown below in Figure 2.39, to obtain the point-biserial correlations for each item, we simply move the 20 items from the left hand box to the Items box on the right, as has been done in this example.

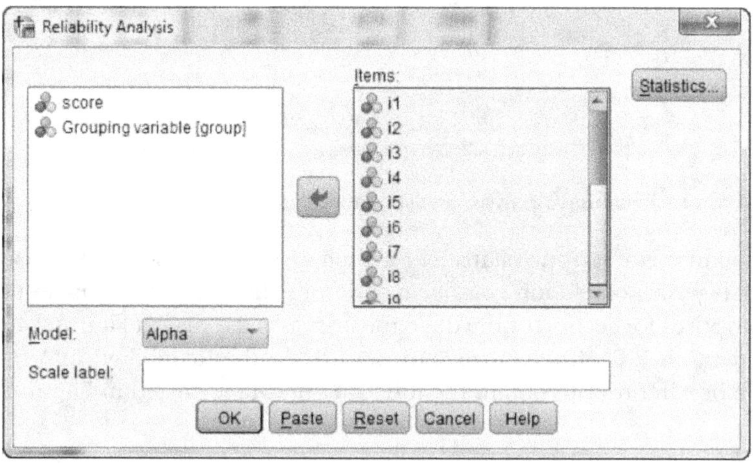

Figure 2.39 Reliability Analysis dialogue box with items selected.

In order to request the calculation of the point-biserial correlation coefficients, click the **Statistics** button.

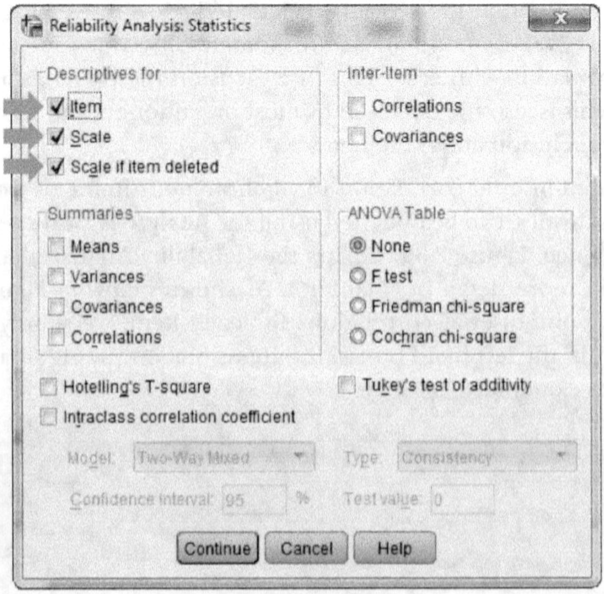

Figure 2.40 Reliability Analysis: Statistics dialogue box.

To obtain the descriptive statistics for each item and the scale, as well as the point-biserial correlation coefficients, we will check the three boxes under Descriptives for section of the dialogue box, as is the case in Figure 2.40. We can then click **Continue** in this box, and **OK** in the Reliability Analysis dialogue box in order to obtain the following output reported in Figure 2.41.

Item Statistics			
	Mean	Std. Deviation	*N*
i1	.91	.290	2000
i2	.61	.489	2000
i3	.51	.500	2000
i4	.32	.466	2000
i5	.36	.479	2000
i6	.67	.469	2000
i7	.59	.492	2000
i8	.51	.500	2000
i9	.79	.405	2000
i10	.81	.392	2000
i11	.54	.499	2000
i12	.48	.500	2000
i13	.21	.405	2000
i14	.84	.369	2000
i15	.78	.412	2000
i16	.59	.492	2000
i17	.59	.492	2000
i18	.36	.479	2000
i19	.36	.480	2000
i20	.35	.476	2000

Item-Total Statistics				
	Scale Mean if Item Deleted	Scale Variance if Item Deleted	Corrected Item-Total Correlation	Cronbach's Alpha if Item Deleted
i1	10.25	12.777	.312	.716
i2	10.55	12.239	.301	.715
i3	10.65	11.985	.367	.709
i4	10.84	12.783	.152	.728
i5	10.80	12.302	.291	.716
i6	10.48	12.091	.367	.709
i7	10.57	11.956	.385	.707
i8	10.64	11.957	.376	.708
i9	10.36	12.606	.256	.719
i10	10.35	12.376	.354	.711
i11	10.62	12.457	.227	.722
i12	10.68	12.198	.304	.715
i13	10.95	12.800	.187	.724
i14	10.32	12.627	.283	.717
i15	10.37	12.355	.339	.712
i16	10.57	12.247	.296	.715
i17	10.57	12.300	.280	.717
i18	10.80	12.638	.188	.725
i19	10.80	12.250	.305	.714
i20	10.81	12.368	.272	.717

Scale Statistics			
Mean	Variance	Std. Deviation	*N* of Items
11.16	13.507	3.675	20

Figure 2.41 Point-biserial correlation coefficients, and item and scale descriptive statistics for Dichotomous Items scale.

The resulting output includes the point-biserial correlation between each item and the corrected total with the target item excluded, as well as descriptive statistics for the individual items and the scale as a whole, an estimate of the Cronbach's Alpha reliability coefficient for the total scale, and an estimate of alpha with each item deleted. The issue of reliability and Cronbach's alpha will be discussed in much greater detail in Chapter 3. Note that in Figure 2.41 only the item and scale descriptive statistics, along with the point-biserial correlation tables are included. From this output, we can ascertain the proportion of correct responses to each item (item difficulty) by referring to the Mean column in the Item Statistics table. This table also includes the item standard deviation (Std. Deviation), and the number of respondents to each item (N). The item discrimination estimates in the form of point-biserial correlations appear in the Item-Total Statistics table (Corrected Item-Total Correlation). This latter table also includes the mean, variance, and Cronbach's Alpha of the total scale if the item were to be deleted.

To judge the quality of individual items, we can examine the reliability estimate for the scale scores when each of the items is deleted. If these item specific Alpha values are lower than the total scale value of 0.73, we can conclude that the item contributes positively to the overall consistency of the scale. On the other hand, when the Alpha value for the item deleted is higher than for the total scale (or, 0.73 in this case), we would conclude that the item might actually be detracting from the overall consistency of the scale. In such cases, these items also have lower item discrimination (point-biserial correlation) values.

In this example, Item 1 (among others) appears to contribute positively toward the overall reliability, because the item level value of 0.716 is lower than the total of 0.726. Only for Item 4 did the reliability improve (albeit very slightly) when the item was deleted from the scale. However, it would be unwise of the scale developer to delete an item solely based on the information obtained from an empirical item analysis. Both content and numerical information should be considered when adding and deleting items. References exist (e.g., Haladyna, 1999) for discussion on developing quality items using multiple sources of information.

The previously described Reliability command sequence can also be used with ordinal data, such as the Likert Scale responses described above and seen below with sample results.

Item Statistics			
	Mean	Std. Deviation	*N*
V1	4.12	.550	1533
V2	3.75	.686	1533
V3	4.00	.573	1533
V4	3.99	.608	1533
V5	4.00	.579	1533
V6	4.06	.545	1533
V7	3.95	.665	1533
V8	3.89	.636	1533
V9	3.90	.622	1533
V10	3.80	.678	1533
V11	3.94	.616	1533
V12	4.06	.586	1533
V13	3.94	.675	1533
V14	3.80	.743	1533
V15	4.04	.593	1533
V16	3.79	.741	1533
V17	3.86	.696	1533
V18	3.60	.776	1533
V19	4.01	.603	1533
V20	3.85	.695	1533

Item-Total Statistics				
	Scale Mean if Item Deleted	Scale Variance if Item Deleted	Corrected Item-Total Correlation	Cronbach's Alpha if Item Deleted
V1	74.21	60.893	.589	.916
V2	74.58	59.671	.577	.916
V3	74.33	60.273	.635	.915
V4	74.34	60.113	.612	.915
V5	74.33	60.158	.641	.915
V6	74.27	60.839	.601	.916
V7	74.38	59.377	.628	.915
V8	74.44	59.520	.645	.914
V9	74.43	60.238	.583	.916
V10	74.53	59.722	.579	.916
V11	74.39	59.498	.671	.914
V12	74.27	60.090	.641	.915
V13	74.39	60.480	.507	.918
V14	74.54	60.037	.492	.918
V15	74.29	59.917	.652	.914
V16	74.54	59.792	.516	.918
V17	74.47	60.350	.502	.918
V18	74.73	60.337	.441	.920
V19	74.32	59.935	.638	.915
V20	74.48	59.692	.566	.916

Scale Statistics			
Mean	Variance	Std. Deviation	*N* of Items
78.33	66.254	8.140	20

Figure 2.42 Point-biserial correlation coefficients, and item and scale descriptive statistics for Polytomous Items scale.

Interpretation of the resulting output is comparable to that for the dichotomous items. Thus we do not add information on this interpretation.

Chapter Summary

This chapter introduced some statistical procedures to conduct item analyses based on CTT. These analyses serve as a first step in the examination of the psychometric properties of scale scores. The analyses represent an easy manner in which to estimate the difficulty and discrimination parameters of items and overall reliability for internal consistency. As you have learned, the calculation of the indices is efficient and easy. We have discussed some suggested guidelines, as well, for determining item quality. This allows you, as a scale developer or user, to understand additional information about which items will remain, be revised, or excluded from the final version of an educational or psychological measure (e.g., motivation, mathematics achievement). Of course, the numeric indices are the easy part in the scale development process. Understanding what is required to revise or replace items must include discussion about content and representativeness of the skills or knowledge measured by the items and how such changes will influence the measurement of the underlying trait or ability. This is where the fun mental space that psychometricians have the opportunity to interact with the experts if various domains. We hope you enjoy playing in these spaces as well with your new knowledge of empirical item analysis. Now that we are familiar with CTT and IRT models, let us move to item analysis in Chapter 2 with these ideas in mind. We also want you to be aware that many of our datasets and code are available to download at the website for this book (https://labs.wsu.edu/psychometric/resources/).

3

Reliability

Introduction

In Chapter 1 we reviewed the basic ideas underlying classical test theory (CTT). The fundamental equation underlying CTT is

$$X = T + E, \tag{3.1}$$

where X is the observed score on a test or measure for an individual, T is the individual's true score (i.e., true ability) on the construct of interest, and E is random error. This random error encompasses all factors that might influence the observed score, other than an examinee's true ability. In Chapter 1 we also provided examples of what might encompass error, including examinee fatigue and mood, as well as environmental variation such as the temperature and noise in the room where the test is administered, and finally factors specific to the test such as the items selected for inclusion. The random nature of error leads to a number of truisms about the relationships among X, T, and E, concluding in the definition of reliability as the ratio of true score to observed score variance, or

Applied Psychometrics Using SPSS and AMOS, pages 47–73

$$\rho_{xx} = \frac{\sigma_T^2}{\sigma_T^2 + \sigma_E^2}. \quad (3.2)$$

While this definition of reliability has proven quite useful theoretically, in practice it is not possible to obtain either σ_T^2 or σ_E^2. Therefore, researchers have had to develop methods for estimating reliability using information that is available from an actual test administration. This chapter will focus on a variety of these methods, describing their theoretical underpinnings and demonstrating how to use them in actual practice with SPSS software. In addition, the reader will be provided with examples using both dichotomous and polytomous data.

Prior to describing methods for estimating reliability, we first need to consider what such estimates actually tell us. A classic definition of reliability states that it is the consistency of scores on an instrument that is given repeatedly to the same individual many times (Crocker & Algina, 1986). Of course in practice this is rarely if ever possible because (a) there would be learning effects such that one test administration would influence the next, thus changing the construct being measured, and (b) the construct itself might change naturally over time. For these reasons we must estimate reliability most often with a single or perhaps two administrations. A question of some interest is regarding what these reliability estimates actually mean. Quite often, researchers reporting reliability estimates will describe the reliability of the instrument as if it is a static value independent of the particular sample from which the data were collected. However, a more recent discussion of this issue, as well as recommendations for reporting reliability estimates, have suggested that reliability estimates (as opposed to the theoretical construct described above) must be described as being data specific (Thompson, 2003). In other words, for each sample that is given the instrument of interest, an estimate of reliability should be calculated and this estimate should be explicitly linked to that sample only, rather than reported as applying to the instrument across samples (Eason, 1991). Throughout the remainder of this chapter, we will strive to describe example results in this way.

Measures of Internal Consistency

One very common set of reliability estimates is based on relationships among individual items. More specifically, covariances among the items are used to construct a statistic that reflects consistency of measurement for the entire scale. If we consider each item, X_j to be a kind of miniature test of a common construct of interest (e.g., math achievement), then the degree to which these items are related to one another reflects the consistency of the scale as a whole (i.e., stronger inter-item correlations indicate greater overall consistency of the instrument). This logic has been used by researchers to suggest a number of such coefficients.

KR-20

Perhaps the most popular estimate of internal consistency is Cronbach's α and its dichotomous item response version, the Kuder Richardson-20 (KR-20). We will first present the special case of the KR-20 with dichotomous data and then generalize to Cronbach's α. The equation for KR-20 is:

$$\left(\frac{K}{K-1}\right)\left[1-\frac{\Sigma_{k=1}^{p}(p_k q_k)}{S_{\text{Total}}^2}\right] \tag{3.3}$$

where

K = Total number of items on the instrument
p_k = Proportion of individuals with correct response to item k
q_k = Proportion of individuals with incorrect response to item k
S_{Total}^2 = Variance of the scores on the test

Thus, each item's variance ($p_k\, q_k$) is calculated and then compared to the variance of the total test score. As mentioned above, KR-20 is really just a special case of Cronbach's α, and as such we can obtain it using the SPSS functions for computing the latter.

As an example, let's consider again the 20-item test for which we obtained item difficulty and discrimination values in Chapter 2. Remember that each item was coded as either 1 (correct) or 0 (incorrect). While in those examples we used only 10 examinees for pedagogical purposes, in this case we will estimate KR-20 for the entire sample of 2,000 examinees using SPSS. In order to obtain the estimate of total scale reliability, as well as descriptive statistics for the individual items, and an estimate of the scale reliability when a particular item is deleted, we would use the following sequence of windows in SPSS. We would first select **Analyze** from the SPSS menu bar, and then select **Scale** and **Reliability Analysis**. We will then be presented with the following window:

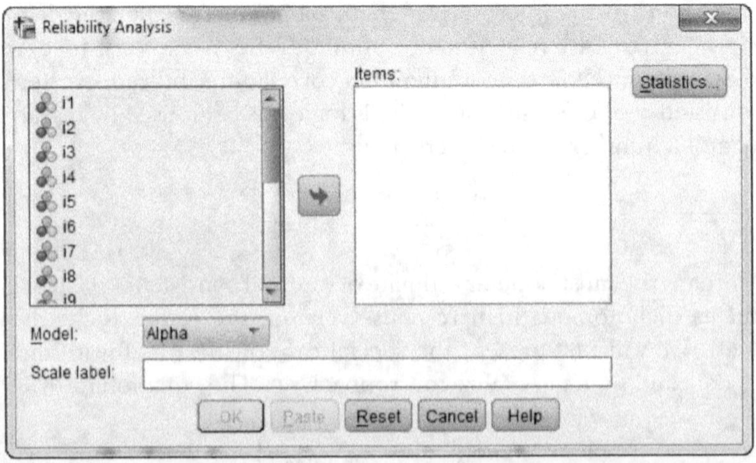

The variables in the dataset appear in the left side window. In this case, all 20 variables correspond to the 20 items of interest. In order to obtain a reliability estimate for the entire scale, we will need to move the items into the right side window, labeled Items. To do this, we simply highlight the 20 variables and then click on the arrow pointing to the Items window so that our dialogue box now looks like:

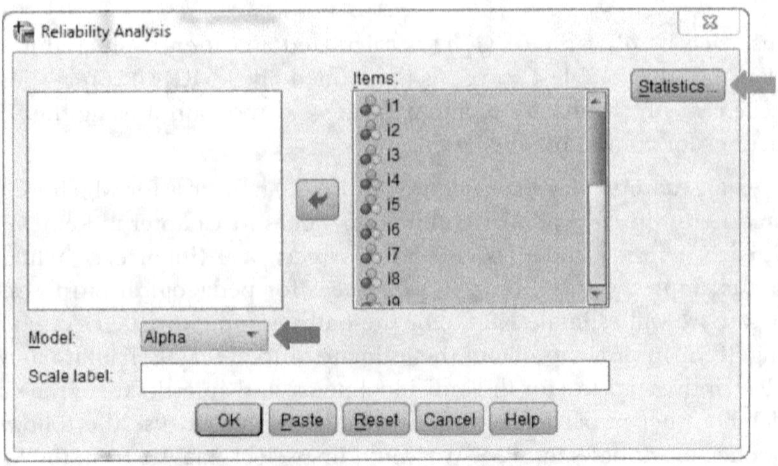

By default Cronbach's α will be calculated for us. We may wish to change the reliability estimate to be calculated, in which case we would simply click on the button indicated by the red arrow above. Among the choices are Split-half, Guttman (which provides several additional estimates of internal consistency), parallel, and strictly parallel. We will not investigate all of these in the book, but do encourage the interested reader to delve more deeply into this topic.

Once we have selected the items constituting the scale, we will then want to select the statistics of interest by clicking the **Statistics** box indicated by the green arrow. The result will be the following dialogue box.

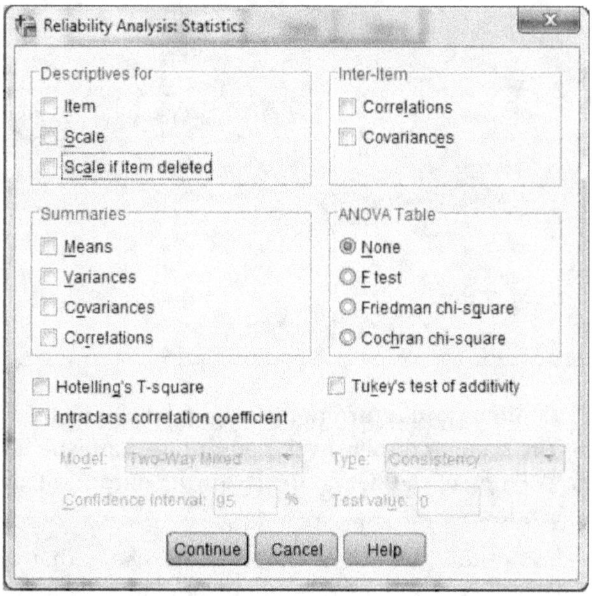

We can simply click the boxes next to each statistic that we would like to see. In general, we may want to see descriptive statistics for each item (mean and standard deviation), along with descriptive statistics for the scale, and for the scale if each item is deleted. Should we want any other statistics, we simply need to click the appropriate boxes.

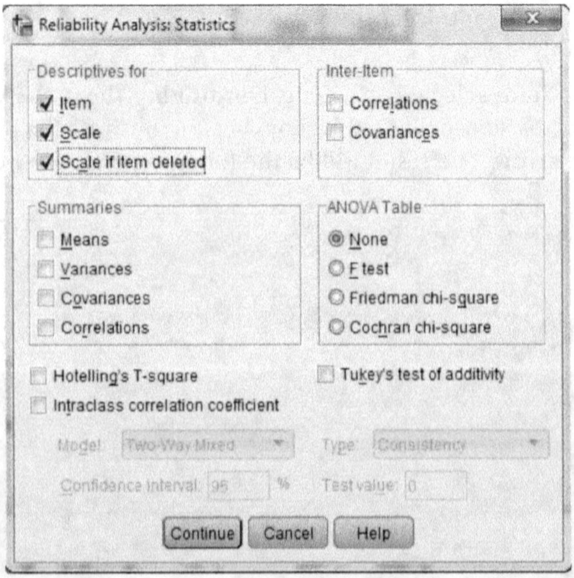

We then click **Continue** and return to the original dialogue box. If we would like a title for the scale to display in the output, we can type it in the Scale label window. We then click **OK**, and the following output will appear in the SPSS Output window.

First we should note that SPSS will paste the syntax that we could use to run the analysis, rather than the menu sequence. This syntax can be very helpful if we want to replicate the analysis at some point in the future, either with this sample or with a new set of data.

```
RELIABILITY
  /VARIABLES=i1 i2 i3 i4 i5 i6 i7 i8 i9 i10 i11 i12 i13 i14 i15
i16 i17 i18 i19 i20
  /SCALE('20 Item Test') ALL
  /MODEL=ALPHA
  /STATISTICS=DESCRIPTIVE SCALE
  /SUMMARY=TOTAL.
```

Reliability

Scale: 20 Item Test

Case Processing Summary

		N	%
Cases	Valid	2000	100.0
	Excluded[a]	0	.0
	Total	2000	100.0

[a] Listwise deletion based on all variables in the procedure.

Reliability Statistics	
Cronbach's Alpha	*N* of Items
.726	20

Item Statistics			
	Mean	Std. Deviation	*N*
i1	.91	.290	2000
i2	.61	.489	2000
i3	.51	.500	2000
i4	.32	.466	2000
i5	.36	.479	2000
i6	.67	.469	2000
i7	.59	.492	2000
i8	.51	.500	2000
i9	.79	.405	2000
i10	.81	.392	2000
i11	.54	.499	2000
i12	.48	.500	2000
i13	.21	.405	2000
i14	.84	.369	2000
i15	.78	.412	2000
i16	.59	.492	2000
i17	.59	.492	2000
i18	.36	.479	2000
i19	.36	.480	2000
i20	.35	.476	2000

Item-Total Statistics				
	Scale Mean if Item Deleted	Scale Variance if Item Deleted	Corrected Item-Total Correlation	Cronbach's Alpha if Item Deleted
i1	10.25	12.777	.312	.716
i2	10.55	12.239	.301	.715
i3	10.65	11.985	.367	.709
i4	10.84	12.783	.152	.728
i5	10.80	12.302	.291	.716
i6	10.48	12.091	.367	.709
i7	10.57	11.956	.385	.707
i8	10.64	11.957	.376	.708
i9	10.36	12.606	.256	.719
i10	10.35	12.376	.354	.711
i11	10.62	12.457	.227	.722
i12	10.68	12.198	.304	.715
i13	10.95	12.800	.187	.724
i14	10.32	12.627	.283	.717
i15	10.37	12.355	.339	.712
i16	10.57	12.247	.296	.715
i17	10.57	12.300	.280	.717
i18	10.80	12.638	.188	.725
i19	10.80	12.250	.305	.714
i20	10.81	12.368	.272	.717

Scale Statistics			
Mean	Variance	Std. Deviation	*N* of Items
11.16	13.507	3.675	20

Based on these results we would conclude that for this sample, the KR-20 reliability estimate (labeled as Cronbach Coefficient Alpha) of the test is approximately 0.73. In addition to providing the KR-20 value, SPSS also produces descriptive statistics for each of the items, including the number of examinees (*N*), the proportion of 1's (Mean), and the standard deviation for each item (Std. Deviation). In the table labeled "Item-Total Statistics," we see information about how the scale mean, the scale variance, and KR-20 (alpha) would change were each item to be removed from the scale. In addition, this table also provides the Corrected Item-Total Correlation, which is simply the correlation between the total test score (sum of the items) with the item removed, and the item response itself. As a side note, this sum of the other items answered correctly is frequently referred to as the "rest score," meaning it is the score obtained from the rest of the items. The higher this correlation, the more strongly associated the individual item is with the construct being measured by the other items. In addition, the value of alpha is calculated including the other items. For example, were Item 1 to be excluded from the scale, the value of KR-20 (Alpha column) would be 0.72. We can use this table to ascertain whether any of the items have a markedly deleterious impact on the overall reliability of the scale with this sample. If KR-20 increases substantially when a single item is removed, as compared to when all items are included, we might conclude that this item is potentially problematic and should be investigated further to determine if it exhibits any anomalies with regard to difficulty or discrimination, or if it seems to have any wording problems. In this example, none of the items appear to be problematic in this regard. In general, with a large number of items, it will be unlikely that we will find removal of a single item to have a dramatic impact on the estimate of KR-20. The final table in this set of output includes descriptive statistics for the total scale score.

In addition to obtaining a point estimate for KR-20, it is also possible to construct a confidence interval for this value, thus providing us with greater information about the population parameter itself. In other words, much as with a confidence interval for the mean, we will be able to say that we are 95% certain the actual reliability in the population from which the sample was drawn is between the upper and lower bounds of the confidence interval. There are a number of proposed methods for calculating these intervals, including approaches based on transforming α so that it is approximately normally distributed in which case standard critical values can be used to construct the interval (Bonett, 2002; Hakstain & Whalen, 1976).

Other researchers have developed methods that avoid the transformation of α, including an approach by Feldt (1965) based on the *F* statistical distribution, two variants of this *F* approach (Koning & Franses, 2003), and a method developed by Iacobucci and Duchanchek (2003) that uses item covariances. Maydeu-Olivares, Coffman, and Hartmann (2007) developed a method that does not require any assumptions about the distribution of α. Using a simulation study, they found that their asymptotically distribution free (ADF) approach might be optimal in many situations. We can obtain Feldt's confidence interval for α based upon the *F* statistic by first accessing the **Reliability** window under **Analyze ▶ Scale**, and moving the items to the right hand box, as usual.

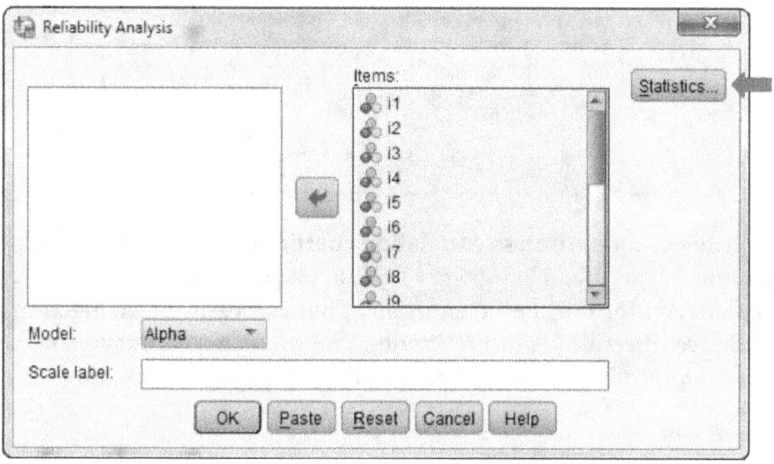

We will then click on the **Statistics** box to obtain the following window.

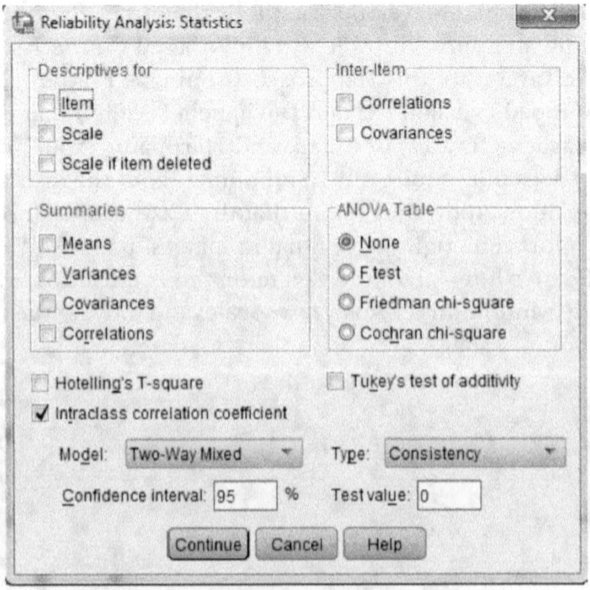

We will select the **Intraclass correlation coefficient** box, with the **Two-Way Mixed** model, and the **Consistency** type, as shown here. The default confidence interval for the coefficient is 95%, but can easily be changed in the Confidence interval box in the window. We then click **Continue**, and then **OK** on the preceding window. The resulting output appears below.

```
RELIABILITY
  /VARIABLES=i1 i2 i3 i4 i5 i6 i7 i8 i9 i10 i11 i12 i13 i14 i15
i16 i17 i18 i19 i20
  /SCALE('ALL VARIABLES') ALL
  /MODEL=ALPHA
  /ICC=MODEL(MIXED) TYPE(CONSISTENCY) CIN=95 TESTVAL=0.
```

Reliability

Notes		
Output Created		28-AUG-2014 12:32:01
Comments		
Input	Data	C:\research\SPSS psychometric book\data\ex2.sav
	Active Dataset	DataSet7
	Filter	<none>
	Weight	<none>
	Split File	<none>
	N of Rows in Working Data File	2000
	Matrix Input	

Missing Value Handling	Definition of Missing	User-defined missing values are treated as missing.
	Cases Used	Statistics are based on all cases with valid data for all variables in the procedure.
Syntax		RELIABILITY /VARIABLES=i1 i2 i3 i4 i5 i6 i7 i8 i9 i10 i11 i12 i13 i14 i15 i16 i17 i18 i19 i20 /SCALE('ALL VARIABLES') ALL /MODEL=ALPHA /ICC=MODEL(MIXED) TYPE(CONSISTENCY) CIN=95 TESTVAL=0.
Resources	Processor Time	00:00:00.00
	Elapsed Time	00:00:00.03

Scale: ALL VARIABLES

Case Processing Summary			
		N	%
Cases	Valid	2000	100.0
	Excluded[a]	0	.0
	Total	2000	100.0
[a] Listwise deletion based on all variables in the procedure.			

Reliability Statistics	
Cronbach's Alpha	*N* of Items
.726	20

Intraclass Correlation Coefficient

	Intraclass Correlation[b]	95% Confidence Interval: Lower Bound	95% Confidence Interval: Upper Bound	F Test With True Value 0: Value	df1	df2	Sig
Single Measures	.117[a]	.108	.126	3.652	1999	37981	.000
Average Measures	.726[c]	.708	.743	3.652	1999	37981	.000

Two-way mixed effects model where people effects are random and measures effects are fixed.

[a] The estimator is the same, whether the interaction effect is present or not.
[b] Type C intraclass correlation coefficients using a consistency definition. The between-measure variance is excluded from the denominator variance.
[c] This estimate is computed assuming the interaction effect is absent, because it is not estimable otherwise.

Based on these results, we are 95% confident that the actual KR-20 value for the population from which our sample was drawn lies between approximately 0.71 and 0.74. The interested reader is encouraged to learn more about the various methods for calculating these confidence intervals, as well as the various comparisons of these approaches in order to make a decision regarding which seems optimal for a given application.

If we do not wish to make any assumptions about the distribution of Cronbach's α, rather than Feldt's method demonstrated above, we can use the bootstrap approach instead. In general, the bootstrap methodology involves the resampling of individuals from our actual sample, with replacement in order to create *B* samples of size *N*, where *B* is typically a large number (e.g., 1,000 or more). For each of the *B* samples, the statistic of interest (e.g., α) is calculated, thereby creating a sampling distribution for the statistic. In this case, the standard deviation is then calculated as an estimate of the standard error for the statistic, which can then be used in constructing the confidence interval. The following SPSS macro was written by David Marso for calculating the bootstrap confidence interval for Cronbach's α.

```
*Author:David Marso.
/*************************************************************/
/* SPSS Macro:                                               */
/* Bootstrapped Confidence Interval for Cronbach's Alpha     */
/* Requires three arguments:                                 */
/* NSAMP: the number of boootstrap samples                   */
/* VARLIST:The set of variables comprising the scale         */
/* INTWID : The confidence interval (95 = 95% CI )           */
/* Example : !CA_BOOT NSAMP 2000                             */
/* / VARLIST V1 TO V10                                       */
/* / INTWID 95                                               */
/*                                                           */
/* NOTE: This macro creates and deletes two files in the     */
/* current working directory: 'c:\research\SPSS psychometric
   book\' and                                                */
/* You will need to change this directory to match the
   directory on your                                         */
/* computer where you keep the data. Note that it appears in
   several                                                   */
/* locations in the macro                                    */
/* 'BOOTSAMP.SAV'. The working data file is saved            */
/* as 'RAWDATA.SAV' and then retrieved so it becomes         */
/* the active file after the macro has completed.            */
/*************************************************************/

DEFINE !CA_BOOT (NSAMP !CHAREND('/')
/VARLIST !CHAREND('/')
/ INTWID !CMDEND ).

*0 Save original data after tagging ID *.
COMPUTE BOOTID=$CASENUM.
SAVE OUTFILE 'c:\research\SPSS psychometric book\RAWDATA.SAV'.

*1 Find the sample size and create a MACRO for it *.
COMPUTE NOBREAK=1.
AGGREGATE OUTFILE * / PRESORTED / BREAK=NOBREAK / N=N.
```

```
WRITE OUTFILE 'c:\research\SPSS psychometric book\outfile.out'
/ 'DEFINE !NCASE ( ) ',N,' !ENDDEFINE '.
EXECUTE.
SET ERRORS OFF.
INCLUDE 'c:\research\SPSS psychometric book\outfile.out'.
SET ERRORS ON.

*2 Build bootstrap samples *.
VECTOR #SUBJ( !NCASE).
LOOP SAMPLE=1 TO !NSAMP.
* Initialize a vector of case indicators *.
+ LOOP #I=1 TO !NCASE.
+ COMPUTE #SUBJ(#I)=0.
+ END LOOP.

*3 Mark each case the number of times it must be sampled *.
+ LOOP #ITER=1 TO !NCASE.
+ COMPUTE INDEX=TRUNC(UNIFORM(!NCASE))+1.
+ COMPUTE #SUBJ(INDEX)=#SUBJ(INDEX)+1.
+ END LOOP.

*4 Write out the cases for each bootstrap sample and a weight *.
+ LOOP BOOTID=1 TO !NCASE.
+ DO IF #SUBJ(BOOTID) > 0.
+ COMPUTE BOOTWGT=#SUBJ(BOOTID) .
+ XSAVE OUTFILE 'c:\research\SPSS psychometric book\BOOTSAMP
.SAV' / KEEP SAMPLE BOOTID BOOTWGT.
+ END IF.
+ END LOOP.
END LOOP.
EXECUTE.

*5 Attach the original data using a TABLE lookup *.
GET FILE 'c:\research\SPSS psychometric book\BOOTSAMP.SAV'.
SORT CASES BY BOOTID.
MATCH FILES FILE * / TABLE 'c:\research\SPSS psychometric book\
RAWDATA.SAV' / BY BOOTID.

*6 Weight by the number of times cases is in each sample *.
WEIGHT BY BOOTWGT.

*7 Compute Coefficient Alpha for each sample *.
COMPUTE SCALE = SUM(!VARLIST).
AGGREGATE OUTFILE *
/ BREAK SAMPLE
/ !VARLIST SCALE=SD(!VARLIST SCALE).
DO REPEAT V=!VARLIST SCALE.
```

```
COMPUTE V=V**2.
END REPEAT.

COMPUTE NV=NVALID(!VARLIST).
COMPUTE C_ALPHA =(NV/(NV-1))*(1-(SUM(!VARLIST)/SCALE)).

* 8 Extract the lower and upper confidence limits for Alpha *.
SORT CASES BY C_ALPHA.
COMPUTE #=#+1.
COMPUTE CPCT=#/!NSAMP.
COMPUTE #IW=!INTWID/100.
SELECT IF (CPCT <=(1-#IW)/2) OR (CPCT >= 1-(1-#IW)/2 ).
COMPUTE TAG=CPCT > (1-#IW)/2.
MATCH FILES FILE *
/ FIRST=TOP / LAST=BOT
/ BY TAG
/ KEEP C_ALPHA CPCT TAG.
SELECT IF (NOT (TAG) AND BOT) OR (TAG AND TOP).
DO IF TAG.
COMPUTE LCL=LAG(C_ALPHA).
COMPUTE UCL=C_ALPHA.
PRINT /!QUOTE(!CONCAT(!INTWID,"% CI for Cronbach's Alpha"))
/!QUOTE(!CONCAT("Based on ",!NSAMP," Samples")) /"LCL=",LCL,'
UCL=',UCL .
END IF.
EXECUTE.
SELECT IF TOP.
EXECUTE.
ERASE FILE 'c:\research\SPSS psychometric book\BOOTSAMP.SAV'.
ERASE FILE 'c:\research\SPSS psychometric book\outfile.out'.
GET FILE 'c:\research\SPSS psychometric book\RAWDATA.SAV'.
!ENDDEFINE.
```

In order to run the macro, we first need to type it into an SPSS syntax window, which we can open under **File ► New ► Syntax**. We then highlight the macro, and click **Run ► All** from the syntax window menu bar. Once the macro has been compiled, we would then type the following line at the bottom of the syntax window, below the macro itself.

```
!CA_BOOT NSAMP=1000 / VARLIST i1 TO i20 / INTWID 95 .
```

We then highlight this line, and select **Run ► Selection** in the menu bar. The following output will appear.

```
95% CI for Cronbach's Alpha
Based on 1000 Samples
LCL= .71 UCL= .74
```

This final result is extremely close to the interval provided using the Feldt method, and presented above, suggesting that the data do conform to the assumption underlying the parametric method.

Cronbach's α for Ordinal Data

As mentioned previously, KR-20 is a special case of Cronbach's α when the item responses are dichotomous. When the items are polytomous in nature, we can express α in a more general way as

$$\left(\frac{K}{K-1}\right)\left[1-\frac{\Sigma_{k=1}^{p} S_k^2}{S_{\text{Total}}^2}\right] \quad (3.4)$$

where

K = Total number of items on the instrument
S_k^2 = Variance of item k

Note that this equation is really no different than for the KR-20. In that case, the variance estimate for an item was simply pq. Using SPSS, we can obtain a for polytomous data in much the same way that we did for the dichotomous items. In order to demonstrate the estimation of a in this context, we will use the polytomous data that was first introduced in Chapter 2. In this example, we had data for 20 items from respondents who were asked to rate the current President of the United States on a variety of job tasks, with ratings being as follows: *Strongly Disagree* (1), *Disagree* (2), *Neutral* (3), *Agree* (4), and *Strongly Agree* (5).

In using such ordinal polytomous items, we must ensure that the nature of the questions is unidirectional. The reader is encouraged to refer to Chapter 6 to learn about this issue, and the need to recode items to ensure that they all have response patterns in the same direction. Assuming that the items are indeed unidirectional, we can use the reliability function in SPSS once again to obtain an estimate of α. The command sequence in SPSS will be identical to what we saw with the dichotomous data. The resulting output appears below:

```
RELIABILITY
  /VARIABLES=V1 V2 V3 V4 V5 V6 V7 V8 V9 V10 V11 V12 V13 V14 V15
V16 V17 V18 V19 V20
  /SCALE('Presidential items') ALL
  /MODEL=ALPHA
  /STATISTICS=DESCRIPTIVE SCALE
  /SUMMARY=TOTAL.
```

Reliability		
Notes		
Output Created		26-AUG-2014 09:05:34
Comments		
Input	Data	C:\research\SPSS psychometric book\data\poly1.sav
	Active Dataset	DataSet3
	Filter	<none>
	Weight	<none>
	Split File	<none>
	N of Rows in Working Data File	1533
	Matrix Input	
Missing Value Handling	Definition of Missing	User-defined missing values are treated as missing.
	Cases Used	Statistics are based on all cases with valid data for all variables in the procedure.
Syntax		RELIABILITY /VARIABLES=V1 V2 V3 V4 V5 V6 V7 V8 V9 V10 V11 V12 V13 V14 V15 V16 V17 V18 V19 V20 /SCALE('Presidential items') ALL /MODEL=ALPHA /STATISTICS=DESCRIPTIVE SCALE /SUMMARY=TOTAL.
Resources	Processor Time	00:00:00.03
	Elapsed Time	00:00:00.04

Scale: Presidential items			
Case Processing Summary			
		N	%
Cases	Valid	1533	100.0
	Excluded[a]	0	.0
	Total	1533	100.0

[a] Listwise deletion based on all variables in the procedure.

Reliability Statistics	
Cronbach's Alpha	*N* of Items
.920	20

Item Statistics			
	Mean	Std. Deviation	*N*
V1	4.12	.550	1533
V2	3.75	.686	1533
V3	4.00	.573	1533
V4	3.99	.608	1533
V5	4.00	.579	1533
V6	4.06	.545	1533
V7	3.95	.665	1533
V8	3.89	.636	1533
V9	3.90	.622	1533
V10	3.80	.678	1533
V11	3.94	.616	1533
V12	4.06	.586	1533
V13	3.94	.675	1533
V14	3.80	.743	1533
V15	4.04	.593	1533
V16	3.79	.741	1533
V17	3.86	.696	1533
V18	3.60	.776	1533
V19	4.01	.603	1533
V20	3.85	.695	1533

Item-Total Statistics				
	Scale Mean if Item Deleted	Scale Variance if Item Deleted	Corrected Item-Total Correlation	Cronbach's Alpha if Item Deleted
V1	74.21	60.893	.589	.916
V2	74.58	59.671	.577	.916
V3	74.33	60.273	.635	.915
V4	74.34	60.113	.612	.915
V5	74.33	60.158	.641	.915
V6	74.27	60.839	.601	.916
V7	74.38	59.377	.628	.915
V8	74.44	59.520	.645	.914
V9	74.43	60.238	.583	.916
V10	74.53	59.722	.579	.916
V11	74.39	59.498	.671	.914
V12	74.27	60.090	.641	.915
V13	74.39	60.480	.507	.918
V14	74.54	60.037	.492	.918
V15	74.29	59.917	.652	.914
V16	74.54	59.792	.516	.918
V17	74.47	60.350	.502	.918
V18	74.73	60.337	.441	.920
V19	74.32	59.935	.638	.915
V20	74.48	59.692	.566	.916

Scale Statistics			
Mean	Variance	Std. Deviation	*N* of Items
78.33	66.254	8.140	20

We can see that the reliability estimate of this measure for the sample is quite high, at 0.92. In addition, there are not any items which, when removed, yield a markedly higher or lower value of α. We might also find it helpful to obtain the 95% confidence interval for α, using the menu command sequence previously described. The results appear below.

Intraclass Correlation Coefficient							
		95% Confidence Interval		*F* Test With True Value 0			
	Intraclass Correlation[b]	Lower Bound	Upper Bound	Value	df1	df2	Sig
Single Measures	.364[a]	.347	.383	12.470	1532	29108	.000
Average Measures	.920[c]	.914	.926	12.470	1532	29108	.000

Two-way mixed effects model where people effects are random and measures effects are fixed.

[a] The estimator is the same, whether the interaction effect is present or not.

[b] Type C intraclass correlation coefficients using a consistency definition. The between-measure variance is excluded from the denominator variance.

[c] This estimate is computed assuming the interaction effect is absent, because it is not estimable otherwise.

The resultant output shows that for all methods of calculating the intervals, the population value of α lies roughly between 0.914 and 0.926. We can also obtain the bootstrap confidence interval for a using the syntax demonstrated previously.

```
95% CI for Cronbach's Alpha
Based on 1000 Samples
LCL= .91 UCL= .93
```

Once again, the bootstrap confidence interval is very similar to that based on the *F* statistic.

Split-Half Reliability

Split-half reliability estimation is unlike the internal consistency approach just described in that it focuses on larger units of analysis than the individual item. To use this method, one administers the instrument to a sample and then takes the completed items and divides them into two equally sized halves. The intent is to make the two halves equivalent in terms of factors that might influence item response, such as item difficulty, content, and location in the instrument itself (i.e., near the front, in the middle, or near the end). These two halves are then scored individually, and the correlation between the scores is calculated. This correlation can be viewed as an estimate of the reliability of the two halves in that we assume they represent parallel forms of the same measure. However, this correlation reflects the reliability estimate for an instrument that is half as long as the actual one to be used, because we have split it in half. Therefore, we need to make a correction to this value to reflect reliability for the full instrument with our sample. The correction, which is known as the Spearman–Brown correction is calculated as:

$$SB = \frac{2r_{H1,H2}}{1+r_{H,1H2}}, \tag{3.5}$$

where $r_{H1,H2}$ is the correlation coefficient between the two halves.

Before examining how to calculate the split-half reliability estimate using the Spearman–Brown formula in SPSS, we need to consider strategies for creating the two halves. One very commonly used approach is to divide the instrument into odd and even components. A variation of this approach requires the researcher to first order the items based on their difficulty value and then assign them into odd and even halves, working down the list of item difficulty values. A final method is to simply randomly assign items to one half or the other without regard to their position in the test. No one approach has been shown to be optimal, and the odd–even split tends to be very popular, perhaps in part because it is easy to carry out, is likely to be random with respect to item difficulty, and ensures that items from all parts of the test (beginning, middle, and end) are included in both halves. This last issue would be particularly important for longer times assessments where fatigue and speededness may have very real impacts on test performance.

In the following example with SPSS, we will use the 20 dichotomous item measure discussed above, splitting the items into odd and even halves. SPSS has a built in function for estimating the split-half reliability coefficient, using the Spearman–Brown correction. This function can be found in the reliability window where we began this chapter, with Cronbach's Alpha.

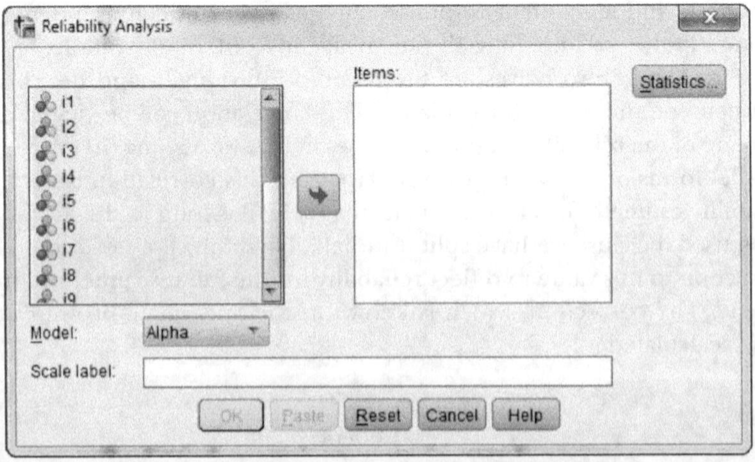

We must move the items from the left window to the right in the dialogue box. We can then change the model to Split-half using the pull down menu, as in the example dialogue box below.

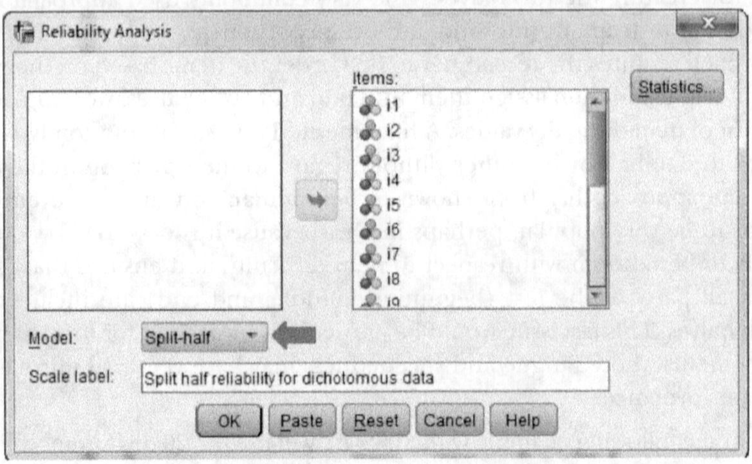

By default, the SPSS command will divide the instrument into the first half and second half when calculating the scores to be correlated. Below, we will see how this can be changed using SPSS syntax. To begin, however, we will use the default settings. Once we have selected the **Split-half** model, we can click **OK** to produce the following output.

```
DATASET ACTIVATE DataSet1.
GET
  FILE='C:\research\SPSS psychometric book\data\ex2.sav'.
```

```
DATASET NAME DataSet5 WINDOW=FRONT.
RELIABILITY
  /VARIABLES=i1 i2 i3 i4 i5 i6 i7 i8 i9 i10 i11 i12 i13 i14 i15
i16 i17 i18 i19 i20
  /SCALE('Split half reliability for dichotomous data') ALL
  /MODEL=SPLIT.
```

Reliability		
Notes		
Output Created		26-AUG-2014 12:18:27
Comments		
Input	Data	C:\research\SPSS psychometric book\data\ex2.sav
	Active Dataset	DataSet5
	Filter	<none>
	Weight	<none>
	Split File	<none>
	N of Rows in Working Data File	2000
	Matrix Input	C:\research\SPSS psychometric book\data\ex2.sav
Missing Value Handling	Definition of Missing	User-defined missing values are treated as missing.
	Cases Used	Statistics are based on all cases with valid data for all variables in the procedure.
Syntax		RELIABILITY /VARIABLES=i1 i2 i3 i4 i5 i6 i7 i8 i9 i10 i11 i12 i13 i14 i15 i16 i17 i18 i19 i20 /SCALE('Split half reliability for dichotomous data') ALL /MODEL=SPLIT.
Resources	Processor Time	00:00:00.02
	Elapsed Time	00:00:00.01

```
[DataSet5] C:\research\SPSS psychometric book\data\ex2.sav
```

Scale: Split half reliability for dichotomous data			
Case Processing Summary			
		N	%
Cases	Valid	2000	100.0
	Excluded[a]	0	.0
	Total	2000	100.0

[a] Listwise deletion based on all variables in the procedure.

Reliability Statistics			
Cronbach's Alpha	Part 1	Value	.624
		N of Items	10[a]
	Part 2	Value	.536
		N of Items	10[b]
	Total *N* of Items		20
Correlation Between Forms			.535
Spearman–Brown Coefficient	Equal Length		.697
	Unequal Length		.697
Guttman Split-Half Coefficient			.697

[a] The items are: i1, i2, i3, i4, i5, i6, i7, i8, i9, i10.
[b] The items are: i11, i12, i13, i14, i15, i16, i17, i18, i19, i20.

From these results, we see that the Spearman–Brown Split-half reliability coefficient is 0.697, with a correlation between the two halves of 0.535. Within each half, the Cronbach's Alpha values were 0.624 and 0.536, respectively. As can be seen in the footnotes at the bottom of the table, "form" A of the test consisted of items 1–10, and "form" B consisted of items 11–20. Dividing the test in this manner is not typically optimal, because in some cases items are ordered from easy to difficult (e.g., intelligence tests), and for longer tests later items may not receive the full attention of the examinees, or may even not be completed by all examinees. The odd–even splitting strategy is much more often used, for reasons cited above. In order to divide the test in this fashion and then calculate the Split-half reliability coefficient, we can take the syntax provided by SPSS and appearing above for the default approach, and edit it to the following.

```
DATASET ACTIVATE DataSet1.
GET
FILE='C:\research\SPSS psychometric book\data\ex2.sav'.
DATASET NAME DataSet5 WINDOW=FRONT.
RELIABILITY
/VARIABLES=i1 i2 i3 i4 i5 i6 i7 i8 i9 i10 i11 i12 i13 i14 i15
i16 i17 i18 i19 i20
/SCALE('Split half reliability for dichotomous data') ALL
/MODEL=SPLIT.
```

The difference in this syntax and the default is that we manually list the odd items first, followed by the even ones. Thus, when SPSS uses the first half of the items in the list to create the first half scale, it is actually using the odd items.

Reliability		
Notes		
Output Created		26-AUG-2014 12:47:07
Comments		
Input	Data	C:\research\SPSS psychometric book\data\ex2.sav
	Active Dataset	DataSet5
	Filter	<none>
	Weight	<none>
	Split File	<none>
	N of Rows in Working Data File	2000
	Matrix Input	C:\research\SPSS psychometric book\data\ex2.sav
Missing Value Handling	Definition of Missing	User-defined missing values are treated as missing.
	Cases Used	Statistics are based on all cases with valid data for all variables in the procedure.
Syntax		RELIABILITY /VARIABLES=i1 i2 i3 i4 i5 i6 i7 i8 i9 i10 i11 i12 i13 i14 i15 i16 i17 i18 i19 i20 /SCALE('Split half reliability for dichotomous data') i1 i3 i5 i7 i9 i11 i13 i15 i17 i19 i2 i4 i6 i8 i10 i12 i14 i16 i18 i20/ /MODEL=SPLIT.
Resources	Processor Time	00:00:00.00
	Elapsed Time	00:00:00.01

Scale: Split half reliability for dichotomous data			
Case Processing Summary			
		N	%
Cases	Valid	2000	100.0
	Excluded[a]	0	.0
	Total	2000	100.0

[a] Listwise deletion based on all variables in the procedure.

Reliability Statistics			
Cronbach's Alpha	Part 1	Value	.566
		N of Items	10[a]
	Part 2	Value	.555
		N of Items	10[b]
	Total *N* of Items		20
Correlation Between Forms			.599
Spearman–Brown Coefficient	Equal Length		.749
	Unequal Length		.749
Guttman Split-Half Coefficient			.749

[a] The items are: i1, i2, i3, i4, i5, i6, i7, i8, i9, i10.
[b] The items are: i11, i12, i13, i14, i15, i16, i17, i18, i19, i20.

We can see from these results that adjusting the correlation using the Spearman–Brown equation made quite a difference in our estimate of reliability as compared to a test that is only half as long. The SB value of 0.75 is slightly larger than the Cronbach's α of 0.72 that we discussed earlier, and higher than the default Split-half value as well.

Test–Retest Reliability

In some applications, a researcher is particularly interested in the temporal stability of scores from an instrument. In other words, they would like to know whether individuals administered a measure at one point in time will tend to produce similar scores at a later point in time. An index measuring this relationship over time is often referred to as a coefficient of stability, as well as test–retest reliability (Raykov & Marcoulides, 2011). The estimate itself is simply the correlation coefficient between the scores at times 1 and 2. Therefore, a major difference between test–retest reliability and the measures of internal consistency and split-half reliability discussed previously is that the former focused on relationships among individual items or sets of items from one test administration, while the latter focuses on the relationship between total scores on the instrument from two points in time.

As an example, a researcher is interested in the stability of a measure of coping competence for adolescents. She administers a coping competence measure to a sample of 312 children aged 14 to 16 years at two points in time, separated by 3 weeks. Of these 312 individuals, 274 provided both scores and thus will provide data for the calculation of the correlation coefficient. To obtain the correlation coefficient between scores at time 1 and time 2 using SPSS, we would first click on the following menu sequence: **Analyze ► Correlate ► Bivariate**, which yields the following window.

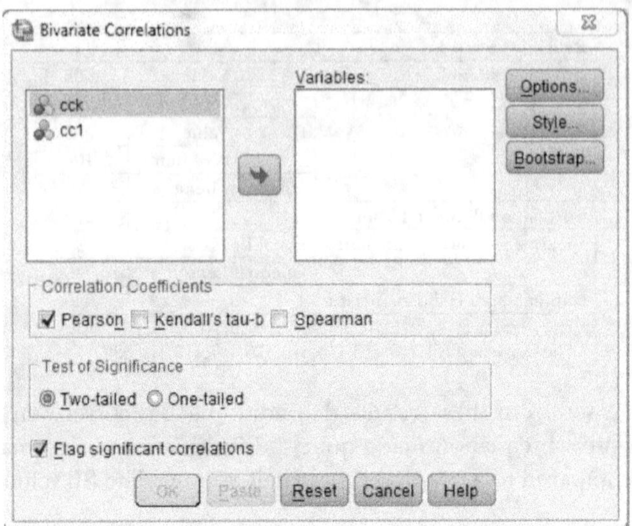

The coping competence scores for Kindergarten (cck) and First Grade (cc1) must then be moved to the variables box.

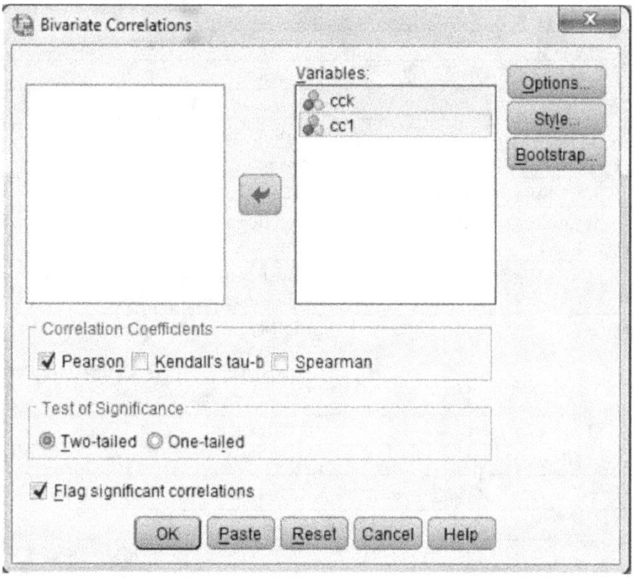

By default, Pearson's correlation coefficient is calculated. We also have the option to get nonparametric estimates of the correlation, including Kendall's tau and Spearman's Rho. However, for the current application with a large sample and continuous data, we can comfortably use Pearson's *r*. We click **OK** and obtain the following output.

```
GET
  FILE='C:\research\SPSS psychometric book\coping.sav'.
DATASET NAME DataSet6 WINDOW=FRONT.
CORRELATIONS
  /VARIABLES=cck cc1
  /PRINT=TWOTAIL NOSIG
  /MISSING=PAIRWISE.
```

Correlations		
Notes		
Output Created		26-AUG-2014 13:07:17
Comments		
Input	Data	C:\research\spss psychometric book\coping.sav
	Active Dataset	DataSet6
	Filter	<none>
	Weight	<none>
	Split File	<none>
	N of Rows in Working Data File	312
Missing Value Handling	Definition of Missing	User-defined missing values are treated as missing.
	Cases Used	Statistics for each pair of variables are based on all the cases with valid data for that pair.
Syntax		CORRELATIONS /VARIABLES=cck ccl /PRINT=TWOTAIL NOSIG /MISSING=PAIRWISE.
Resources	Processor Time	00:00:00.02
	Elapsed Time	00:00:00.05

Correlations			
		cck	ccl
cck	Pearson Correlation	1	.755**
	Sig. (2-tailed)		.000
	N	304	274
ccl	Pearson Correlation	.755**	1
	Sig. (2-tailed)	.000	
	N	274	281

** Correlation is significant at the 0.01 level (2-tailed).

The correlation between the two measures is 0.755, indicating a positive relationship such that individuals who had higher scores at time 1 (i.e., those with greater coping competence) also had higher scores at time 2. This correlation is statistically significant, as the *p*-value is less than 0.0001, and as mentioned above the total sample involved in the calculation of the correlation coefficient was 274.

When using test–retest reliability, the researcher must consider how long to allow between administrations of the instrument. There are not agreed upon guidelines for how long this should be, and indeed authors generally suggest that this time period must depend to a large extent on the perceived stability of the trait being measured. The interested reader is encouraged to refer to excellent discussion on this issue that appear in both Raykov and Marcoulides (2011) and Crocker and Algina (1986). In general, the researcher must allow sufficient time so that the subjects do not remember specific item responses and thus simply mimic their previous behavior on the instrument, but not so much time that the trait itself changes. Therefore, use of this technique for estimating reliability requires that the researcher be able to justify its use by demonstrating that the trait should not have changed during the interval, and that there are not memory or other related effects.

Chapter Summary

The issue of reliability is central to educational and psychological measurement. Whether viewed through the prism of CTT as a measure of error, or more generally as the degree of score consistency, reliability of a scale score is one of the pillars upon which psychometrics is built. In nearly every instance where a researcher makes use of a measure, (s)he will need to estimate and report its reliability for the sample at hand. This value, along with validity evidence (Chapter 5) will serve as the primary means by which the quality of the scale for the current sample is judged. As we have seen in Chapter 3, there are multiple ways in which reliability can be estimated. Certainly the most common approach is based on internal consistency, particularly using Cronbach's a. However, other methods may be more appropriate for a given situation, such as test–retest when the temporal stability of the scale is at issue. In addition, there are a number of methods for estimating reliability that were not discussed in this chapter, either because they are somewhat outdated or useful in very specialized conditions. Nonetheless, the interested reader is encouraged to further investigate these alternative methods for estimating reliability. Finally, as with many statistical analyses, the use of confidence intervals, where possible, is highly recommended. Such intervals provide greater information regarding the population parameter value than does a simple point estimate. In Chapter 4, we consider an alternative method for estimating reliability using information from analysis of variance (ANOVA) models, in an approach known as generalizability theory. This methodology can be applied to items on a scale, or to scores provided by raters or judges. As we shall see, while the end goal of generalizability theory is the same as that of the statistics discussed here, the statistical theory underlying the two approaches is quite different.

4

Generalizability Theory

Introduction

In Chapter 3, we discussed the estimation of reliability indices in terms of internal consistency (e.g., Cronbach's alpha) and correlations between scores on parts (e.g., split-halves reliability) or the entire (e.g., test–retest reliability) instrument (e.g., survey). In this chapter, we describe evaluating reliability from a very different perspective, and one that is linked more closely to the fundamental equation in CTT than were the other estimates of reliability described previously. This alternative approach to estimating reliability is known as generalizability theory (GT), and as we will see below, it is based upon a framework embedded in a commonly used statistical model, the analysis of variance (ANOVA).

Recall, that the fundamental CTT equation is

$$X = T + E, \tag{4.1}$$

Applied Psychometrics Using SPSS and AMOS, pages 75–93

where reliability was defined as the ratio of true score variance (σ_T^2) to observed score variance (σ_x^2). When using traditional methods for estimating reliability, error (E) was dealt with only implicitly. It was known to have an impact on the scores, and could be seen in the relative magnitude of reliability estimates, such that greater measurement error would be associated with lower reliability. However, no attempt was made in this paradigm to quantify error. On the other hand, GT seeks to address measurement error directly by estimating its magnitude and using this estimate in conjunction with information about the observed score to calculate an estimate of reliability. The GT framework also provides a basis to quantify different sources of error, thus providing more information regarding the nature of the observed scores. Therefore, for example, error associated with the items on a test will be distinguishable from error associated with different test administrations (presuming the instrument is administered to subjects on multiple occasions). As will be shown, GT also proves useful for assessing inter-rater reliability.

G-Studies/D-Studies

Before examining the details of GT, we must first learn some of the nomenclature specific to its practice. In this context, a score on some instrument is thought of as coming from a *universe* of all possible scores for this same individual on this particular test. In other words, we consider the current instrument to be only one of an infinite number of possible such instruments that could be used to measure the trait(s) of interest (e.g., argumentative writing). The entire measurement scenario is made up of multiple *facets,* such as the examinee(s) being assessed and the items comprising the instrument. Depending on the instrument and administrative conditions, among others, facets can include: raters (e.g., teachers, judges), measurement occasion (or time), and the instrument type (e.g., portfolio, writing sample). Within this framework, each facet is assumed to uniquely contribute to the observed score, and an aim of a GT study is to estimate what portion of the score is associated with each facet. This estimation of the relative contribution of each facet to the total score is done in what is known as a *G-study.* The goal of a GT study, then, is to isolate the unique contribution of each facet to the total score, in the form of explained variance. Thus, the researcher will identify the facets that are hypothesized to contribute to the scores and then use a variance components analysis to quantify the unique contribution of each.

Once the score variances associated with the facets are estimated, the researcher will then use these in a *D-study.* The purpose of the D-study is to generalize the results to the universe of interest. More specifically, the researcher will identify all facets to which they would like to generalize the instrument. This universe of generalization will include the number of individuals being measured, the number of items, raters, measurement occasions, for example. The purpose of the measurement will also be considered in the D-study. Thus, the goal of rank ordering individuals based on their scores (i.e., norm referenced assessment) will be treated differently at this stage than will the goal of identifying individuals whose score is above (or below) some cut value (i.e., criterion-referenced assessment). In addition, in the D-study the information obtained from the G-study can be used to compare the relative reliability of the measure under different conditions with respect to the facets.

Variance Components

The actual estimation of the unique error contributed by each facet is done using variance components analysis, which is drawn from the ANOVA statistical paradigm. Using variance components analysis, it is possible to decompose an observed score into its constituent parts (e.g., items, individuals). For didactic purposes, let us consider a situation in which 100 students were asked to create portfolios reflecting their work in a class over the course of an academic semester. Say the portfolios included a collection of student work samples, including: homework assignments, journal reflections, in-class assignments, tests, and a final project (e.g., paper). Each portfolio received scores from four individual raters (e.g., trained university faculty) who evaluated each student portfolio. Based on a four-point holistic scoring scale (i.e., 1–4), each rater assigned a score to each student's portfolio, where: 1 = *Below basic,* 2 = *Basic,* 3 = *Proficient,* and 4 = *Excellent.* In addition to a holistic rating, analytic scores were provided across individual aspects of the portfolios, including the quality of the design and the professionalism of the presentation, among others. For programmatic purposes (e.g., training raters), the researcher collecting the data would like to estimate the reliability of the ratings.

To begin, let us consider only the holistic ratings (we will examine analytic scores later). The facets involved in this rating are the students (i.e., persons) and the raters (e.g., university faculty). In addition, we will assume that there remains some left over variation in scores that is not associated with either the student creating the portfolio or the rater assigning the score, which we will refer to as the residual. We can then think of the score (x_{pi}) for a given person from a given rater as

$$x_{pi} = \mu + p + r + pr. \tag{4.2}$$

We can further define these terms so that μ is the overall mean score across all persons and raters, which we can think of as the "typical" score for any student/rater combination. The term p refers to the person effect on the score (i.e., proficiency of student creating the portfolio), r is the rater effect (i.e., how easy or difficult an individual rater is in scoring portfolios), and pr is the residual. We will have more to say about the residual later. These individual effects can be described in terms of the actual scores, as we see below.

$$p = \mu_p - \mu; \tag{4.3}$$

Mean score of person p across raters.

$$r = \mu_r - \mu; \tag{4.4}$$

Mean score given by rater r across persons.

$$pr = x_{pi} - \mu_p - \mu_r + \mu; \tag{4.5}$$

Remainder of score after the effects of person and rater are removed.

The residual in this model, which is actually the interaction between rater and person, can be viewed as unsystematic error associated with the holistic score. It represents remaining error in the scores that is not accounted for by the two systematic components: person and rater. From this equation, it is clear why proper identification of all relevant and measureable facets is so important. If such a facet is not explicitly included in the model, it will be implicitly accounted for in the residual. As we will see, a large residual term is associated with lower reliability.

Each of the terms described above has associated with it a mean and variance. For example, the mean of p is 0 with a variance of

$$\sigma_p^2 = E(\mu_p - \mu)^2, \tag{4.6}$$

and the mean of r is also 0 with a variance of

$$\sigma_r^2 = E(\mu_r - \mu)^2. \tag{4.7}$$

The mean of the residual is 0 as well, with a variance of

$$\sigma_{pr}^2 = E(x_{pi} - \mu_p - \mu_r + \mu)^2. \tag{4.8}$$

It is possible, in turn, to express the variance of the observed score as

$$\sigma_x^2 = \sigma_p^2 + \sigma_r^2 + \sigma_{pr}^2. \tag{4.9}$$

Thus, we can now think of variation in the observed ratings for our sample as a function of variation due to persons, raters, and residual (or unsystematic variability).

We can estimate each of these variances using a statistical modeling method known as variance components analysis, which is based in ANOVA. In considering Equation 4.9, we can see how closely aligned it is to the fundamental equation in CTT, where the observed score was viewed as a function of true score and error, and reliability was the ratio of true score variance to observed score variance. Our next step will be to determine which components in Equation 4.9 correspond to true score and which correspond to error.

Equation 4.9 refers to the population parameter values associated with GT. However, researchers never actually have access to the population, and thus must use samples drawn from the population to estimate population parameters. This is where ANOVA proves to be useful in the context of GT. Specifically, we can use variance components analysis to derive estimates for each of the terms in Equation 4.9, which in turn can be used to estimate reliability of the measure. For example, the variance component for σ_p^2, the portion of variance in observed scores due to the persons being measured is

$$\frac{MS_p - MS_{pr}}{n_r}. \tag{4.10}$$

Here, MS_p is the mean square for persons, which is the sum of the squared differences between the mean for each individual across the four raters, and the overall mean rating, divided by the number of persons in the sample minus 1. MS_{pr} is the mean square of the residual, often referred to as the mean square error, and n_r is the number of raters. Similarly, the variance component for the rater is

$$\frac{MS_r - MS_{pr}}{n_p}, \tag{4.11}$$

where MS_r is the mean square for the rater and n_p is the number of persons that were rated. The variance component for σ_{pr}^2 is simply MS_{pr}. We will not delve into the subject of variance components estimation in more detail, however, the interested reader is encouraged to pursue such detail in references including Brennan (2001) and Shavelson and Webb (1991), among others.

Generalizability Coefficient/Phi Coefficient

In the previous chapter, we described several statistics that could be used to estimate test score reliability. These differed both in terms of how they were calculated (e.g., split half versus internal consistency) as well as how they might be used. In the latter case, for instance, we saw that researchers interested in the temporal stability of a measure (e.g., Time 1 to Time 2) might be particularly interested in estimating a test–retest reliability coefficient. On the other hand, when an instrument may be administered only once for a given group of individuals (e.g., students), measures of internal consistency might be more appropriate.

In the case GT, there also exist multiple estimates of reliability, which differ in terms of how the researcher might expect to use the instrument vis-à-vis the individuals being measured. For instance, if the purpose of the instrument is to make relative decisions about the individuals being assessed, such as which portfolios to use to make programmatic decisions as compared to other measures (e.g., norm-referenced assessments), then the researcher will use the generalizability coefficient (G-coefficient). *G* is defined as

$$G = \frac{\sigma_p^2}{\sigma_p^2 + \frac{\sigma_{pr}^2}{n_r}}, \tag{4.12}$$

where all terms are as described above. This statistic is directly analogous to reliability as described in Chapter 3

$$\text{(i.e.,} = \frac{\sigma_T^2}{\sigma_T^2 + \sigma_E^2}\text{).}$$

Thus, in GT, true score variance is equivalent to the variance in observed score due to the persons being measured, while error is equivalent to the residual variance adjusted for the number of raters. We can see that if the number of raters increases, the estimate of error decreases and *G* becomes larger. Of course, this would presume that the quality of the new raters is the same as that of the raters used to estimate the variance components.

A second estimate of reliability in the context of GT is useful when the instrument is used for absolute decisions about the individuals. This statistic is calculated as

$$\phi = \frac{\sigma_p^2}{\sigma_p^2 + \frac{\sigma_{pr}^2}{n_r} + \frac{\sigma_r^2}{n_r}}. \tag{4.13}$$

Note that the difference between Equations 4.12 and 4.13 is the inclusion of the variance due to the raters in the denominator. In other words, when we are interested in using an instrument to make absolute decisions about individuals, error includes both the interaction of persons and raters, as well as the raters themselves. The inclusion of raters is logical in this context because we are no longer only interested in ranking individuals based on their performance, in which case the effect of raters is not important since it will impact each individual to the same extent. However, when we need to determine whether, for example, an individual's portfolio meets a cut-score value so that they pass the assignment, the impact of raters becomes very important. The presence of relatively low scoring (harder) raters will lead to fewer individuals meeting the cut-value, while relatively high scoring (easier) raters will lead to more individuals meeting the standard. It is also clear from Equations 4.12 and 4.13 that ϕ will nearly always be lower than G.

Example 1: One Facet Crossed Design

Let us now consider the analysis of this one-facet crossed design using SPSS. In order to do so, we make use of SPSS syntax written by Mushquash and O'Connor (2006) that allows for a wide variety of GT designs. The macro is available to download at the website for this book. In this example, we consider the simplest GT design, in which each portfolio is rated on a single element (quality of the design) by each judge. Because each judge rates each portfolio, we call this a fully crossed design, in contrast to a nested design in which each judge rates only some of the portfolios. The data for this analysis are organized into 100 rows representing the individual portfolios (or persons) and 4 columns representing the raters (i.e., each rater's scores provided in column for each student). As noted above, scores are given on a 1 to 4 scale. Data for the first 5 subjects appear in Figure 4.1.

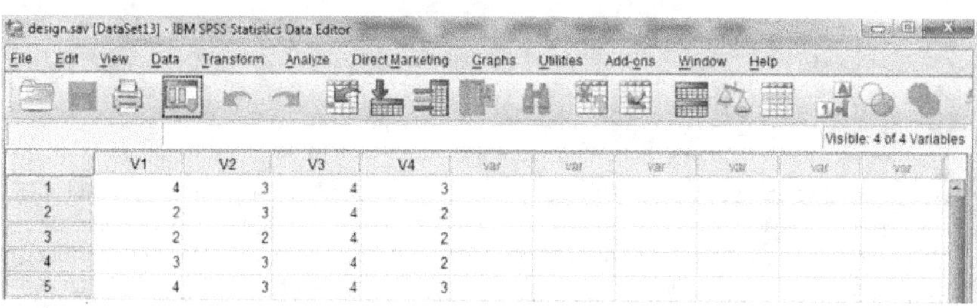

Figure 4.1 First five observations of the design.sav file.

These data were first saved as a SPSS dataset and then read in using the following command sequence. The following lines appear at the top of the SPSS script file entitled `G1design.sps`, in which the GT program is written. The remainder of the syntax appears below these lines, and the entire program can be found on the website for the book. These specific lines are all well explained at the beginning of the macro provided by Mushquash and O'Connor, and appear below. The syntax file itself can be opened through the **File ► Open ► Syntax** menu sequence. Note that the lines set behind * are comments designed for the syntax user. In order to run the program, after making the appropriate changes to the commands below, we simply use the command sequence **Run ► All**.

```
* G1.sps for Generalizability Theory analyses

set printback = off.
matrix.

* There are two main ways of entering data into this program.

* Method 1: You can specify the data to be analyzed on a
  GET statement, as in the example below. On the GET statement,
  the data matrix must be named SCORES (as in the example);
  "FILE = *" will use the currently active SPSS data set;
  "FILE = C:\filename" will use the specified SPSS data file on
  your computer. The * beside the GET command below converts the
  command into a comment. To use the GET command, remove
  the * that appears before GET; specify the data for analysis
  on FILE =; and specify the variables for analysis on VARIABLES =.

GET scores / file = * /variables = all / missing = omit.

* Enter the number of levels/conditions of Facet 1 (e.g., # of
  items).
compute nfacet1 = 4.

* Enter the number of levels/conditions of Facet 2 (e.g., # of
  occasions);
  You can ignore this step for single-facet designs.
compute nfacet2 = 1.

* For two-facet designs, Facet 1 is the facet with the fastest-
  changing conditions in the columns of your data matrix. For
  example, if the first 10 columns/variables contained the data for
  10 different items measured on occasion 1, and if the next 10
  columns/variables contained the data for the same 10 items
  measured on occasion 2, then items would be the fastest-changing
  facet. As you slide from one column to the next across the data
  matrix, it is the item levels that change most quickly. You would
  therefore enter a value of "10" for NFACET1 and a value of "2"
```

```
  for NFACET2 on the above statements.

* Enter the design of your data on the "COMPUTE TYPE =" statement
  below:
  enter "1" for a single-facet fully-crossed design, as in P * F1
  enter "2" for a single-facet nested nested design, as in F1 : P
  enter "3" for a two-facet fully-crossed design, as in P * F1 * F2
  enter "4" for a two-facet nested design, as in P * (F1 : F2)
  enter "5" for a two-facet nested design, as in (F1 : P) * F2
  enter "6" for a two-facet nested design, as in F1 : (P * F2)
  enter "7" for a two-facet nested design, as in (F1 * F2) : P
  enter "8" for a two-facet nested design, as in F1 : F2 : P.
compute type = 1.

* Enter D-study values for Facet 1; enter the values inside curly
  brackets, and place a comma between the values.
  compute dfacet1 = {1,2,3,4}.

* Enter D-study values for Facet 2; enter the values inside curly
  brackets, and place a comma between the values. You can ignore
  this step for single-facet designs.
  compute dfacet2 = {1,2,3,4,5}.

* At the very bottom of this file, after the END MATRIX statement,
  is a GRAPH command that can be used to plot the results for the
  D-study values that you specified above. Specify the data that
  you would like to plot by entering the appropriate number on the
  COMPUTE GRAPHDAT statement:
  enter "1" for relative error variances;
  enter "2" for absolute error variances;
  enter "3" for G-coefficients;
  enter "4" for phi coefficients.
compute graphdat = 3.

* End of user specifications. Now just run this whole file.
*****************************************************************
```

The `GET scores / file = * /variables = all / missing = omit.` line indicates that the open file will be used, through the `file=*` statement. If we wanted to use a file that is not open, we would simply put its path here. When using the open data option, it is easiest if the target file is the only one open. All of the variables in the dataset will also be included in the analysis. If we wanted to use only a subset of the variables in a file, they would be listed in this line after the `variables=` subcommand. As shown, the code indicates that there are 4 levels to facet 1 (the only facet of interest in this analysis), which correspond to the 4 raters. The 2 in the next line of code is not meaningful as we do not have a second facet, thus we can leave it as is. The next command tells SPSS that we have a single facet fully-crossed design, which is why the second facet command is ignored. Next, we must indicate what values of facet 1 we would like to explore in the D-study portion of our analysis. This is tantamount to indicating for how many raters we would like to obtain estimates of reliability. In this case, we are requesting D-study results for 1, 2, 3, 4, and 5 raters. Again, there is a command for requesting similar information for a D-study involving facet 2, which is not meaningful here. Finally, we indicate what type of graph we would like to see for our D-study. Specifically, we can obtain a scatter plot of one of four different values on the *y*-axis against the number of raters on *x*. Option 1 plots the relative error variance, which is the denominator of the *G* coefficient value, or error when we are interested in comparing individuals with one another. Option 2 plots the absolute error variance, the denominator of ϕ while options 3 and 4 plot each of the reliability estimates, respectively. Thus, if our primary interest is in ordering the portfolios based on their scores, we may be most interested in option 1 or 3, while if we are primarily interested in determining whether the portfolios have met a given standard of performance, we would select either option 2 or 4. For this example, we elected to obtain a plot of the *G* coefficient values, as our interest is in comparing the relative quality of the portfolios with one another. Following is the output from running this syntax for design.sav.

```
Run MATRIX procedure:


GENERALIZABILITY THEORY ANALYSES:

Design Type 1: single-facet fully-crossed design, as in P * F1

Number of persons/objects ('P'):
   100

Number of levels for Facet 1 ('F1'):
   4

ANOVA Table:
             df          SS         MS    Variance    Proport.
P        99.000      91.610       .925        .173        .232
F1        3.000     101.970     33.990        .338        .453
P*F1    297.000      69.530       .234        .234        .314

Error Variances:

    Relative    Absolute
        .059        .143

G-coefficients:

           G         Phi
        .747        .547

D-Study:
Entered D-Study values for Facet 1:
   1  2  3  4  5
```

```
Entered D-Study values for Facet 2:
  1  2  3  4  5

In the D-study results below, the levels of Facet 1 appear in the
first column, and the levels of Facet 2 appear in the first row.

D-Study Absolute Error Variances
     .000    1.000
    1.000     .572
    2.000     .286
    3.000     .191
    4.000     .143
    5.000     .114

D-Study Relative Error Variances
     .000    1.000
    1.000     .234
    2.000     .117
    3.000     .078
    4.000     .059
    5.000     .047

D-Study G Coefficients
     .000    1.000
    1.000     .425
    2.000     .596
    3.000     .689
    4.000     .747
    5.000     .787

D-Study Phi Coefficients
     .000    1.000
    1.000     .232
    2.000     .377
    3.000     .476
    4.000     .547
    5.000     .602
----- END MATRIX -----
```

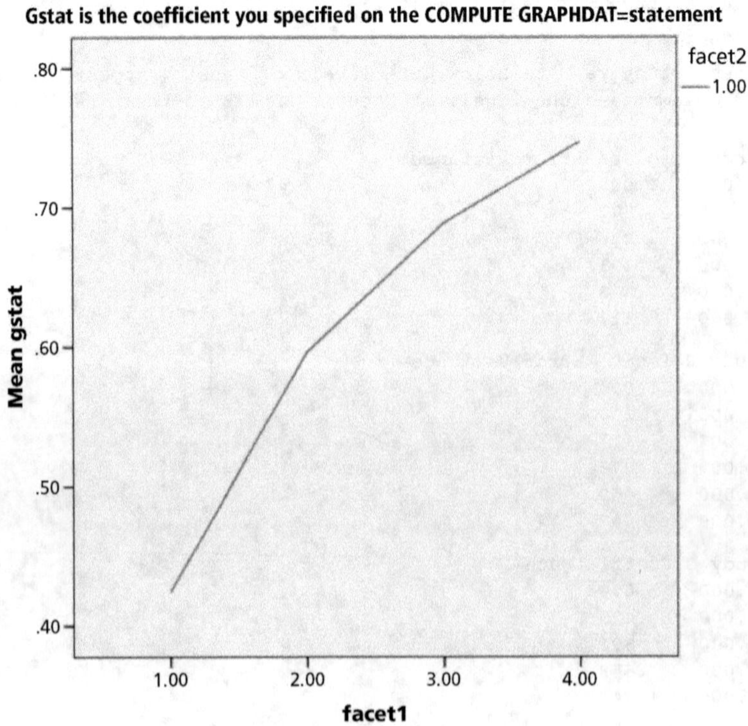

Let us inspect the output to determine what we have learned about the portfolio ratings. First, we see that the number of persons and number of raters (levels for facet 1) are correct, indicating that the data were read in properly. We then see the ANOVA Table, which contains the variance components estimates for each term in the analysis. The first column includes the name of the variable for which estimates were obtained, persons (P), raters (F1), and the interaction of persons by raters (P*F1). Next, we see the degrees of freedom for each of these terms. This value is the number of persons 100 – 1 = 99 (P), the number of raters 4 – 1 = 3 (F1), and the number of persons × the number of raters 300 – 3 = 297 (P * F1). The sum of squares (SS) are sample estimates of the quantities in Equations 4.6, 4.7, and 4.8, while the mean squares (MS) are the $\frac{SS}{df}$. The variance components values are as defined in Equations 4.10 and 4.11, above. We can calculate these by hand very simply using the information from the table:

$$\frac{MS_p - MS_{pr}}{n_r} = \frac{0.92 - 0.23}{4} = 0.17 \text{ and } \frac{MS_r - MS_{pr}}{n_p} = \frac{33.99 - 0.23}{100} = 0.34.$$

Remember that the variance component for the interaction is simply equal to the MS. Finally, this table reports the proportion of total variance in the ratings accounted for by each of the terms. Thus, the proportion of variance in the ratings due to differences in scores among the 100 individual portfolios is

$$\frac{0.17}{0.17+0.34+0.23}=0.23.$$

We can obtain the proportion of rating variance accounted for by raters and the interaction in the same fashion. The next table includes the relative and absolute error variances, which correspond to the denominators of the G and ϕ values, respectively. Following this, we see the estimates for G and ϕ for the 4 raters included in this sample. These correspond to the estimates of reliability for relative and absolute decisions for the current sample of raters and persons.

Taken together, these results indicate that the largest segment of variability in ratings is due to differences among the raters themselves, while the least amount of variation is attributed to differences among the persons. In general, this would not be a positive outcome because it indicates that the measurement mechanism (raters) and unexplained variance (interaction) account for more variation in the design scores than do differences among the individual portfolios themselves. In general, we would prefer to see most of the variation being due to the portfolios, as it is an estimate of T in the context of CTT. In addition, the error variance for the absolute case is much greater than for the relative case, leading to the great difference in G and ϕ. This difference in error variances is reflective of the large variability in the scores provided by the raters (e.g., faculty) towards students' portfolios.

The output for the D-study begins by showing the values for the facets that we are interested in examining. Remember that we asked to see reliability estimates for 1, 2, 3, 4, and 5 raters, a fact which is reflected in the *Entered D-Study values for Facet 1:* table. The next two tables include the absolute and error variances for different numbers of raters, from 0 to 5, which is what we requested. We can see that in each case, as we increase the number of raters, the amount of error decreases. Remember that these error variances correspond to the denominators in Equations 4.12 and 4.13, respectively. Similarly, the final two tables in the D-study output reflect the G and ϕ values for different numbers of raters. For both statistics the estimate of reliability increases with more raters, and that in the case of G having 4 or more raters results in reliability estimates greater than 0.7. On the other hand, in the case of ϕ, the reliability estimate does not approach 0.7 even for as many as 5 raters. The graph provides a graphical representation of how *G* changes when the number of raters is increased.

One issue that is important to note is that we work under an assumption that the quality of the additional raters is the same as those in the current sample. If they are not as well trained or are drawn from a different population, then we cannot be sure that they will produce similar quality ratings to those in the sample. In turn, we cannot be sure that the scores will be similar, and thus the variance accounted for due to raters may change. Test developers face a similar issue when they add items to an instrument. In order for the estimates of variance obtained from the original sample to be applicable, they must ensure that the quality of the additional items is equivalent to that of the current set of items. Consequently, when this is not the case, the results of the D-study are not meaningful.

Example 2: Two Facet Crossed Design

Let us now consider a somewhat more complex research design, including more than one facet. When data were collected on the portfolios described above, raters provided scores for 7 different dimensions, including student reflection on their own work, the rationale for the elements included: the design, environmental factors, the mechanics of the portfolio, the professionalism of the product, and quality of the artifacts. In this case, the researcher is interested in estimating the reliability of the entire scale, rather than a single rated aspect. Therefore, we will need to include a second facet to our design, which includes information about the different tasks. The dataset that we use now includes 28 columns and 100 rows, reflecting the 4 raters' scores on the seven tasks for 100 students. The first five observations appear as:

```
4 3 4 3 4 3 3 2 4 3 4 3 4 4 4 3 4 3 3 3 4 3 3 3 4 3 3 2
3 2 2 3 2 1 3 1 2 3 4 2 2 2 4 2 3 3 2 3 3 3 3 3 1 1 1 1
3 2 3 3 2 2 3 2 2 2 4 2 3 3 4 3 2 3 2 3 3 2 3 3 3 3 4 2
3 2 3 2 3 1 3 1 3 3 4 2 2 4 3 2 3 3 3 2 3 3 3 2 3 2 4 2
3 2 2 2 3 2 2 2 4 3 4 3 4 3 4 3 3 3 3 3 4 3 3 3 3 3 4 3
```

Our interest here is in estimating the reliability of the entire set of measures, rather than a single component, as we did previously with design.

In order to conduct this analysis, we will use the GT syntax file once again, the header commands of which appear below.

```
* G1.sps for Generalizability Theory analyses

set printback = off.
matrix.

* There are two main ways of entering data into this program.

* Method 1: You can specify the data to be analyzed on a
  GET statement, as in the example below. On the GET statement,
  the data matrix must be named SCORES (as in the example);
  "FILE = *" will use the currently active SPSS data set;
  "FILE = C:\filename" will use the specified SPSS data file on your
  computer. The * beside the GET command below converts the
  command into a comment. To use the GET command, remove
  the * that appears before GET; specify the data for analysis
  on FILE =; and specify the variables for analysis on VARIABLES =.
  GET scores / file = * /variables = all / missing = omit.

* Enter the number of levels/conditions of Facet 1 (e.g., # of items).
compute nfacet1 = 4.

* Enter the number of levels/conditions of Facet 2 (e.g., # of
  occasions); You can ignore this step for single-facet designs.
compute nfacet2 = 7.

* For two-facet designs, Facet 1 is the facet with the fastest-
  changing conditions in the columns of your data matrix. For
  example, if the first 10 columns/variables contained the data for
  10 different items measured on occasion 1, and if the next 10
  columns/variables contained the data for the same 10 items
  measured on occasion 2, then items would be the fastest-changing
  facet. As you slide from one column to the next across the data
  matrix, it is the item levels that change most quickly. You would
  therefore enter a value of "10" for NFACET1 and a value of "2"
  for NFACET2 on the above statements.

* Enter the design of your data on the "COMPUTE TYPE =" statement
  below:
  enter "1" for a single-facet fully-crossed design, as in P * F1
  enter "2" for a single-facet nested nested design, as in F1 : P
  enter "3" for a two-facet fully-crossed design, as in P * F1 * F2
  enter "4" for a two-facet nested design, as in P * (F1 : F2)
  enter "5" for a two-facet nested design, as in (F1 : P) * F2
  enter "6" for a two-facet nested design, as in F1 : (P * F2)
  enter "7" for a two-facet nested design, as in (F1 * F2) : P
  enter "8" for a two-facet nested design, as in F1 : F2 : P.
compute type = 3.

* Enter D-study values for Facet 1; enter the values inside curly
  brackets, and place a comma between the values.
compute dfacet1 = {1,2,3,4,5}.
```

```
* Enter D-study values for Facet 2; enter the values inside curly
  brackets, and place a comma between the values. You can ignore
  this step for single-facet designs.
compute dfacet2 = {1,2,3,4,5,6,7}.

* At the very bottom of this file, after the END MATRIX statement,
  is a GRAPH command that can be used to plot the results for the
  D-study values that you specified above. Specify the data that
  you would like to plot by entering the appropriate number on the
  COMPUTE GRAPHDAT statement:
  enter "1" for relative error variances;
  enter "2" for absolute error variances;
  enter "3" for G-coefficients;
  enter "4" for phi coefficients.
compute graphdat = 3.

* End of user specifications. Now just run this whole file.
*****************************************************************
```

Once again, we indicate that the first facet consists of 4 levels corresponding to the raters, while we now have a second facet with the 7 portfolio components that were rated. We indicate that we have a two-facet fully crossed design (type = 3), and that we would like to see reliability estimates for raters 1 through 5, and for each of the seven components to be measured. We also request the scatter plot of the *G*-coefficient values associated with different numbers of raters and components to rate.

```
Run MATRIX procedure:

GENERALIZABILITY THEORY ANALYSES:

Design Type 3: two-facet fully-crossed design, as in P * F1 * F2

Number of persons/objects ('P'):
  100

Number of levels for Facet 1 ('F1'):
  4

Number of levels for Facet 2 ('F2'):
  7

ANOVA Table:
```

	df	SS	MS	Variance	Proport.
P	99.000	638.741	6.452	.197	.243
F1	3.000	371.053	123.684	.165	.203
F2	6.000	147.700	24.617	.042	.052
P*F1	297.000	217.912	.734	.075	.092
P*F2	594.000	240.871	.406	.049	.060
F1*F2	18.000	135.960	7.553	.073	.090
P*F1*F2	1782.000	374.326	.210	.210	.259

```
Error Variances:
   Relative   Absolute
       .033       .083

G-coefficients:
          G        Phi
       .856       .704

D-Study:

Entered D-Study values for Facet 1:
  1  2  3  4  5

Entered D-Study values for Facet 2:
  1  2  3  4  5  6  7

In the D-study results below, the levels of Facet 1 appear in the
first column, and the levels of Facet 2 appear in the first row.

D-Study Absolute Error Variances
     .000    1.000    2.000    3.000    4.000    5.000    6.000    7.000
    1.000     .614     .427     .365     .334     .315     .302     .293
    2.000     .353     .236     .198     .178     .167     .159     .153
    3.000     .266     .173     .142     .126     .117     .111     .106
    4.000     .222     .141     .114     .100     .092     .087     .083
    5.000     .196     .122     .097     .085     .078     .073     .069

D-Study Relative Error Variances
     .000    1.000    2.000    3.000    4.000    5.000    6.000    7.000
    1.000     .334     .204     .161     .140     .127     .118     .112
    2.000     .191     .114     .089     .076     .068     .063     .059
    3.000     .144     .084     .065     .055     .049     .045     .042
    4.000     .120     .069     .052     .044     .039     .036     .033
    5.000     .106     .060     .045     .038     .033     .030     .028

D-Study G Coefficients
     .000    1.000    2.000    3.000    4.000    5.000    6.000    7.000
    1.000     .371     .491     .550     .586     .609     .626     .638
    2.000     .508     .633     .690     .722     .743     .758     .769
    3.000     .578     .700     .753     .783     .802     .815     .825
    4.000     .622     .740     .790     .817     .835     .847     .856
    5.000     .651     .766     .813     .840     .856     .868     .876

D-Study Phi Coefficients
     .000    1.000    2.000    3.000    4.000    5.000    6.000    7.000
    1.000     .243     .316     .351     .372     .385     .395     .402
    2.000     .359     .455     .500     .525     .542     .554     .563
    3.000     .426     .533     .582     .610     .627     .640     .649
    4.000     .471     .583     .634     .663     .681     .694     .704
    5.000     .502     .618     .670     .699     .718     .731     .741

----- END MATRIX -----
```

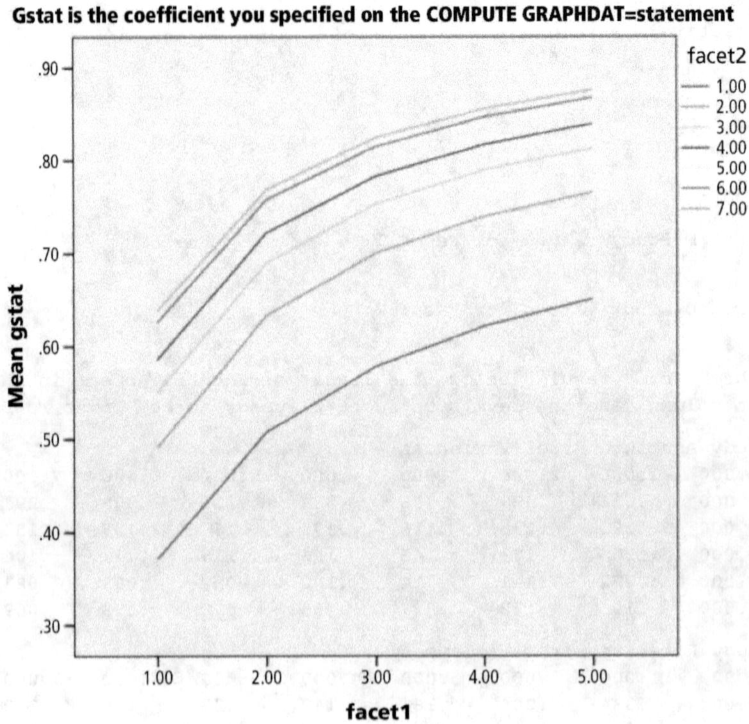

As before, we see that the first three aspects of the output simply restate the structure of our data, with 100 persons, 4 raters, and 7 rated components. Next, we see the ANOVA table, which includes the variance component values along with the proportion of variance for which each term accounts. In this case, Persons accounted for approximately a quarter of the variance in ratings, as did the interaction of person by rater by component. Only rater accounts for nearly as much, at 20%. None of the other model terms explain even 10% of the variation in ratings. This result is very different from the findings for design alone, where together the rater and interaction of rater and person accounted for over 75% of score variance. In contrast, in this situation they account for approximately 40%. In addition, we can see that both the relative and absolute error variances are much smaller in this two-facet analysis than they were when we only examined design scores, particularly in the absolute case. As a result, the G and ϕ values are both higher for this more complex design. For this design, these coefficients are calculated as follows:

$$G = \frac{\sigma_p^2}{\sigma_p^2 + \frac{\sigma_{pr}^2}{n_r} + \frac{\sigma_{pc}^2}{n_c} + \frac{\sigma_{prc}^2}{n_c n_r}} \tag{4.14}$$

and

$$\phi = \frac{\sigma_p^2}{\sigma_p^2 + \frac{\sigma_{pr}^2}{n_r} + \frac{\sigma_{pc}^2}{n_c} + \frac{\sigma_{prc}^2}{n_c n_r} + \sigma_r^2 + \sigma_c^2 + \sigma_{rc}^2}. \tag{4.15}$$

All terms in these models are as defined previously, with the addition of σ_c^2, which is the variance due to the component being rated, n_c the number of components being rated, and interactions of the number of components being rated with the raters (n_c), and with the persons and raters (σ_{prc}^2).

When considering the D-study, again we see familiar output with regard to the number of levels that we requested for each of the facets under consideration. Following this, SPSS produces a table containing the absolute error variance values for each combination of number of raters and components to be rated. For example, if we were to have only a single rater and one component, the absolute error variance would be 0.61. On the other hand, if we had 5 raters scoring 7 components, the absolute error variance would drop to 0.07. Similarly, in the next table we have information on the relative error variance values. The pattern is quite similar, with decreases in error variance concomitant with increases in either the number of raters or the number of scored components. Finally, the macro provides us with both *G* and ϕ values for varying combinations of the levels that we requested for the two facets of interest. If, therefore, we would like to ensure a *G* value of 0.8 or higher, we should have at minimum 3 components to score and 5 raters, but would be better off with no fewer than 3 raters and at least 5 components. The graph relating the number of facet levels with *G* provides similar results. Note that facet 1 (raters) appears along the *x*-axis and facet 2 (components) is represented by separate lines in the plot.

Chapter Summary

Generalizability theory allows a researcher to address measurement error directly, estimate its magnitude, and use this estimate in conjunction with information about the observed score to calculate an estimate of reliability. A clear advantage it has over other reliability estimates (e.g., alpha) is that the GT framework provides a basis to quantify different sources of error. This, in turn, provides more information regarding the nature of the observed scores. Our simple examples demonstrate that GT is useful for assessing inter-rater reliability and is a common use. The reader is encouraged to think broadly how such a method could be used to separate error in various situations to enhance the accuracy of the measurement of human capabilities. And with that, we will move away from reliability to validity.

5

Validity

Introduction

Validity assessment is both at the core of measurement theory and perhaps the most difficult aspect of applied measurement and psychometrics to investigate. Quite simply, the validation of an instrument involves determining the extent to which obtained scores represent the intended measured trait (e.g., academic achievement, motivation) to build an argument based on theory and empirical evidence to support score-based inferences and actions. Early in the development of measurement theory, validation was treated as primarily a statistical problem involving the correlation of a target measurement to be validated with a criterion that was known, or believed strongly, to be associated with the construct. Later, this statistical methodology extended to the use of factor analysis to investigate whether an instrument's internal structure, based on obtained data, corresponded to its theoretical model. For example, empirical questions pertaining to whether a measure of reading aptitude was as three dimensional as the theory said it should be, could be investigated. Therefore, within this paradigm, validity assessment was primarily the discussion of statistical methodology.

Applied Psychometrics Using SPSS and AMOS, pages 95–167

More recently, the notion of instrument validation has changed direction rather dramatically, perhaps most clearly embodied in the work of Messick (1989), who described the importance of theory in the examination of test score validity. Perhaps the key feature of this change in how validity is considered, is the change in focus from the instrument itself to the interpretations and uses of scores from that instrument. As outlined by Kane (2006), scale validation can be characterized by three key principles:

1. The theory underlying the instrument and what it measures must precede any assessment of test score validity.
2. Validation involves a directed program of research and not a single study.
3. Competing theories as to the behavior of the measure must be considered when validity is assessed.

Key throughout the validation process is what Kane terms the interpretive argument, or the theory of how and what is being measured by the scale. This argument is quite separate from the statistical evidence for or against the validity argument of an instrument and, thus, it must be steeped in the relevant literature.

According to these considerations, the issue of validity is now centered on test score use and inferences rather than on the instrument itself. Thus, we might say that using scores obtained from a college entrance exam to predict freshman year academic performance is valid, but we cannot say that the college entrance exam itself is valid. Indeed, taking this idea a step further, use of the college entrance exam score can be valid in some contexts (e.g., predicting cumulative freshman GPA), but not in others (e.g., determining remedial course placement). While the score itself may be valid for predicting how well a student will perform in her first year of college, it may be quite meaningless as a tool for predicting how well the same person will do in their first job four years later. Thus, the validity of a particular score is conditional on its purpose, which takes us back to the interpretive argument that should be developed before and during scale development. The theory underlying the instrument, which is based in the relevant literature, must inform how we use and interpret scores from it.

There are two important concepts to consider when addressing issues of test score validity. The first is the extent to which a selected set of scale or test, items or measured behaviors (e.g., classroom engagement) adequately measure the intended construct (e.g., achievement motivation). Any particular instrument can only include a sample of items from the universe of all possible items that could be used to operationalize the construct domain.

Construct coverage occurs when the items comprising an instrument represent the universe of all possible items. Problems with validity emerge when the coverage is seriously incomplete or biased away from key domains (e.g., phonological awareness, comprehension) of the construct (e.g., literacy). For example, construct underrepresentation occurs when a set of scale items provide an incomplete assessment of the intended measured trait. This could occur when a Grade 6 mathematics assessment includes only three items, thus limiting the potential of the measure to adequately measure students' mathematical problem-solving ability.

The second important concept in validation is what Kane (2006) termed nomothetic span, which is the relationship of scores on the instrument to scores on other measures, or to other manifestations of the construct. For example, the nomothetic span of scores on the college entrance exam would include their relationship to performance in the freshman year of college. Validation, then, involves combining theory and descriptive (often though not always statistical) evidence to examine both the construct coverage of the instrument, and the nomothetic span of the scores to answer the following questions:

1. To what extent do the items actually measure the construct?
2. Are scores on the instrument useful for their intended purpose?

Perhaps the final words in this section should be left to Zumbo (2007), who said that validity has evolved from simply analyzing data with discrete statistical procedures, to integrating such statistical evidence with theoretical arguments to develop a complete picture of how well the instrument does what it is purported to do.

Types or Sources of Validity Evidence

Traditionally, the investigation of validity evidence has been divided into several discrete types, such as: content, criterion, and construct. As previously stated, though they are discrete in terms of their application, these types should not be viewed as separate, but rather employed together with theory in order to demonstrate to what extent scores from a measure are useful for their intended purpose. In this chapter, we provide general descriptions of these validity types and demonstrate the use of statistical procedures to gather relevant empirical evidence to substantiate the interpretation and use of scores for their designated purposes (e.g., predictive).

Initial investigations of validity typically begin with an examination of the degree to which scale items adequately represent the intended measured construct. Indeed, this assessment of *content validity* begins during the phase of instrument development. It continues through the administration of the instrument to individuals (e.g., students) from the target population. Content validation is focused on ensuring that the items selected to comprise an instrument provide acceptable content coverage of the measured trait. Content validity is generally investigated by subject matter experts (e.g., teachers) familiar with the content domain (e.g., mathematics) being assessed, as well as the target population (e.g., 3rd grade students, college students). The primary responsibility of the content experts is to review and assess item quality to ensure that the items provided acceptable coverage of the content domain (e.g., Grade 6 mathematics). We will not discuss this aspect of validation further in this book as it does not usually involve much, if any, in the way of statistical analysis. However, this lack of coverage in the text should not be interpreted as our demeaning the importance of content validation. To the contrary, it is, in many ways, the key component of validity assessment.

A second source of instrument validation is criterion-related validity, which falls with the broad category of evidence of associations with other variables. *Criterion validity* involves examination of the relationship between scores obtained from the target measure (the one for which we want to assess validity) to those gathered from one or more instruments theorized to measure the same or a similar construct. Most often, criterion-related validity is measured with a correlation coefficient (e.g., Pearson product moment) between scores obtained from the target and criterion measures. An example would be the correlation between scores obtained from a newly developed measure of literacy achievement to an existing measure of students' literacy outcomes. The direction and magnitude of the correlation provides statistical evidence on the relationship between the scores, which can be used for developing and testing theories.

Depending on the use(s) of obtained scores, gathering criterion-related validity evidence typically falls into two categories: concurrent and predictive. First, *concurrent validity* seeks to investigate the degree to which two measures designed to measure a similar trait yield similar scores. It is the condition that the target and criterion measures are designed to assess a similar construct (e.g., academic achievement, psychological distress). Gathering concurrent validity evidence is based on the administration of the target and criterion measure simultaneously to judge correspondence between resultant scores. It would be expected that two measures designed to measure the same trait would yield scores that report a strong, positive correlation. *Predictive validity* is the second type of criterion-related validity. As suggested by the name, it is concerned with the degree to which scores obtained from a target measure (e.g., college aptitude test) can be used to predict examinees' performance on some future criterion, such as college freshman GPA or employee job performance. Like concurrent validity, predictive validity is generally evaluated using correlational techniques. Both concurrent and predictive validity seek to gather empirical evidence on the degree to which scores obtained from a target measure relate to those obtained from a criterion measure. The primary difference is the time in which scores on the criterion measure have been obtained, either at the same time as the target measure or at a designated time in the future.

Although criterion validity is often assessed through the use of correlations, it can also take the form of expected differences between qualitatively distinct groups (e.g., low and high risk readers) on the target measure, such as a literacy assessment. *Discriminant groups validity* is used to judge the degree to which an instrument yields scores that differentiate between two or more groups hypothesized to have differential performance, such as the ability of a depression inventory to distinguish between individuals with and without clinical depression. This type of test score validity evidence is typically assessed through the use of group mean comparisons using a *t*-test or analysis of variance (ANOVA). For example, the overall average scores of a clinical sample would be expected to be statistically greater than those obtained on a non-clinical sample on a diagnostic measure (e.g., depression), indicative of the presence of higher clinical symptoms (e.g., anxiety, loss of interest).

The third common type of validity, and the type that has grown in importance over the last 20 years, is *construct validity*. Put simply, construct validation focuses on the extent to which obtained scores correspond with the theory used to guide scale development. Given the increased primacy of theory in scale validation, it is easy to see why construct validity, which heavily emphasizes contextualizing statistical evidence into existing theory, is central to substantiating the interpretation and use of scores for decision-making purposes (e.g., diagnostic, placement). Indeed, some authors (e.g., Messick, 1989) have argued that all other types of validity evidence can be thought of as a part of construct validity. Statistical approaches to assessing construct validity are many and varied, because the concept itself is highly varied. For example, factor analytic procedures can be used to investigate the correspondence between an instrument's dimensionality to the theoretical structure of the measured construct used during the initial stages of scale development. In addition, relationships between the latent (or unobserved) scores on the measure and some criterion (i.e., criterion validity) may also be used in construct validation.

However, often with construct validity we must go further than simply showing that our measure is correlated with another measure purportedly of the same (or a similar construct). Rather, we must also show that the target measure behaves in theoretically sound ways when it comes to gauging its relationships with variables to which it should *not* be related. This concept is referred to as *discriminant validity* and has traditionally not been part of criterion-related validity. Nonetheless, inspecting the degree to which scores obtained from a target measure relate to dissimilar measures can be very important. For example, it would be expected that scores on a measure of college students' achievement motivation would be negatively correlated with scores on a measure of academic dishonesty. In summary, construct validity evidence is truly all encompassing, taking into account a myriad of evidence on the functioning of obtained scores, and thereby potentially providing the most compelling evidence for scale validation.

Finally, it is important to comment on the relationship between test score validity and reliability. To recall Chapter 3, test score reliability refers to test score consistency, or the degree to which scores are absent of error. Thus, reliability seeks to determine the magnitude of measurement error in obtained scores, with lower reliability estimates associated with greater measurement error. This relationship is particularly evident in generalizability theory, where measurement error can be directly quantified. As such, low reliability estimates indicate greater measurement error and will, consequently, be associated with lower estimates of validity. This is true regardless of the type of validity evidence we seek to gather. The reason perhaps can be most clearly seen in the assessment of criterion validity, which often takes the form of a correlation coefficient between a target and criterion measure. Raykov and Marcoulides (2011) show that the correlation between the target and criterion measures cannot be as large as the correlation between the observed and true scores on the target, which is the reliability of the score obtained on the target measure. Alternatively, if the target instrument score contains a great deal of random error, its correlation with any other measure, including the criterion, will be lower. Thus, high reliability is a prerequisite condition to achieving high validity, though not sufficient towards this end. As such, low test score reliability will ensure low test score validity, while high test score reliability will not necessarily result in high test score validity. While perhaps not as intuitively obvious, a similar relationship exists between the amount of random error present in the data and factor analytic results. Given the relationship between reliability and validity, they cannot be considered disjointed ideas. Instead, they should be viewed as separate but related aspects of the statistical properties of scores obtained on measuring instruments that must be considered together when evaluating the interpretation and use of scores.

In the next section, we demonstrate the correction for attenuation, which provides an estimate of the correlation between true scores on the target and criterion measures, after accounting for the reliability of each measure. This adjustment may prove particularly useful when variation in the target or criterion measure lead to low validity coefficient estimates.

Concurrent Validity

To contextualize our discussion of concurrent validity, let's consider an example in which a new measure of extraversion has been developed based on emerging research findings. Say the resultant scale consists of 30 items instead of the 50 items that comprise the widely used existing scale. An attractive feature of the new instrument is less administration time than the previously used instrument due to a reduced number of items. Through scale development, content validity was based on input from a panel of experts regarding the scale's theoretical underpinnings, item quality, and the alignment of items to the extraversion construct. At this stage, the researcher is prepared to gather empirical evidence on the utility of obtained scores from the new extraversion measure. One piece of validity evidence that might be particularly useful is the correlation of scores from the new scale with those obtained from the existing 50-item measure of extraversion. If the correlation, or validity coefficient (Crocker & Algina, 1986), is relatively large and positive, then it can be concluded that the new, shorter measure does appear to measure the same construct as the existing (criterion) measure of extraversion.

Typically, in a criterion validity study, a sample of individuals from the target population is administered both the target and criterion measures simultaneously. Subsequently, obtained scores across the measures are correlated to inspect the magnitude and direction of their relationship (e.g., moderate and positive). For this example, a sample of 411 college students was administered both instruments. Of these individuals, 383 completed all of the items for both scales, allowing for calculation of scores on each measure. The data are contained in the SPSS file, `concurrent_validity.sav`. To obtain the Pearson correlation (validity coefficient) using SPSS, we would select **Analyze** from the menu bar, and then **Correlate** and **Bivariate** to obtain the following window:

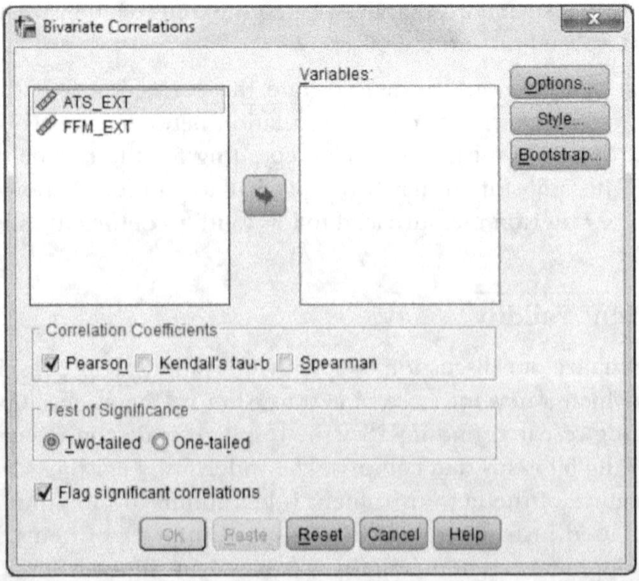

All of the variables in the dataset appear in the left side window, and Pearson's *r* correlation coefficient is the default. First, we will highlight the variables of interest, and move them into the Variables window.

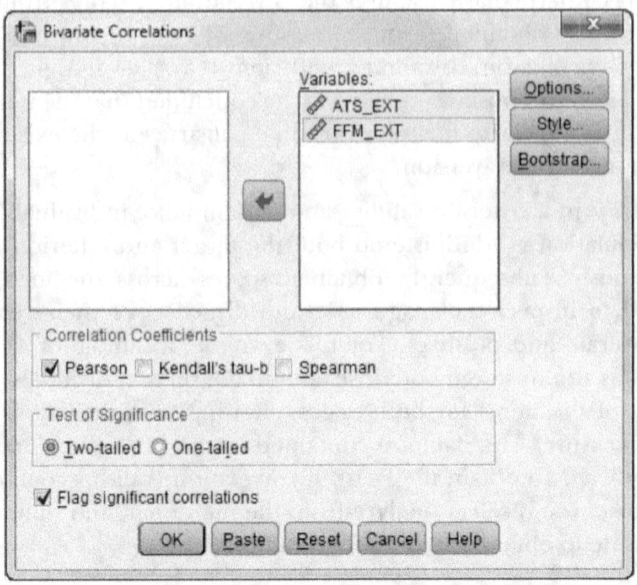

We can click the **Options** button to obtain the following window.

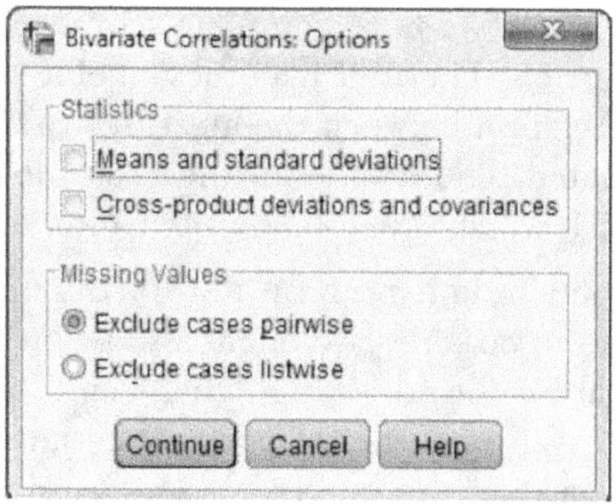

Note that by default missing data are excluded pairwise, meaning that for each pair of variables for which correlations are requested, individuals with missing data on one or both are excluded from the calculation of Pearson's *r*. In contrast, listwise deletion would result in the exclusion from calculation of all Pearson's *r* values of individuals with missing data on any of the variables to be included in a calculation of a correlation coefficient. In this case, because only two variables are involved, pairwise and listwise deletion will yield the same results. In addition, we can request the calculation of means and standard deviations, as well as the cross-product deviations and covariances matrix for the variables. In this case, we will check the **Means and standard deviations** box. The resulting output appears below.

Correlations

Descriptive Statistics

	Mean	Std. Deviation	*N*
ATS_EXT	4.3723	.77343	389
FFM_EXT	25.57	6.609	411

Correlations

		ATS_EXT	FFM_EXT
ATS_EXT	Pearson Correlation	1	.568**
	Sig. (2-tailed)		.000
	N	389	383
FFM_EXT	Pearson Correlation	.568**	1
	Sig. (2-tailed)	.000	
	N	383	411

** Correlation is significant at the 0.01 level (2-tailed).

As shown, the output includes descriptive statistics for each variable, followed by the correlation matrix. Note that 411 individuals completed all items on the new instrument (ats_ext), and 383 completed all items on the criterion (ffm_ext). Pearson's *r* for the two variables is then based on the

383 individuals for whom we have complete scores on both instruments, yielding a value of 0.568. The null hypothesis being tested is that in the population, the correlation between the measures (ρ) is 0, indicating that the scores are unrelated. The *p*-value for the *z* statistic testing this hypothesis is less than 0.0001, which is well below the typical α threshold of 0.05.

In addition to obtaining hypothesis test for the null hypothesis of no correlation between the variables, we might also be interested in obtaining a confidence interval for the correlation coefficient in the population. As with confidence intervals for other statistics, such an interval provides us with information regarding the range of values within which the population correlation value is likely to be. There are a few technical issues that should be dealt with when discussing confidence interval results for *r*. The *p*-value for Pearson's *r* is obtained using the equation

$$t = \sqrt{n-2}\sqrt{\left(\frac{[r^2]}{[1-r^2]}\right)}. \tag{5.1}$$

The resulting value is then compared to the *t* distribution with $n-2$ degrees of freedom. To construct the confidence interval for the correlation coefficient, Fisher (1915) developed a transformation of *r* to the standard normal distribution, leading to what is commonly known as Fisher's *z* transformation. It takes the following form

$$z_r = .5\ln\left(\frac{1+r}{1-r}\right). \tag{5.2}$$

The distribution of z_r tends toward the normal as the sample size increases. The upper and lower bounds of the confidence interval of ρ can then be obtained through the use of z_r. Once Fisher's transformation has been conducted, lower and upper bounds of the 95% confidence interval in the standard normal scale are obtained as follows:

$$\begin{aligned} Z_L &= z_r - z_{0.975}\sqrt{\frac{1}{n-3}} \\ Z_U &= z_r + z_{0.975}\sqrt{\frac{1}{n-3}} \end{aligned} \tag{5.3}$$

Here, *n* is the total sample size, and $z_{0.975}$ is the value of the standard normal distribution at the 97.5th percentile. If the researcher was interested in obtaining a 90% confidence interval she would use $z_{0.95}$. After these values are obtained on the standard normal distribution scale, they are then converted back to the standard normal as such:

$$r_L = \frac{e^{2Z_{L-1}}}{e^{2Z_{L+1}}}$$
$$r_U = \frac{e^{2Z_U} - 1}{e^{2Z_U} + 1} \tag{5.4}$$

One issue with the sample estimate of the population correlation is that it is somewhat negatively biased as a result of its slightly negative skewed distribution. The previous equations do not take into account this bias, which is most pronounced for smaller sample sizes. In an effort to counter the effects of this negative bias, Keeping (1962) developed an adjustment to the correlation that can also be applied to the estimates of the upper and lower bounds of the confidence interval. This correction takes the form

$$bias(r) = \left(\frac{r}{2(n-1)}\right). \tag{5.5}$$

The bias correction term is then used in calculating the confidence interval as follows:

$$Z_L = z_r - bias(r) - z_{0.975}\sqrt{\frac{1}{n-3}} \tag{5.6}$$

The bias corrected correlation estimate is then calculated as:

$$r_{adj} = \frac{e^{2Z_r - bias(r)} - 1}{e^{2Z_r - bias(r)} + 1}. \tag{5.7}$$

To obtain the *Z* transformation confidence interval for ρ, we can use the `!rhoCI` SPSS macro developed by Weaver and Koopman (2014). The macro can be obtained at the website for this book, along with the example data file used here. Prior to using the macro, the user will first need to run the following syntax in the SPSS syntax window, much as we did in Chapter 3 for the confidence interval of Cronbach's α.

```
FILE HANDLE MacroDefinition /NAME="C:\research\SPSS
psychometric book\rhoCI.SPS".
FILE HANDLE TheDataFile /NAME="C:\research\SPSS psychometric
book\data\concurrent_validity.sav".
```

This code tells SPSS where the macro and the data file can be found, and assigns them the names `MacroDefinition` and `TheDataFile`, respectively.

The Insert File command in SPSS then needs to be used in order to compile the macro. This only needs to be done once in each SPSS session.

```
INSERT FILE ="C:\research\SPSS psychometric book\rhoCI.SPS".
```

The next lines to be run are designed to keep the macro code itself from appearing in the output window.

```
SET PRINTBACK = OFF. /* Suppress output.
INSERT FILE = "MacroDefinition".
SET PRINTBACK = ON. /* Turn output back on.
```

We are now ready to call the macro, for which we will use the following lines in the SPSS syntax window:

```
NEW FILE.
DATASET CLOSE all.
GET FILE = "TheDataFile".
DATASET NAME raw.
!rhoCI DataSetName = raw
 /Vars = ats_ext ffm_ext
/ConfidenceLevel = 95.
```

First, note that the name we assigned the file earlier, `TheDataFile`, appears in the `GET FILE` command. This data file is then called raw, which SPSS will use in the actual macro call. We don't need to change any of the first four lines of syntax. In the actual macro call, we will need to indicate the names of the variables to include in the analysis on the `/Vars` line, and we can indicate the level of confidence that we would like (95% in this example) on the final line. If we do not include the `/ConfidenceLevel` line, the default of 95% will be used. Taken together, the syntax for running the `!rhoCI` macro appears below:

```
FILE HANDLE MacroDefinition /NAME="C:\research\SPSS
psychometric book\rhoCI.SPS".
FILE HANDLE TheDataFile /NAME="C:\research\SPSS psychometric
book\data\concurrent_validity.sav".
INSERT FILE ="C:\research\SPSS psychometric book\rhoCI.SPS".

SET PRINTBACK = OFF. /* Suppress output.
INSERT FILE = "MacroDefinition".
SET PRINTBACK = ON. /* Turn output back on.
```

```
NEW FILE.
DATASET CLOSE all.
GET FILE = "TheDataFile".
DATASET NAME raw.
!rhoCI DataSetName = raw
 /Vars = ats_ext ffm_ext
/ConfidenceLevel = 95.
```

After their initial use, the commands through the `SET PRINTBACK` line do not need to be run again.

From the output, we see that the 95% confidence interval for the population correlation between the two variables is 0.496 to 0.632, meaning that we are 95% confident that the population correlation between ATS_EXT and FFM_EXT lies between 0.496 and 0.632. Thus, based on both the significant hypothesis test and on the fact that the confidence interval does not include 0, we can conclude that there is a significant positive correlation between the new measure of extraversion and the criterion, and the best sample estimate we have of this value is 0.568.

Pearson Correlations With 95% Confidence Intervals*

	X	*Y*	*r*	Lower	Upper	*p*	*n*	Notes
1	ATS_EXT	ATS_EXT	1.000	.	.	.	389	
2	ATS_EXT	FFM_EXT	.568	.496	.632	.000	383	
3	FFM_EXT	ATS_EXT	.568	.496	.632	.000	383	
4	FFM_EXT	FFM_EXT	1.000	.	.	.	411	

* With PAIRWISE deletion.

SPSS affords us with an alternative for calculating the confidence interval of the correlation coefficient through the use of the bootstrap. Recall from Chapter 3 that the bootstrap methodology involves the repeated random resampling of individuals from the original sample and the calculation of the target statistic (the correlation in this case) for each of these bootstrap samples. From this distribution, a confidence interval can be created either by identifying the appropriate percentiles in the bootstrap distribution of correlation values (e.g., the 2.5th and 97.5th for the 95% confidence interval), or through the bias corrected and accelerated (BCa) bootstrap, which corrects biases known to exist with the bootstrap in some cases (Wilcox, 2009). The bootstrap option is available through the standard menu that we used to obtain the confidence interval as described above.

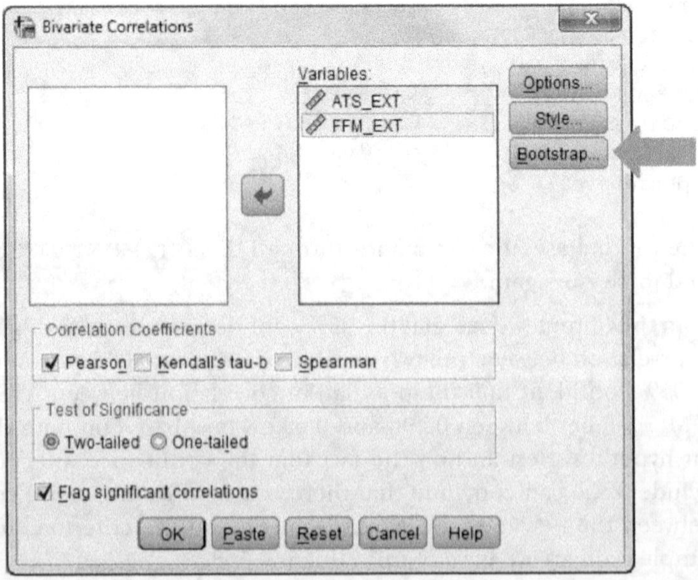

The bootstrap window itself appears below. Here we must indicate that we would like for the bootstrap to be performed by clicking on the **Perform bootstrapping** box. We then must indicate how many bootstrap samples we would like, with the default being 1,000. We can leave the seed for the Mersenne Twiser random number generator alone, and set our desired level of confidence, with the default being 95%. Finally, we must determine which of the two bootstrap methods to use for obtaining the confidence interval, with the default being the bootstrap. We will use both and compare the results with one another, and with the *Z* transformation confidence interval.

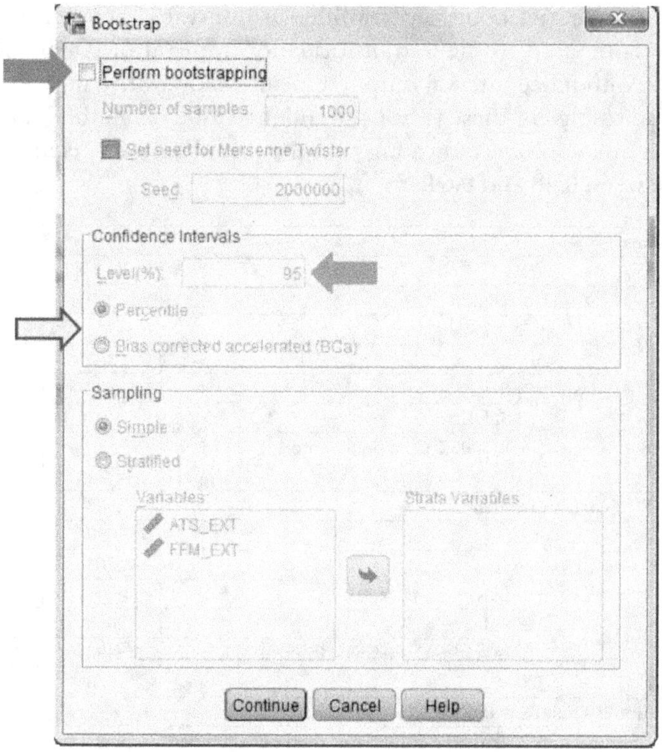

Output for the percentile bootstrap confidence interval appears below.

Correlations					
				ATS_EXT	FFM_EXT
ATS_EXT	Pearson Correlation			1	.568**
	Sig. (2-tailed)				.000
	N			383	383
	Bootstrap[a]	Bias		0	.000
		Std. Error		0	.039
		95% Confidence Interval	Lower	1	.489
			Upper	1	.639
FFM_EXT	Pearson Correlation			.568**	1
	Sig. (2-tailed)			.000	
	N			383	383
	Bootstrap[b]	Bias		.000	0
		Std. Error		.039	0
		95% Confidence Interval	Lower	.489	1
			Upper	.639	1

** Correlation is significant at the 0.01 level (2-tailed).
[a] Unless otherwise noted, bootstrap results are based on 1,000 bootstrap samples.

The 95% percentile bootstrap confidence interval is between 0.489 and 0.639, as compared to the Z transformation interval of 0.496 and 0.632. The BCa confidence interval output appears below, with values of 0.480 to 0.638. The results for these various confidence interval methods are all very similar to one another, indicating that the population correlation is likely to fall between 0.48 and 0.64.

Correlations

				ATS_EXT	FFM_EXT
ATS_EXT	Pearson Correlation			1	.568**
	Sig. (2-tailed)				.000
	N			383	383
	Bootstrap[a]	Bias		0	–.001
		Std. Error		0	.039
		BCa 95% Confidence Interval	Lower	.	.480
			Upper	.	.638
FFM_EXT	Pearson Correlation			.568**	1
	Sig. (2-tailed)			.000	
	N			383	383
	Bootstrap[a]	Bias		–.001	0
		Std. Error		.039	0
		BCa 95% Confidence Interval	Lower	.480	.
			Upper	.638	.

** Correlation is significant at the 0.01 level (2-tailed).

[a] Unless otherwise noted, bootstrap results are based on 1,000 bootstrap samples.

Once the validity coefficient has been obtained, a natural question is, "What does this value mean?" In this case, we know that it is significantly different from 0, but beyond this is there anything else that we can say about the magnitude of this value? One approach to interpreting correlation coefficients in general is to refer to the guidelines for interpretation provided by Cohen (1988), who created the following heuristic to be used in the absence of guidance in the literature:

$$\text{Small effect: } 0.1 \leq r < 0.3$$

$$\text{Medium effect: } 0.3 \leq r < 0.5$$

$$\text{Large effect: } r \geq 0.5$$

Thus, based on Cohen's guidelines, the relationship between the new extraversion measure and the criterion measure of extraversion is of a large magnitude. In other words, there appears to be fairly strong evidence as to the criterion validity of the score on the new extraversion measure. Of course, it is preferable to ground the interpretation within the literature when available, as Cohen suggests.

In addition to obtaining the correlation value, it is often desirable to calculate the coefficient of determination (r^2) when considering the validity coefficient. This value expresses the proportion of variation in the criterion that is accounted for by the new (target) measure. For the current problem, if we use the bias corrected correlation value, r^2 is $0.568^2 = 0.323$. This indicates that the new measure accounts for approximately 32% of the variability in the old measure. It is a decision for the researcher as to how important or large is the relative magnitude of this value, and the information it yields on the quality of the newly created instrument.

Concurrent validity can also focus on relationships between the instrument of interest and a criterion to which it should not be theoretically related. In this instance, a finding of a relatively large relationship would be indicative of measurement problems. In our example, the researcher knows that theoretically speaking extraversion is conceptually different from a desire to be popular among a social group. However, the researcher also knows that if items on the extraversion scale are not written accurately, they could inadvertently assess subjects' desire to be popular with others, rather than the intended construct of extraversion. For this reason, the researcher is interested in determining whether the new measure also exhibits evidence of divergent validity with regard to popularity. As noted earlier in the chapter, divergent validity refers to the relative lack of relationship between the target instrument and a criterion with which it should not be related theoretically. In this example, the subjects were administered a measure of their desire for popularity in addition to the two extraversion scales. Using the command window as described above, in conjunction with the following call to the !rhoCI macro, we obtain the following output.

```
!rhoCI DataSetName = raw
 /Vars = ats_ext ffm_ext
/ConfidenceLevel = 95.
```

Correlations			
		ATS_EXT	SCQ_POP
ATS_EXT	Pearson Correlation	1	–.001
	Sig. (2-tailed)		.977
	N	389	386
SCQ_POP	Pearson Correlation	–.001	1
	Sig. (2-tailed)	.977	
	N	386	418

Pearson Correlations With 95% Confidence Intervals*								
	X	*Y*	*r*	Lower	Upper	*p*	*n*	Notes
1	ATS_EXT	ATS_EXT	1.000	.	.	.	389	
2	ATS_EXT	SCQ_POP	–.001	–.101	.098	.977	386	
3	SCQ_POP	ATS_EXT	–.001	–.101	.098	.977	386	
4	SCQ_POP	SCQ_POP	1.000	.	.	.	418	
* With PAIRWISE deletion.								

One would expect that with divergent validity the correlation between the target (new extraversion) measure and the divergent construct (popularity) to be lower than the correlation between the target measure and the convergent criterion, or existing, measure of extraversion. Indeed, in this example we see that this is the case. The correlation between the new extraversion measure and popularity seeking is –0.001, which is lower than the correlation between new and old extraversion measures. Furthermore, inspection of results indicates that the correlation of –0.001 is not statistically significant from 0, based on the hypothesis test and confidence interval. Thus, we have some evidence of divergent validity and can be reasonably sure that the new measure is not mistakenly assessing a desire for popularity.

Considerations in Concurrent Validity Assessment

There are several issues to consider when investigating concurrent validity. These are important considerations because they can impact both the magnitude and interpretation of the validity coefficient (see Crocker and Algina, 1986, and Raykov and Marcoulides, 2011, for further discussion of these). First, and perhaps most important, the selection of the criterion is critical. In general, the criterion must be well-established as being directly associated with the construct of interest (referred to as the "ultimate" by Raykov and Marcoulides, 2011), or at the very least, as a very reasonable measure of the construct. The selection and argument in favor of the criteria is based upon a thorough review of the literature in the area of interest, and consideration of existing evidence of the reliability and validity of the criterion measure scores. In the case of divergent validity, selection of the criterion is perhaps even more difficult than for the convergent situation, because it may not be completely clear what a related but different construct should be. In the current example, the researcher was able to cite literature indicating that extraversion and a desire for popularity can be confused, but are different. Therefore, information that the new extraversion scale is unrelated to the desire for popularity provides validity evidence for the new scale by dissociating it from this nuisance construct. However, evidence that the new extraversion measure is unrelated to intelligence would not be valuable in an argument for validity. This is because there is no theoretical basis to suggest that extraversion and intelligence can be confused with one another on theoretical grounds.

A second important issue is the sample size used to estimate the validity coefficient. Specifically, smaller samples can lead to more unstable correlation estimates, and potentially more influenced by outliers present in the data. Therefore, researchers must carefully examine the characteristics of the sample when conducting concurrent validity studies, including, among others: sample size, distribution of values on variable, and skewness/kurtosis. The distributions of the variables of interest represent a third concern in conducting concurrent validity studies. In particular, if the variables are both categorical in nature, such as ordinal ratings, then Spearman's rank–order correlation (by selecting the **Spearman** check box in the **main correlation coefficient** menu box) would be more appropriate than Pearson's *r*. If both variables are dichotomous, then the phi coefficient (found in the **Crosstabs** menu box under the **Statistics** button) would be preferred, whereas if one variable is dichotomous and the other continuous, we would use the biserial or point biserial correlations, previously described in Chapter 2.

The reliability of scores from the target and criterion measures will also have an impact on the magnitude of the validity coefficient. In particular, as previously discussed, scores with relatively low reliability will yield lower correlation coefficients. Indeed, Raykov and Marcoulides (2011) demonstrate analytically that the correlation between the target and criterion is a lower bound for the correlation between their true scores. The lower the reliability, the further the correlation between the observed measures will be from the correlation between the true scores, which represents the actual validity coefficient. In response, researchers may employ the correction for attenuation using the observed correlation coefficient as well as the reliability estimates for each of the measures. This correction provides an estimate of the correlation coefficient between the true scores, as opposed to the observed score correlation value. The correction for attenuation is calculated as

$$\frac{r_{x,y}}{\sqrt{\rho_x \rho_y}} \tag{5.8}$$

where ρ_x is the reliability estimate for measure *x*, ρ_y is the reliability estimate for measure *y*, and $r_{x,y}$ is the correlation between the two observed scores, *x* and *y*. For the current example, Cronbach's α was 0.79 and 0.87, respectively, for the new and old extraversion scales. Taking the bias corrected correlation of 0.62, we calculate the correlation between the measures, corrected for attenuation to be

$$\frac{0.568}{\sqrt{0.79(0.87)}} = \frac{0.568}{\sqrt{0.69}} = \frac{0.568}{0.83} = 0.684.$$

Raykov and Marcoulides recommend considering both the observed and corrected correlation estimates when assessing criterion validity evidence.

Predictive Validity

Predictive validity is similar to concurrent validity with the difference being with the timing in which the criterion score is obtained relative to the score from the target measure. For concurrent validity studies, both the target and criterion measures are typically administered simultaneously; for predictive validity studies, the criterion measure score is obtained at some point in time after the target measure has been administered. For example, the target of a predictive validity study could be the score on a college entrance exam, with the criterion being academic performance after completion of the freshmen year. In that case, the validity coefficient would be the correlation between the exam score and the freshman year GPA. In other respects, the interpretation and treatment of this correlation coefficient would be similar to what we saw with the concurrent validity coefficient described above.

Using SPSS to conduct a predictive validity study, consider an instance in which data were being collected on a coping competence measure for a sample of children at the beginning of Kindergarten and again for the same children at the beginning of first grade. The initial measure was completed by parents and was designed to measure a child's general ability to cope with everyday stressors. In this context, the score should represent this coping competence construct prior to the beginning of formal schooling. The second measure was completed by each child's first grade teacher in the beginning of the school year. In this study, the goal is to measure children's ability to cope with everyday stressors after a year of formal schooling. For the predictive validity study, the focus is whether scores on the measure obtained prior to Kindergarten can be used to predict childrens' coping competence in the school setting (first grade).

To obtain the predictive validity coefficient, we will use the standard approach for obtaining a Pearson correlation coefficient for a pair of variables, including the menu box and the `!rhoCI` macro. As shown, the SPSS command sequence and the calling of the macro are essentially identical to that used in the previous concurrent validity example. In this case, the two variables of interest are CcK (coping competence at the beginning of Kindergarten) and Cc1 (coping competence at the beginning of first grade).

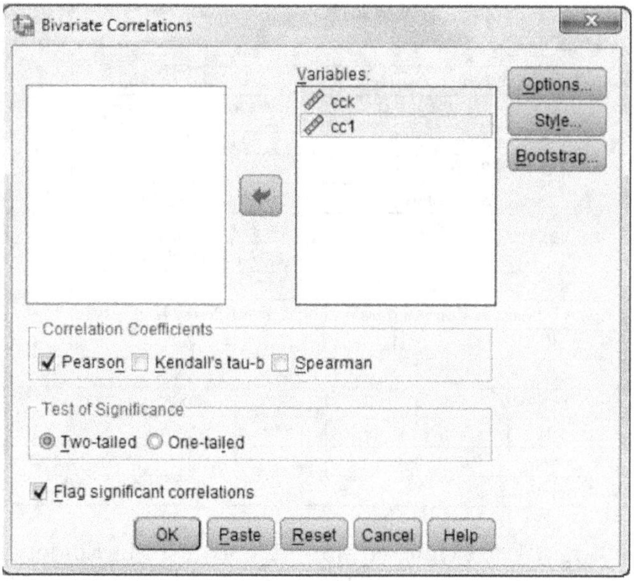


```
FILE HANDLE MacroDefinition /NAME="C:\research\SPSS
psychometric book\rhoCI.SPS".
FILE HANDLE TheDataFile /NAME="C:\research\SPSS psychometric
book\data\predictive_validity.sav".

* Use INSERT FILES to run the macro definition syntax.
* Note that this only needs to be done once per SPSS session.

INSERT FILE =
"C:\research\SPSS psychometric book\rhoCI.SPS".

* The SET PRINTBACK OFF line prevents the macro definition from
* being echoed in the user's output window.

SET PRINTBACK = OFF. /* Suppress output.
INSERT FILE = "MacroDefinition".
SET PRINTBACK = ON. /* Turn output back on.

NEW FILE.
DATASET CLOSE all.
GET FILE = "TheDataFile".
DATASET NAME raw.

!rhoCI DataSetName = raw
 /Vars = cck cc1
/ConfidenceLevel = 95.
```

Correlations

		cck	ccl
cck	Pearson Correlation	1	.755**
	Sig. (2-tailed)		.000
	N	304	274
ccl	Pearson Correlation	.755**	1
	Sig. (2-tailed)	.000	
	N	274	281

** Correlation is significant at the 0.01 level (2-tailed).

Pearson Correlations With 95% Confidence Intervals*

	X	*Y*	*r*	Lower	Upper	*p*	*n*	Notes
1	cck	cck	1.000	.	.	.	304	
2	cck	ccl	.755	.699	.802	.000	274	
3	ccl	cck	.755	.699	.802	.000	274	
4	ccl	ccl	1.000	.	.	.	281	

* With PAIRWISE deletion.

Of the original 304 children who were assessed in Kindergarten, 274 also participated in first grade. There were also an additional 7 children who were measured in first grade, but who did not have scores in Kindergarten. The Pearson's correlation coefficient for the two measures is 0.755. The 95% confidence interval is approximately 0.70 to 0.80, meaning that we are 95% confident that the actual correlation between the measures lies between those two values. Finally, the coefficient of determination is $0.755^2 = 0.570$, indicating that scores obtained prior to Kindergarten account for 57% of the variation in the first grade coping competence score. More precisely, 57% of the variance in Grade 1 scores is associated with the variance in Kindergarten scores.

Discriminant Groups Validity

As mentioned in the above description of the various types of validity evidence, discriminant groups validity can be thought of as a type of criterion validity evidence or associations with other variables validity evidence. In this case, the criterion of interest is a known group (e.g., diagnosis), rather than another continuous measure, but in most other respects the concept underlying this approach is similar to that in concurrent validity. As an example, consider two reading assessments developed for use among 2nd grade students. These tests are designed to be used together, with one assessing more mechanical aspects of reading (e.g., phonological awareness), whereas the other seeks to assess comprehension and understanding of passages. Higher scores on each instrument are indicative of stronger reading performance. In addition to administering these two measures to the Grade 2 students, we also seek to know whether the students successfully passed a separate norm-referenced, standardized achievement test or not. Theory would suggest that those who passed the standardized reading assessment should have higher mean scores on both of the reading assessments. To assess this hypothesis, we have at least two possibilities for statistical analysis. Given that we have two groups, and the test scores are continuous in nature, we could conduct separate *t*-tests comparing group means. The two groups include those students who passed the standardized reading assessment, and those who did not. However, because the two scores are part of the same assessment, measuring distinct but related aspects of reading aptitude, we may be better served relying on a multivariate comparison of means (i.e., comparing the groups' means on both scores simultaneously) in the form of a multivariate analysis of variance (MANOVA). There is a large literature on the decision of when to apply a univariate (single dependent variable) approach such as a *t*-test or ANOVA versus a multivariate procedure such as MANOVA (e.g., Huberty & Olejnik, 2006; Tabachnick & Fidell, 2007). We will, therefore, not devote time to that issue, other than to say that in the current situation the fact that both scores are theoretically measuring different aspects of the same construct (reading aptitude), coupled with the relatively high correlation between them (0.87) would suggest the use of multivariate analyses rather than a univariate approach.

We will leave the technical details underlying MANOVA and the generally accepted post hoc investigation using discriminant analysis to other texts (see authors noted above). Rather, our focus here will be on carrying out the analysis using SPSS. The dataset for this example is called validity.sav, and the SPSS menu commands for conducting the MANOVA and the follow-up discriminant analysis are **Analysis ► General Linear Model ► Multivariate**, which produces the following window:

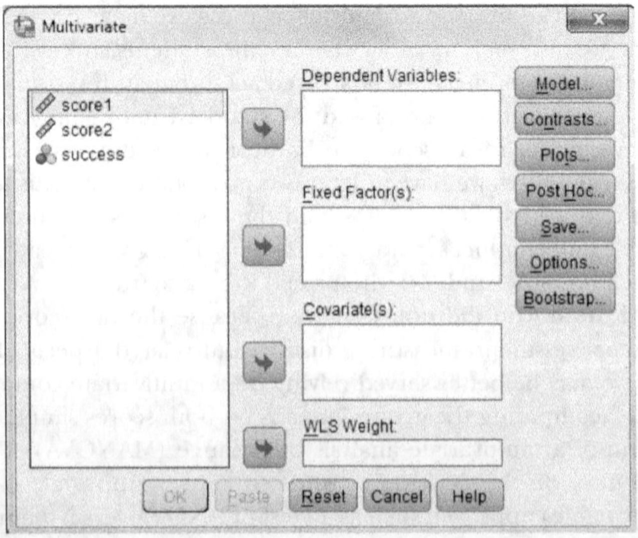

In the Fixed Factors window, we will place the grouping variable, in this case **Success**, which is coded as 1 (Yes) or 0 (No) to indicate whether the students passed the standardized reading exam. In the **Dependent Variables** box we place the two reading aptitude test scores, **score1** and **score2**.

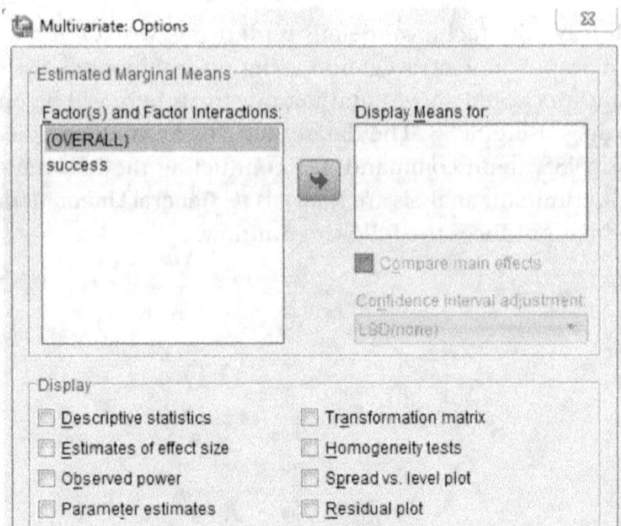

We need to request the means of score1 and score2 for each of the success groups by clicking on the **Options** button.

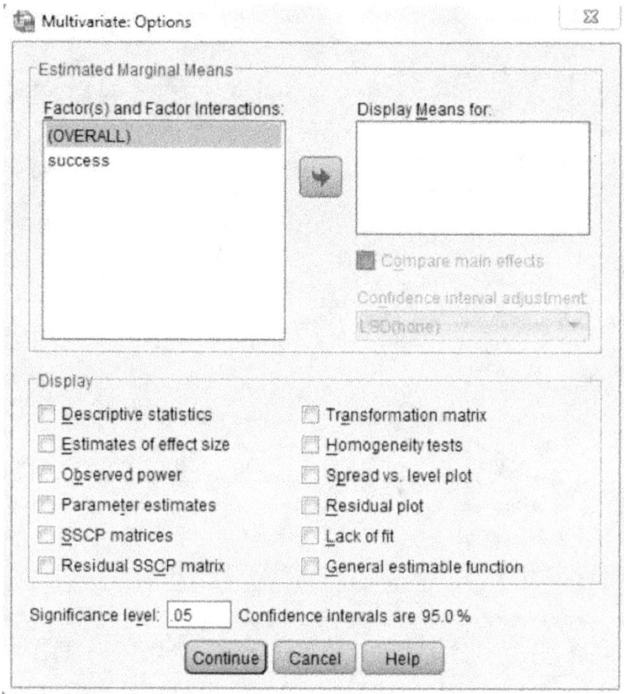

We move the variable success to the **Display Means for** box, in order to obtain the means for both scores for both success groups. In addition, we can request the effect size for the mean differences by checking the **Estimates of effect size** box.

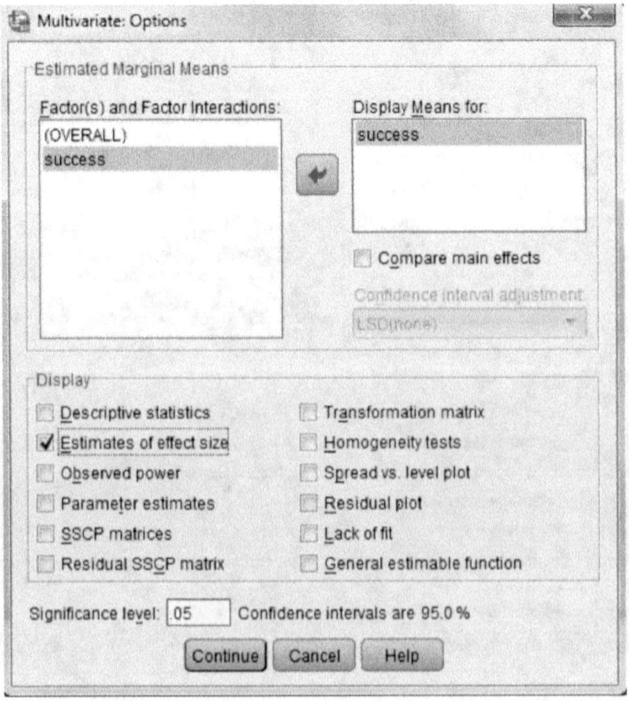

The output for this analysis appears below.

Between-Subjects Factors

		Value Label	*N*
success	.00	No	46
	1.00	Yes	328

Multivariate Tests[a]

Effect		Value	F	Hypothesis df	Error df	Sig.	Partial Eta Squared
Intercept	Pillai's Trace	.970	5920.366[b]	2.000	371.000	.000	.970
	Wilks' Lambda	.030	5920.366[b]	2.000	371.000	.000	.970
	Hotelling's Trace	31.916	5920.366[b]	2.000	371.000	.000	.970
	Roy's Largest Root	31.916	5920.366[b]	2.000	371.000	.000	.970
success	Pillai's Trace	.021	4.026[b]	2.000	371.000	.019	.021
	Wilks' Lambda	.979	4.026[b]	2.000	371.000	.019	.021
	Hotelling's Trace	.022	4.026[b]	2.000	371.000	.019	.021
	Roy's Largest Root	.022	4.026[b]	2.000	371.000	.019	.021

a. Design: Intercept + success

b. Exact statistic

Tests of Between-Subjects Effects

Source	Dependent Variable	Type III Sum of Squares	df	Mean Square	F	Sig.	Partial Eta Squared
Corrected Model	score1	844.888[a]	1	844.888	3.879	.050	.010
	score2	1053.375[b]	1	1053.375	.555	.457	.001
Intercept	score1	2406317.059	1	2406317.059	11049.121	.000	.967
	score2	21308092.37	1	21308092.37	11234.172	.000	.968
success	score1	844.888	1	844.888	3.879	.050	.010
	score2	1053.375	1	1053.375	.555	.457	.001
Error	score1	81015.487	372	217.784			
	score2	705580.264	372	1896.721			
Total	score1	5817614.000	374				
	score2	50616769.00	374				
Corrected Total	score1	81860.374	373				
	score2	706633.639	373				

a. R Squared = .010 (Adjusted R Squared = .008)

b. R Squared = .001 (Adjusted R Squared = -.001)

success

Dependent Variable	success	Mean	Std. Error	95% Confidence Interval	
				Lower Bound	Upper Bound
score1	No	119.826	2.176	115.548	124.105
	Yes	124.402	.815	122.800	126.005
score2	No	360.826	6.421	348.199	373.453
	Yes	365.936	2.405	361.207	370.665

The first table in the SPSS output simply informs us of the sample size (374), that there were two groups in the **Success** variable, taking the values of Yes and No, and that 328 students comprised the Yes group, and 46 students in the No group. Next, the focus of our attention in this example are the MANOVA test results, which appear in the **Multivariate Tests** box. The test statistics appears in the Value column, where we see results for each of 4 multivariate test statistics, including: Pillai's Trace, Wilks' Lambda, Hotelling's Trace, and Roy's Largest Root. Each of these is converted to an *F* statistic with, in this case, 2 and 371 degrees of freedom. The *p*-value for each *F* is 0.019, which is less than the α of 0.05, leading us to reject the null hypothesis. A key question is: What is the null hypothesis in this case? In the case of MANOVA, the null hypothesis is that the multivariate mean does not differ between the groups in the population. Thus, if the groups do, in fact, differ in the population on one mean and not the other, or on both, the null hypothesis should be rejected. And, in fact, in this example we would reject the multivariate null hypothesis, based on the *p*-value (0.019) presented above.

The second table in the output includes the univariate ANOVA results for each score separately. Because we are focusing on the multivariate results because the scores are believed to measure two aspects of a common construct, the univariate results are not of real interest. However, we will briefly review the tables for pedagogical purposes. In particular, we will concentrate on the section of the table associated with the Success variable. There is a separate row for both score1 and score2, and these results include the Type III sum of squares, the degrees of freedom (*df*), the mean square (sum of squares divided by degrees of freedom), the *F* statistic, the *p*-value associated with the *F*, and the Partial Eta Squared effect size. From these results, we can see that there was a statistically significant difference between the success groups for score1 ($p = 0.05$) but not for score2 ($p = 0.457$). However, we would like to emphasize that in this case, we are primarily interested in the MANOVA results, rather than the univariate ANOVA analyses.

The third table that we obtain from SPSS includes the score means for the two success groups, along with the standard error for each, and the 95% confidence interval for the mean. An examination of these results shows that for the sample, the means of both scores were larger for the Yes group. In other words, we see that the means on both scores were larger for those who passed the aptitude test than for those who did not. Therefore, we can conclude based on the univariate results that those who pass the standardized exam have statistically significantly higher means on the first target test, which measures the mechanical aspects of reading. However, the groups' means do not differ on reading comprehension and understanding, measured by score2.

Once the decision regarding the null hypothesis is made, the next question to be addressed is, for which of the variables do the groups differ? The significant MANOVA result does not provide an answer as for which variables the means differ, only that they differ in some respect. Discriminant analysis serves as the standard post hoc investigative analysis for a significant MANOVA. Discriminant analysis can be conducted easily in SPSS using the following menu commands: **Analyze ► Classify ► Discriminant**, with which we obtain the following window.

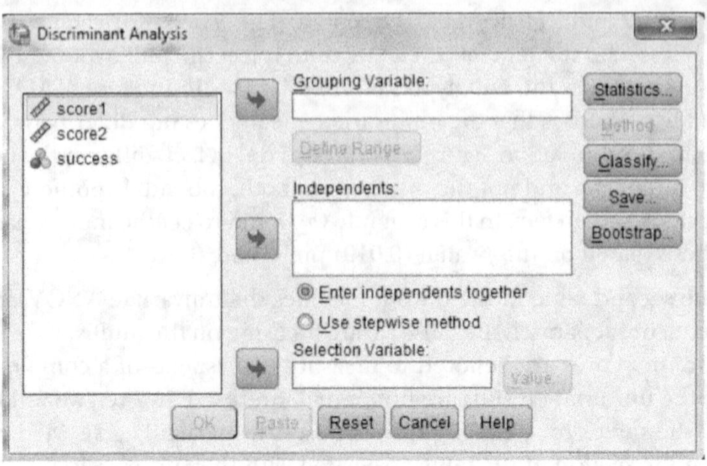

We must define the grouping variable (success), as well as what SPSS calls the independents, which are the outcome variables from the MANOVA, score1 and score2.

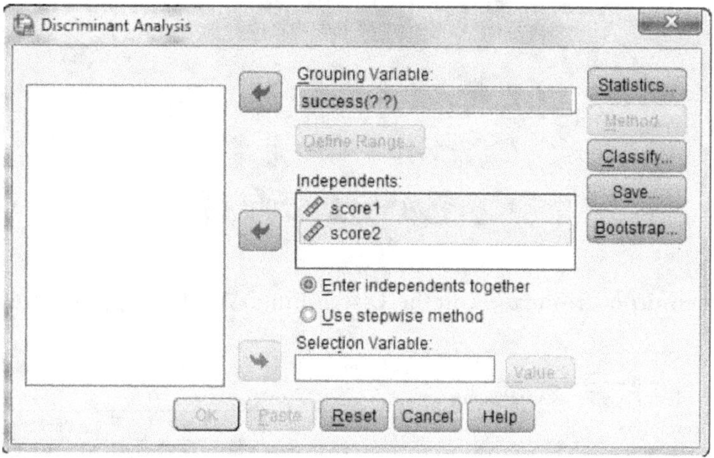

We now need to define the range for the success variable by highlighting it, and clicking on **Define Range...**. We obtain the following window, into which we type the minimum and maximum values of the grouping variable, in this case 0 (No) and 1 (Yes), respectively.

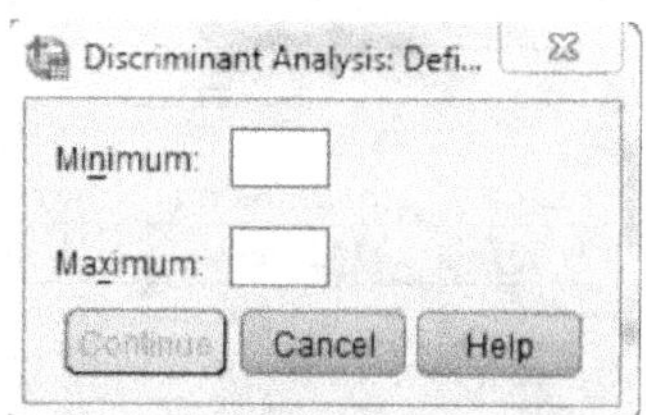

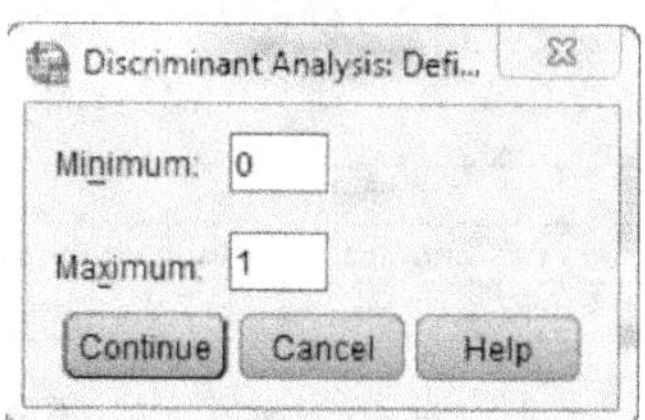

We then click **Continue**.

Under the **Statistics** button in the main Discriminant Analysis window, we can request a number of additional statistics, although for our purposes probably only the Means will be useful.

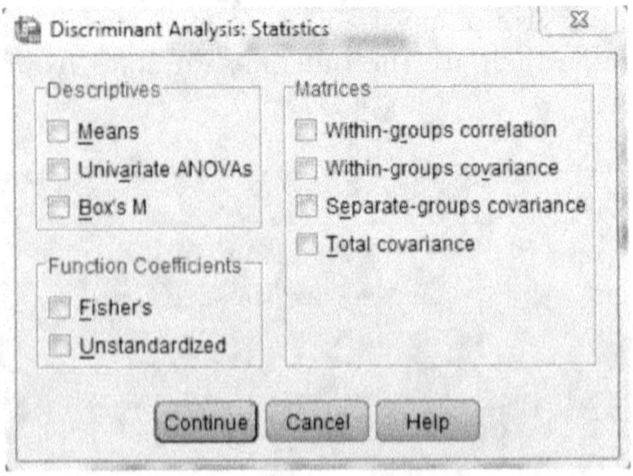

The output from running the Discriminant Analysis appears below.

Discriminant

Analysis Case Processing Summary

Unweighted Cases		*N*	Percent
Valid		374	86.6
Excluded	Missing or out-of-range group codes	8	1.9
	At least one missing discriminating variable	47	10.9
	Both missing or out-of-range group codes and at least one missing discriminating variable	3	.7
	Total	58	13.4
Total		432	100.0

Group Statistics

success		Mean	Std. Deviation	Valid *N* (listwise) Unweighted	Weighted
No	score1	119.8261	13.96552	46	46.000
	score2	360.8261	44.19166	46	46.000
Yes	score1	124.4024	14.86318	328	328.000
	score2	365.9360	43.46251	328	328.000
Total	score1	123.8396	14.81434	374	374.000
	score2	365.3075	43.52540	374	374.000

Analysis 1

Summary of Canonical Discriminant Functions

Eigenvalues

Function	Eigenvalue	% of Variance	Cumulative %	Canonical Correlation
1	.022a	100.0	100.0	.146

a First 1 canonical discriminant functions were used in the analysis.

Wilks' Lambda				
Test of Function(s)	Wilks' Lambda	Chi-square	*df*	Sig.
1	.979	7.965	2	.019

Standardized Canonical Discriminant Function Coefficients	
	Function
	1
score1	2.011
score2	−1.502

Structure Matrix	
	Function
	1
score1	.693
score2	.262
Pooled within-groups correlations between discriminating variables and standardized canonical discriminant functions Variables ordered by absolute size of correlation within function.	

Functions at Group Centroids	
success	Function
	1
No	−.392
Yes	.055
Unstandardized canonical discriminant functions evaluated at group means	

In particular, we are interested in the table labeled Structure Matrix. This table contains what are commonly referred to as structure coefficients, which are the correlations between the individual dependent variables and a linear combination of these variables that maximizes the differences between the two groups. Alternatively, discriminant analysis reports a weight for each dependent variable that when multiplied by the variable and then added to the product of the other dependent variable and its weight, the means of the combination are as different as possible for the two groups (standard canonical discriminant function coefficients). Then, to obtain the structure coefficients, the correlation between each dependent variable and this weighted linear combination is calculated. Large absolute values of these coefficients are indicative of a variable that is strongly related to the significant group difference. While there are no universally agreed upon standards for what constitutes a large value, Tabachnick and Fidell (2007) recommend using 0.32, because its squared value is approximately 0.1, meaning that the linear combination accounts for at least 10% of the variance in the dependent variable. While there are other possibilities for this purpose, we will use 0.32 here. Also, note that the sign of the coefficient is not germane to its relative importance. A negative value simply means that the first group (No in this case) had a smaller mean for that variable than did the second group (Yes). Here we see that score1 has a structure coefficient of 0.693, which is well beyond the threshold of 0.32, while score2 has a value of 0.262. Therefore, we can say that the significant multivariate hypothesis testing result is primarily due to group differences on score1, the measure of mechanical reading skills, and not score2, comprehension and understanding.

What is the final conclusion to be drawn from this analysis? Recall that the goal was to determine whether the reading aptitude measure as a whole, which is made up of the two components represented in score1 and score2, exhibits discriminant groups validity. Theory would suggest that those who passed the standardized reading assessment are better readers than those who did not pass, and thus should perform better on this new measure of reading aptitude. This, of course, is based on the premise that the measure is an appropriate measure of reading. However, these results reveal a somewhat mixed message. That is, the groups did differ on the aptitude measure taken as a whole, and the means for both variables were in the expected direction. However, the discriminant analysis showed that the groups really differed on only score1 and not score2. Does this mean that scores on score1 are valid for interpretation as a student's reading aptitude but those on score2 are not? Consequently, we cannot answer this question definitively. It is possible, for instance, that the standardized reading assessment focuses primarily on lower level reading skills that match more closely those included in score1. In that case, we may have a problem of inadequate construct coverage in the criterion measure. On the other hand, it is also possible that our definition of reading aptitude is too broad, so that there is not a single criterion that is adequate for validation assessment of both instruments. Finally, it is certainly possible that score2 is problematic as an assessment of reading aptitude. However, a single study using one criterion is not sufficient to reach such a conclusion. Perhaps the best we can do with the current results is to consider performance on score1 to be a potentially useful indication of some aspect of reading aptitude, particularly that component that is associated with the standardized test. Similarly, we may tentatively conclude that performance on score2 is not an adequate indicator of reading aptitude *as represented in the standardized reading assessment.* But, we should plan future studies with different criteria and different foci (e.g., construct validity, content validity, predictive validity) to more fully understand this measure.

Construct Validity

Construct validity has become an increasingly important focus of validation researchers over the last two decades. Indeed, the very notion of construct validity as a separate entity came into question as researchers began to view it as a unified theory of validity (Anastasi, 1986; Messick, 1989; Nunnally & Bernstein, 1994). Thus, we can think of concurrent or discriminant groups evidence as facets of the broader construct validity of test scores. This said, there remains a distinct element that is commonly referred to as construct validity evidence, and for which specific statistical tools are employed. In our initial definition of construct validity, we indicated that such evidence is demonstrated when the measure behaves in a theoretically consistent fashion. For example, if theory suggests that an instrument is unidimensional, then a construct validity study using factor analysis could be conducted to empirically examine this claim. Further, if theory also states that this unidimensional construct should be positively correlated with another construct for which measures exist, then the correlation between the two latent variables could be estimated in a structural equation modeling context. Finally, if theory also suggests that the construct is positively associated with observed academic performance, a multitrait multiple indicator (MIMIC) model can be used to empirically test this relationship.

In short, while it is true that the notion of construct validation has expanded to encompass a wide variety of analyses and evidence, there does also remain an aspect of it that is frequently investigated using latent variable modeling, such as factor analysis and structural equation modeling. We will devote much of the remainder of the chapter to demonstrating how these complex latent variable modeling techniques can be utilized in SPSS to investigate construct validity evidence.

Exploratory Factor Analysis as a Tool for Investigating Construct Validity

Our first example of investigating construct validity using latent variable modeling techniques will involve exploratory factor analysis (EFA). EFA is an extremely common tool in the social sciences to examine an instrument's dimensionality. Specifically, it is a data reduction technique that takes a set of observed variables (e.g., scale items) and uses the covariances among them to identify a smaller set of unobserved (latent) variables to explain their interdependency. In the context of construct validation, these latent variables would represent the unobserved constructs (e.g., mathematics ability, achievement motivation) that have been referenced throughout this chapter.

Before going into further detail regarding the technical aspects of EFA and conducting it using SPSS, it is very important to reiterate the crucial role of theory in these analyses. The data reduction that occurs with EFA is completely based upon statistical relationships among the observed data. At the risk of over simplification, the computer has no knowledge of the theory underlying a scale, nor does it know which items should be grouped together based on the scale development principles laid out by those who created the instrument. Thus, the items will be grouped based solely on the covariances among them. The researcher brings theory to bear to these results so that they make sense conceptually. To the extent that this can be done, there is evidence of construct validity. As with all scientific endeavors, there is no guarantee of success a priori, and the researcher must be prepared to acknowledge that the statistical evidence does not match the theory. This lack of agreement may be due to a faulty theory about the nature of the construct, or to statistical issues such as biased sample selection, poor item wording, or problems in instrument administration, among others. Indeed, whether the EFA results buttress the theory or not, it is important to remember that a single study is not definitive, and that construct validation is carried out over many years of research (Kane, 2006).

We emphasize the importance of theory so much because EFA is by definition an exploratory procedure. When we examine confirmatory factor analysis (CFA), we will have the opportunity to explicitly state our theory in statistical terms in the form of a factor model. But with EFA, we essentially take the items and let the statistical algorithm indicate to us how many, and what form the factors will take. Therefore, we need to have a predetermined idea for what this latent variable structure should look like, if theory does in fact hold true. Without such a theory, we may have difficulty coherently explaining the EFA results, or perhaps worse may develop a theoretical explanation based upon our data.

To serve as an example of using EFA for construct validation, let's consider the Scale for Creative Attributes and Behaviors (SCAB), a 20-item instrument designed to assess an individual's propensity for creativity. Each item is measured on a seven-point scale from 1 (*Strongly Disagree*) to 7 (*Strongly Agree*), with statements arranged so that greater agreement corresponds to a more creative outlook. Research has identified 5 separate components (or, dimensions) of creativity: Creative Engagement, Creative Cognition, Spontaneity, Tolerance, and Fantasy. Items on the SCAB are organized so each subscale consists of four items. Whereas theory supports the existence of these 5 dimensions of creativity, empirical evidence is also needed to substantiate these claims. To investigate the latent structure of the SCAB as a way for gathering construct validity evidence, a sample of 413 college students (75.54% females) were asked to complete the instrument (contained in the SPSS dataset scab.sav). Subsequently, an EFA was conducted to ascertain whether the 20 SCAB items grouped together in factors in a manner consistent with the theory described above.

Because factor analysis is a complex statistical procedure with many possible variations, the goal of this discussion is to present only the most commonly used of these variants, while encouraging the interested reader to further investigate the topic. There are a number of excellent books available on the topic (e.g., Brown, 2015; Gorsuch, 1983; Thompson, 2004), and it is our intention that the current description of EFA and SPSS serve as a starting point. EFA involves a series of analyses beginning with initial factor extraction, followed by factor rotation, and concluding with an investigation into the appropriate number of factors for a given sample. While each of these steps represents a distinct analytic thrust, in practice they are conducted more or less simultaneously by the researcher. As a catalyst for discussion of these, we will use the following SPSS commands to access the appropriate window for conducting an EFA on the 20 SCAB items: **Analyze ► Dimension Reduction ► Factor**.

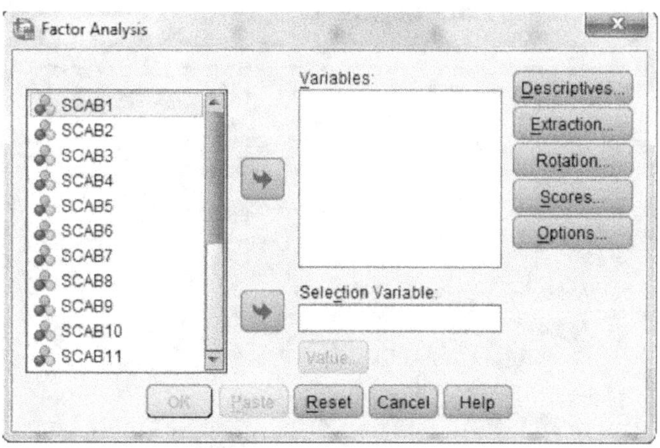

First, we must move all of the variables that we would like to include in the factor analysis to the Variables window.

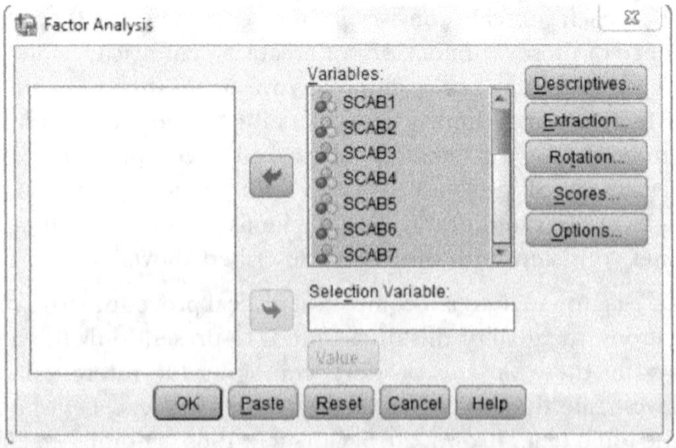

We must then select the type of factor extraction that we would like to use. Factor extraction refers to the initial identification of relationships between the individual indicator variables (items) and the factors, or latent constructs that are believed to underlie the data. The correlation coefficients between the indicators and the factors are known as factor loadings. They serve as perhaps the primary piece of statistical evidence in an EFA because they reveal which indicators are associated with which factors. The initial extraction takes the covariances among the indicators and uses them to estimate factor loadings. We indicate to SPSS which of the methods we would like to use by selecting **Extraction...**.

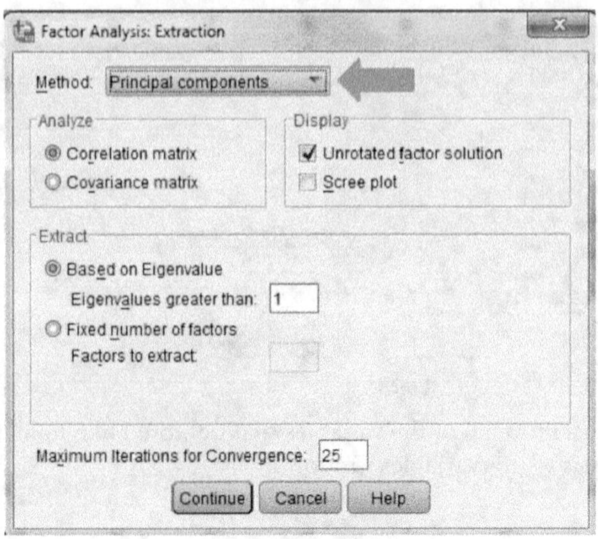

We select the method of extraction using the pull down menu highlighted by the green arrow above. Perhaps the most robust and popular approach is principal axis factoring, which is the one that we will use in this example. Other extraction algorithms available in SPSS are Alpha, Harris, Image, Maximum Likelihood, Generalized Least Squares, and Unweighted Least Squares. Principal components analysis is not strictly speaking factor analysis, and will typically not be the method of choice in such cases. Costello and Osborne (2005) provide a very user-friendly discussion of the utility of these methods for conducting EFA.

In addition to specifying the extraction algorithm, the user can also indicate how the number of factors to extract is to be determined. This can be done using the number of Eigenvalues greater than a specific value (e.g., eigenvalues > 1.00), or the user can indicate how many factors would be preferred to extract. We would recommend this latter approach in nearly all situations. Based on theory, the user can indicate how many factors are expected. In the current case, therefore, we expect 5 factors and would specify this in the Fixed number of factors Factors to extract window, as shown below. Note that we have also checked the **Scree plot** box, which will provide us with a visual representation of the eigenvalues corresponding to each of the extracted factors. The scree plot provides the data analyst another source of information to judge the number of empirical factors underlying a set of scale items.

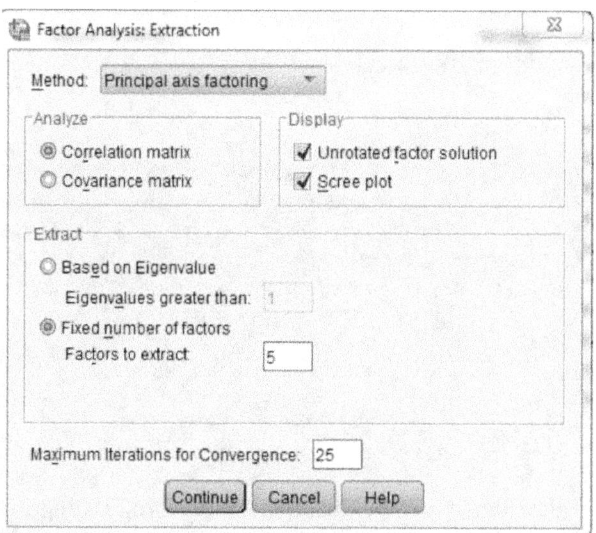

In addition to factor extraction, we must also concern ourselves with the rotation of the factor loadings after their initial extraction. Rotation simply refers to the transformation of the initial loadings using one of several possible methods. But why would we need to transform these initial loadings? The reason for rotation is that the initial factor loading matrix is unlikely to produce a solution that is easily interpretable, in which each indicator is clearly associated with only one factor, a situation known as approximate simple structure. Rather, in practice, we most often find that a given indicator (or, items) will have relatively large loadings with multiple factors, making it difficult to determine with which latent variable the indicator belongs. Rotation is used, therefore, to more clearly associate the indicators with the factors to achieve approximate simple structure. Instead, rotation methodologies all retain the proportion of variation explained in the indicators, even as they alter the individual loadings. In other words, the mathematical quality of the solution, as measured by proportion of variance explained, is not changed, but rather only how that explained variance is apportioned among the various factors. Clearly, much more could be said in this regard, but there is simply not sufficient space. Thus, the interested reader is encouraged to more deeply investigate the notion of rotation using one of the excellent resources that we have previously listed.

There are a number of factor rotation methods available to use to assist with the interpretation of results. The selection of rotation methods can be specified in SPSS by clicking **Rotation...**.

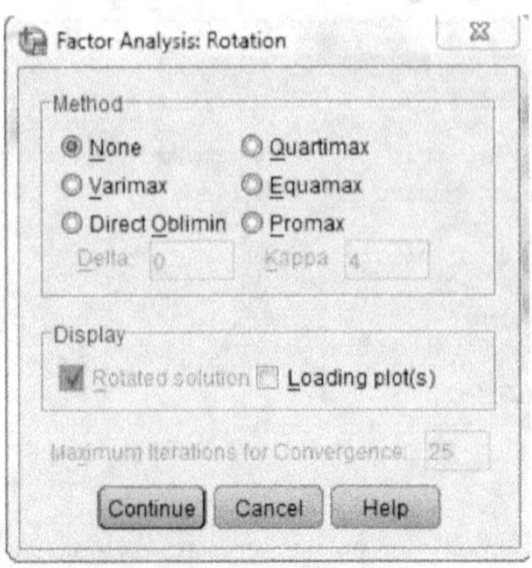

The rotation alternatives can be divided into two broad categories: orthogonal or oblique. Orthogonal factors are forced to be uncorrelated, whereas oblique factors are allowed to be correlated. Within each of these broad families there are multiple options available in SPSS. Within the orthogonal family the most popular rotations that are available in SPSS include: Varimax, Equamax, and Quartimax. Among the oblique rotations, the methods available in SPSS include: Promax and Direct Oblimin. As with extraction methods, there is no universally agreed upon rotation method within the two broad families, or between the families themselves. The decision as to whether one should rely on an orthogonal or oblique rotation is best made through an examination of the inter-factor correlations. Thus, one might begin by using an orthogonal rotation such as Promax, and examine the correlations among the factors. If these are all near 0, then an orthogonal solution might be best, whereas if at least some of them depart from 0, the researcher may elect to use an oblique approach. Within the rotation families, no one method is always best. Perhaps the most popular approaches are Varimax in the orthogonal family, and Promax in the oblique. Perhaps the best advice that we can offer the researcher is to try a few rotation methods and compare the factor loading results. We generally start with Promax as our models have correlated factors. The method that produces the cleanest results, in terms of a simple structure, may be thought of as the best for that particular problem.

The final stage of an EFA is the determination of the number of factors underlying the collective item set. Unfortunately, there is not a single approach for deciding on the optimal number of factors. Rather, much like validity assessment itself, empirical evidence must be evaluated from a variety of sources, most (but not all) statistical in nature. Perhaps one of the oldest and most familiar such approaches (but not one of the best) is the so called eigenvalue greater than 1.00 rule, or Kaiser's little jiffy (e.g., Thompson, 2004). Each factor in the analysis has associated with it an eigenvalue, which is simply a measure of the amount of variation in the indicators associated with it. Kaiser (1958, 1962, 1970) proposed that factors accounting for more variation than was accounted for by a single indicator variable (a value that is always 1 when the data are standardized) should be retained. To use this method, the researcher would simply review the table of eigenvalues and define the optimal number of factors as that for which the last eigenvalue is greater than 1. However, this is not a highly recommended method and should never be used in isolation.

Another option is to visually inspect a scree plot that reports the eigenvalues (on the *y*-axis) by the factor number (on the *x*-axis). The optimal number of factors is then associated with the point where the graph flattens out, which corresponds to a relative lack of explanatory power by the remaining factors. The scree plot is obtained by checking the Scree Plot button in the Extraction window, as demonstrated above. Yet another potential approach is to determine what proportion of the variance in the observed indicators as a whole is explained by each factor, and then stop including factors when the explained variance does not appreciably increase. Another source of information is through the inspection of the residual correlation matrix. Recall that initial factor extraction is based upon covariances among the observed indicators. A byproduct of EFA is the prediction of correlations (standardized covariances) among the indicators. Thus, a factor solution can be termed good when it accurately predicts these correlations. The difference between the actual and predicted correlation matrices is the residual correlation matrix. Thus, for each pair of correlations there exists a residual value. While there is no absolute standard for what is a good residual, general practice has suggested values less than 0.05 or 0.10 (Thompson, 2004). Thus, we would review the residual correlation matrix and if the vast majority of correlations are less than 0.05 (or 0.10), we would conclude that the solution was good. We can obtain the residual correlations in SPSS by first clicking on **Descriptives...**. We then check the **Reproduced** box in the following window.

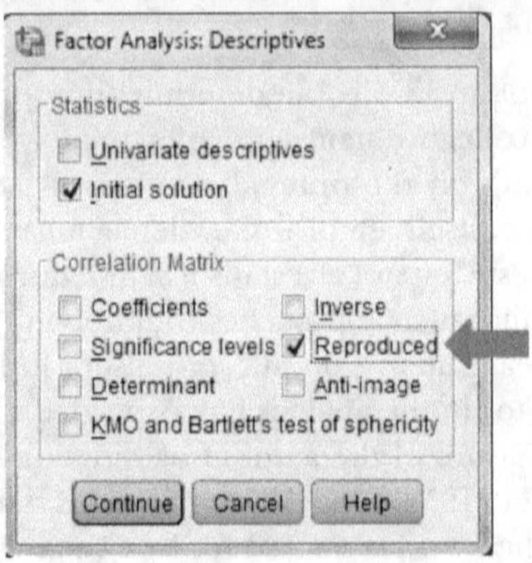

One point to note about each of the methods for determining the optimal number of factors that we described above is that they are descriptive in nature, and thus allow for subjectivity regarding the best solution. For example, how do we decide on what is a sufficiently small number of residual correlations over 0.05, or where the scree plot levels off, or what proportion of variance in the indicators is sufficiently large? To reduce the subjectivity associated with determining the number of factors, statisticians have worked on developing more inferential and/or objective methods. One of these, the chi-square goodness of fit test, is associated with the maximum likelihood method of factor extraction described above. This statistic tests the null hypothesis that the EFA predicted covariances among the indicators is equal to the observed covariances. In one sense, it is similar in spirit to an examination of the residual correlation matrix. However, it goes further by providing an actual significance test. If the null hypothesis is rejected, we would conclude that the EFA solution is not good because the actual and predicted covariances differ beyond chance. While this test holds much promise, it is limited due to its sensitivity to both sample size and the distribution of the indicators. Thus, if the data are not distributed multivariate normal, or the sample is very small (or very large), the chi-square test is not dependable.

A second inferential approach is the use of a parallel analysis (PA) to determine the number of empirical factors (Horn, 1965; O'Connor, 2000). PA is based upon the logic of randomization tests, which are very common in nonparametric statistics. PA requires multiple steps, beginning with the estimation of the EFA solution for the observed data and retaining the eigenvalues. Then, in Step 2 a set of many (e.g., 1,000) random data sets are created based on the same distributional properties as the observed indicators, including: the mean, standard deviation, skewness, and kurtosis. However, within the randomly generated data sets, the indicators are not correlated with one another. The creation of these datasets can be done either through the generation of random values or by randomly mixing indicator values among the observations. As an example of the latter case, the computer would give Subject 1 the indicator 2 value for Subject 103, the indicator 3 value for Subject 15, and so on. In either case, the resultant random dataset shares the distributional characteristics of the observed data with the exception that the indicators are uncorrelated, or orthogonal. For each of the 1,000 randomly generated datasets created an EFA is conducted, the eigenvalues are saved to create a distribution of eigenvalues for the case in which there are no factors underlying the data due to no consistent patterns among the correlations. In Step 3, each eigenvalue from Step 1 is compared with the distribution of eigenvalues based on the random datasets from Step 2. For example, the first eigenvalue obtained from the EFA of the observed data is compared to the distribution of first eigenvalues from Step 2. If the eigenvalues based on the observed data are greater than those based on the random datasets, then the factors are retained. Based on a PA, the number of factors retained is equal to the number of eigenvalues from the actual data greater than those from the randomly generated datasets. While different standards for what is large have been used, perhaps most commonly large refers to the values greater than or equal to the 95th percentile of the parallel distribution, which would correspond to setting an α of 0.05. An example of the use of PA to identify the number of factors is provided later in this chapter. Notably, PA is not available in the SPSS dropdown menu options for conducting EFA. Instead, it must be specified using the SPSS syntax, as demonstrated.

Prior to demonstrating the use of these methods in SPSS, we should discuss just briefly their relative merits. Much research has been conducted comparing the relative accuracy of these various methods with one another. In general, this work has shown that Kaiser's little jiffy, the scree plot, and the proportion of variance explained all perform relatively poorly in terms of accurately identifying the number of factors present (e.g., Thompson, 2004). On the other hand, PA, minimum average partial (MAP), and the residual correlation matrix are generally more effective tools in this regard (Costello & Osborne, 2005; Henson & Roberts, 2006). In addition, particularly for PA, there continues to be revisions and updates to the methodology so that the researcher should check in with the quantitative methods literature on occasion to be sure that he is using the most recent version of this approach.

Based on this overview of EFA, we can now consider applying it to the SCAB data. To recall, theory postulates the presence of 5 factors underlying the 20-item measure, with each factor represented by four items. The following output is based upon the combination of extraction and rotation that we described applying above, namely principal axis factoring with Promax rotation. The first table reports the initial communality estimates, or R^2 values for each indicator, along with the Extraction communalities. These final communality (also represented as h^2) values represent the proportion of variance in the items that are accounted for by the 5 factors. As shown, final communality estimates ranged from .171 (SCAB20) to .836 (SCAB1). These estimates indicate that the variance of several of the indicators are quite well explained by the 5 factor solution (e.g., SCAB1, SCAB4, SCAB7), whereas the solution is not particularly effective for SCAB17 or SCAB20.

Communalities

	Initial	Extraction
SCAB1	.744	.836
SCAB2	.476	.489
SCAB3	.624	.675
SCAB4	.679	.683
SCAB5	.366	.420
SCAB6	.461	.487
SCAB7	.585	.727
SCAB8	.482	.515
SCAB9	.383	.375
SCAB10	.602	.722
SCAB11	.569	.660
SCAB12	.500	.535
SCAB13	.473	.441
SCAB14	.499	.499
SCAB15	.546	.611

SCAB16	.556	.692
SCAB17	.330	.272
SCAB18	.589	.821
SCAB19	.580	.664
SCAB20	.211	.171
Extraction Method: Principal Axis Factoring.		

Next, the eigenvalues and proportion of variance explained by each factor, along with the difference in eigenvalues between each adjacent factors, and the cumulative proportion of variance explained are reported. Based on Kaiser's criterion, 5 factors does appear to be appropriate for this problem, and retaining 5 factors explains essentially all of the variance in the indicators. Thus, we have two pieces of evidence supporting the theoretical 5 factor solution. However, Kaiser's rule is not typically the best rule to follow.

Total Variance Explained

	Initial Eigenvalues			Extraction Sums of Squared Loadings			Rotation Sums of Squared Loadings[a]
Factor	Total	% of Variance	Cumulative %	Total	% of Variance	Cumulative %	Total
1	5.363	26.817	26.817	4.936	24.680	24.680	3.973
2	2.360	11.802	38.619	1.961	9.805	34.485	3.001
3	2.089	10.445	49.064	1.715	8.575	43.061	3.550
4	1.814	9.069	58.133	1.522	7.612	50.672	2.631
5	1.544	7.719	65.852	1.160	5.800	56.473	1.669
6	.979	4.893	70.745				
7	.790	3.949	74.694				
8	.649	3.246	77.940				
9	.626	3.132	81.073				
10	.534	2.670	83.742				
11	.509	2.547	86.290				
12	.435	2.173	88.463				
13	.376	1.878	90.341				
14	.371	1.857	92.198				
15	.360	1.801	93.999				
16	.291	1.455	95.454				
17	.285	1.423	96.878				
18	.242	1.211	98.089				
19	.219	1.094	99.184				
20	.163	.816	100.000				
Extraction Method: Principal Axis Factoring.							
[a] When factors are correlated, sums of squared loadings cannot be added to obtain a total variance.							

The figure below shows the scree plot that graphically shows the eigenvalues for each of the factors reported in the above table. Again, we are looking for the number of factors for which this plot clearly levels out. It would appear that such a point is reached between 5 and 6 factors, again supporting a 5-factor solution.

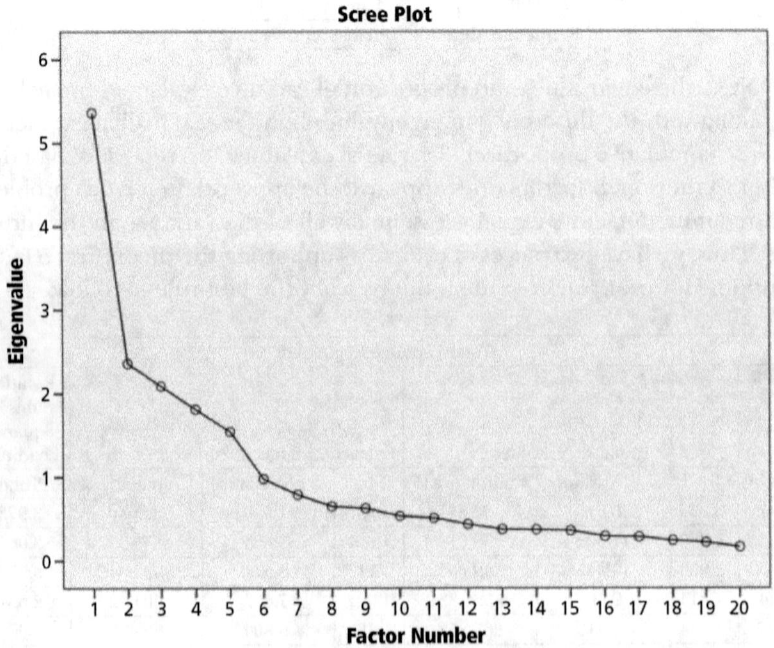

The tables below are provided in the SPSS output and report the unrotated initial factor loadings, the eigenvalues for each of the 5 factors we requested be retained.

Factor Matrix[a]

	Factor				
	1	2	3	4	5
SCAB1	.719	.008	–.372	.148	–.399
SCAB2	.619	–.089	–.241	.057	–.193
SCAB3	.685	–.029	–.280	.142	–.325
SCAB4	.687	.057	–.355	.122	–.261
SCAB5	.432	.149	–.239	–.074	.385
SCAB6	.575	.118	–.072	–.093	.358
SCAB7	.637	.136	–.221	–.093	.495
SCAB8	.591	.084	–.135	–.113	.356
SCAB9	.418	–.401	.131	–.040	.146
SCAB10	.498	–.546	.367	–.201	–.010
SCAB11	.379	–.591	.385	–.115	–.073
SCAB12	.417	–.499	.317	–.110	–.020
SCAB13	.471	.285	.343	–.143	–.012
SCAB14	.548	.293	.324	–.086	–.016
SCAB15	.279	.559	.424	–.133	–.149
SCAB16	.251	.588	.459	–.181	–.198
SCAB17	.481	.061	.085	.171	–.022
SCAB18	.069	.040	.305	.836	.149
SCAB19	.164	–.001	.259	.739	.157
SCAB20	.394	.005	.063	.082	–.074

Extraction Method: Principal Axis Factoring.

[a] Attempted to extract 5 factors. More than 25 iterations required. (Convergence = .002). Extraction was terminated.

We typically do not use the unrotated factor loadings and, therefore, will not discuss them here. Indeed, we can indicate to SPSS that we so not want this table to be printed if we do not want them reported in the output. Instead, we will examine the rotated factor loadings below to determine if these low communalities are harbingers of poor factor loadings. The below table reports the residual correlation matrix (discrepancy between the actual and reproduced matrices).

Reproduced Correlations

		SCAB1	SCAB2	SCAB3	SCAB4	SCAB5	SCAB6	SCAB7	SCAB8	SCAB9	SCAB10	SCAB11	SCAB12	SCAB13	SCAB14	SCAB15	SCAB16	SCAB17	SCAB18	SCAB19	SCAB20
Reproduced Correlation	SCAB1	.836[a]	.619	.747	.748	.237	.285	.331	.317	.184	.192	.137	.170	.197	.270	.088	.067	.349	.001	.068	.301
	SCAB2	.619	.489[a]	.565	.563	.234	.288	.335	.316	.232	.259	.201	.223	.178	.233	.042	.020	.286	-.015	.051	.247
	SCAB3	.747	.565	.675[a]	.670	.223	.281	.320	.309	.208	.229	.176	.202	.202	.269	.086	.065	.335	.031	.094	.288
	SCAB4	.748	.563	.670	.683[a]	.281	.322	.383	.352	.175	.159	.095	.137	.204	.272	.096	.073	.330	.004	.070	.278
	SCAB5	.237	.234	.223	.281	.420[a]	.428	.546	.446	.149	.058	-.035	.031	.170	.203	.055	.023	.175	-.042	.014	.121
	SCAB6	.285	.288	.281	.322	.428	.487[a]	.584	.498	.240	.211	.106	.161	.289	.329	.155	.126	.254	-.002	.063	.188
	SCAB7	.331	.335	.320	.383	.546	.584	.727[a]	.605	.259	.176	.051	.128	.270	.317	.098	.057	.269	-.023	.056	.193
	SCAB8	.317	.316	.309	.352	.446	.498	.605	.515[a]	.252	.219	.110	.167	.268	.309	.117	.086	.251	-.038	.035	.189
	SCAB9	.184	.232	.208	.175	.149	.240	.259	.252	.375[a]	.482	.439	.417	.132	.155	-.068	-.093	.177	.041	.096	.157
	SCAB10	.192	.259	.229	.159	.058	.211	.176	.219	.482	.722[a]	.677	.618	.234	.249	.017	.010	.203	-.046	.027	.201
	SCAB11	.137	.201	.176	.095	-.035	.106	.051	.110	.439	.677	.660[a]	.589	.160	.171	-.035	-.040	.161	.013	.067	.167
	SCAB12	.170	.223	.202	.137	.031	.161	.128	.167	.417	.618	.589	.535[a]	.179	.195	-.011	-.019	.178	.011	.067	.174
	SCAB13	.197	.178	.202	.204	.170	.289	.270	.268	.132	.234	.160	.179	.441[a]	.465	.457	.472	.249	.027	.058	.198
	SCAB14	.270	.233	.269	.272	.203	.329	.317	.309	.155	.249	.171	.195	.465	.499[a]	.468	.477	.295	.074	.107	.232
	SCAB15	.088	.042	.086	.096	.055	.155	.098	.117	-.068	.017	-.035	-.011	.457	.468	.611[a]	.648	.185	.038	.034	.140
	SCAB16	.067	.020	.065	.073	.023	.126	.057	.086	-.093	.010	-.040	-.019	.472	.477	.648	.692[a]	.169	.000	-.006	.130
	SCAB17	.349	.286	.335	.330	.175	.254	.269	.251	.177	.203	.161	.178	.249	.295	.185	.169	.272[a]	.201	.224	.211
	SCAB18	.001	-.015	.031	.004	-.042	-.002	-.023	-.038	.041	-.046	.013	.011	.027	.074	.038	.000	.201	.821[a]	.731	.104
	SCAB19	.068	.051	.094	.070	.014	.063	.056	.035	.096	.027	.067	.067	.058	.107	.034	-.006	.224	.731	.664[a]	.130
	SCAB20	.301	.247	.288	.278	.121	.188	.193	.189	.157	.201	.167	.174	.198	.232	.140	.130	.211	.104	.130	.171[a]
Residual[b]	SCAB1		-.021	-.005	.047	-.001	-.021	.005	.025	-.033	.017	.003	.018	.008	.020	.003	-.011	-.036	.022	-.007	-.054
	SCAB2	-.021		.014	.003	.010	-.025	-.015	.045	.022	-.031	.000	.028	-.007	-.062	.015	.031	.004	-.020	.021	.032
	SCAB3	-.005	.014		-.032	-.022	.030	-.032	.009	.031	.007	-.026	-.029	-.010	.011	-.017	.000	.040	-.004	-.014	.040
	SCAB4	.047	.003	-.032		.032	-.010	.026	-.036	-.035	.016	.021	.005	.022	.001	.010	-.011	-.035	.005	.013	-.044
	SCAB5	-.001	.010	-.022	.032		.009	-.014	.014	-.003	-.025	-.001	.041	.019	-.017	.024	-.015	-.044	.010	9.986E-5	-.005
	SCAB6	-.021	-.025	.030	-.010	.009		.019	-.021	.020	.003	.037	-.048	-.060	-.034	.035	.014	.080	-.010	-.011	.016
	SCAB7	.005	-.015	-.032	.026	-.014	.019		.001	-.055	.010	.010	.006	.005	.020	-.032	-.002	.012	-.008	.007	.016
	SCAB8	.025	.045	.009	-.036	.014	-.021	.001		.054	.012	-.024	-.010	.014	-.004	.009	.018	-.048	.015	.006	-.069
	SCAB9	-.033	.022	.031	-.035	-.003	.020	-.055	.054		.046	-.043	-.016	-.038	-.040	.011	.017	.068	-.002	-.010	.019
	SCAB10	.017	-.031	.007	.016	-.025	.003	.010	.012	.046		.010	-.027	-.015	-.003	.026	.001	-.024	.010	-.005	-.030
	SCAB11	.003	.000	-.026	.021	-.001	.037	.010	-.024	-.043	.010		.034	-.032	-.020	.011	.011	.014	.012	-.012	.003
	SCAB12	.018	.028	-.029	.005	.041	-.048	.006	-.010	-.016	-.027	.034		.073	.018	-.025	-.014	-.053	-.013	.031	-.017
	SCAB13	.008	-.007	-.010	.022	.019	-.060	.005	.014	-.038	-.015	-.032	.073		.147	-.035	-.042	-.093	.024	-.010	-.012
	SCAB14	.020	-.062	.011	.001	-.017	-.034	.020	-.004	-.040	-.003	-.020	.018	.147		-.063	-.047	.004	-.015	.010	.018
	SCAB15	.003	.015	-.017	.010	.024	.035	-.032	.009	.011	.026	.011	-.025	-.035	-.063		.061	.016	.011	-.004	-.012
	SCAB16	-.011	.031	.000	-.011	-.015	.014	-.002	.018	.017	.001	.011	-.014	-.042	-.047	.061		.025	-.012	.011	-.012
	SCAB17	-.036	.004	.040	-.035	-.044	.080	.012	-.048	.068	-.024	.014	-.053	-.093	.004	.016	.025		.008	-.036	.130
	SCAB18	.022	-.020	-.004	.005	.010	-.010	-.008	.015	-.002	.010	.012	-.013	.024	-.015	.011	-.012	.008		.008	-.045
	SCAB19	-.007	.021	-.014	.013	9.986E-5	-.011	.007	.006	-.010	-.005	-.012	.031	-.010	.010	-.004	.011	-.036	.008		.007
	SCAB20	-.054	.032	.040	-.044	-.005	.016	.016	-.069	.019	-.030	.003	-.017	-.012	.018	-.012	-.012	.130	-.045	.007	

Extraction Method: Principal Axis Factoring.

a. Reproduced communalities

b. Residuals are computed between observed and reproduced correlations. There are 15 (7.0%) nonredundant residuals with absolute values greater than 0.05.

The preceding tables report the estimation and residual correlation values. These values can be used as an overall indicator of residual correlation magnitude for each indicator. Specifically, when examining the individual residuals, the goal is to identify the number in the off-diagonal with absolute value greater than our cut-off (e.g., 0.05). In addition, in a footnote to the table, SPSS indicates for us how many, and what percent of the residuals are greater than 0.05. From these results we see that 15 (or, 7%) of the indicators had average residuals greater than the cut-value of 0.05. Thus, we can conclude that these results indicate good fit of the 5 factor model to the data.

Recall that we requested the Promax rotation, which is oblique. The factor loadings and the inter-factor correlation matrix appear below.

Pattern Matrix[a]

	Factor				
	1	2	3	4	5
SCAB1	.980	–.058	–.081	–.018	–.034
SCAB2	.644	.093	.062	–.053	–.038
SCAB3	.842	.018	–.049	–.008	.003
SCAB4	.824	–.092	.065	–.013	–.021
SCAB5	–.003	–.127	.695	–.058	–.027
SCAB6	–.014	.041	.662	.077	.004
SCAB7	–.015	–.044	.884	–.038	–.005
SCAB8	.028	.042	.683	.021	–.033
SCAB9	–.007	.536	.198	–.130	.048
SCAB10	–.017	.858	–.015	.034	–.069
SCAB11	–.006	.852	–.158	–.014	–.004
SCAB12	.008	.744	–.048	–.006	–.003
SCAB13	–.004	.130	.134	.571	–.007
SCAB14	.066	.119	.155	.566	.043
SCAB15	–.027	–.107	–.058	.812	–.010
SCAB16	–.034	–.106	–.117	.877	–.057
SCAB17	.259	.089	.104	.164	.204
SCAB18	–.035	–.049	–.059	–.015	.916
SCAB19	.005	.010	.009	–.031	.816
SCAB20	.249	.122	.028	.130	.096

Extraction Method: Principal Axis Factoring.
Rotation Method: Promax with Kaiser Normalization.

[a] Rotation converged in 5 iterations.

Structure Matrix					
	Factor				
	1	2	3	4	5
SCAB1	.908	.246	.410	.202	.079
SCAB2	.690	.320	.413	.148	.056
SCAB3	.820	.290	.400	.202	.110
SCAB4	.821	.208	.466	.208	.081
SCAB5	.302	.080	.632	.133	.013
SCAB6	.371	.260	.692	.288	.075
SCAB7	.427	.224	.850	.227	.062
SCAB8	.405	.268	.715	.245	.039
SCAB9	.253	.579	.328	.026	.107
SCAB10	.270	.846	.253	.161	.025
SCAB11	.199	.797	.105	.077	.073
SCAB12	.236	.730	.190	.106	.074
SCAB13	.261	.266	.351	.633	.087
SCAB14	.344	.290	.408	.657	.146
SCAB15	.118	.000	.146	.768	.068
SCAB16	.091	−.015	.100	.806	.022
SCAB17	.414	.261	.338	.304	.277
SCAB18	.032	.017	−.017	.059	.899
SCAB19	.111	.098	.077	.073	.814
SCAB20	.353	.249	.248	.236	.160

Extraction Method: Principal Axis Factoring.
Rotation Method: Promax with Kaiser Normalization.

Factor Correlation Matrix					
Factor	1	2	3	4	5
1	1.000	.343	.529	.264	.130
2	.343	1.000	.317	.168	.109
3	.529	.317	1.000	.313	.088
4	.264	.168	.313	1.000	.120
5	.130	.109	.088	.120	1.000

Extraction Method: Principal Axis Factoring.
Rotation Method: Promax with Kaiser Normalization.

In general, the first step involves an examination of the inter-factor correlation matrix. As shown, the factors reported low to high (> 0.50) correlations. Therefore, it is not reasonable to consider an orthogonal rotation. We will return to these correlations shortly when we use these results to assess the construct validity of the SCAB.

There are two loading matrices associated with oblique rotations. The first is referred to by SPSS as the Pattern matrix (semipartial correlations), which represents the correlation between each indicator and factor, with the association of the other factors removed. For example, the loading value of 0.980 for SCAB1 on Factor 1 is the correlation between the item and the factor with the impact of Factors 2 through 5 removed (or, partialed out). On the other hand, the structure matrix (correlations) reports the correlations between the indicators and factors without partialing out the other factors. In this sense, it can be interpreted as a Pearson product moment correlation. Each of these matrices convey important information pertaining to the factor solution. In practice, however, the pattern matrix might be slightly more commonly used because it represents the unique relationships between factors and indicators. For this reason, we will focus on these loadings, rather than on the structure matrix.

Interpretation of factor loading matrices is perhaps the most important aspect of using EFA in construct validation because it provides a measure of the relationship between items and factors. Importantly, a favorable factor solution does not definitively "prove" that the construct(s) exists as hypothesized, but it does provide some evidence that this may be the case. Recall earlier in the chapter we mentioned that a variable loads onto a factor if the absolute value of its loading is greater than 0.32 (Tabachnick & Fidell, 2007). A cross-loading occurs when an indicator (e.g., item) loads on more than one factor. In the instances in which an indicate reports a cross-loading or does not load on any factor are problematic. This is because these indicators represent potential problems in terms of the number of factors and/or qualities of the indicators themselves (e.g., item wording). An item that reports a cross-loading or does not load on any factor should be considered for removal from the instrument with content considerations being of primary concern. In the event that this occurs with many items, the researcher will need to reconsider the factor solution.

The pattern matrix provides the information used to proceed with interpreting the meaning of the empirical factors. As shown, SCAB1 is most strongly related with Factor 1, with almost no association with the other factors. Thus, we would say that SCAB1 loads onto Factor 1 in addition to the following items: SCAB2, SCAB3, and SCAB4. No other indicator loads onto Factor 1, and none of the first four indicators load onto any of the other factors. This result is supportive of the theory underlying the SCAB, which proposed that items 1–4 together constitute the engagement subscale. Similarly, Items 5–8 all load on Factor 3, whereas Items 9–12 (spontaneity) load together on Factor 2. Upon further inspection of the pattern coefficients, Items 13–16 (tolerance) load on Factor 4, and Items 18 and 19 (fantasy) load on Factor 5. Notably, Items 17 and 20, which should measure fantasy, do not load on any factors. We might remember that these items both exhibited low communality estimates, suggesting that they are not well explained by the 5 factor solution.

Taken together, the results suggest that the theory underlying the SCAB was largely supported. This is due to the observation that four of the five factors were clearly identified by the EFA, and the fifth factor was partially supported. Items 17 and 20 warrant further inspection to determine why they did not conform to the hypothesized theoretical structure of the instrument. It is possible that they are not well written and, thus, confusing to respondents. It is also possible that for the particular sample used in the study they are not appropriate, but that they might be appropriate for another sample. Finally, while perhaps not likely, it is also possible that some aspect of the instrument's administration to this sample led to problems on these items. What the researcher should not do is remove these items from the scale altogether, based on this single study. While these results point out potential problems with the items, even while generally supporting the construct validity of the SCAB, they cannot be taken as definitive proof that the items are fatally flawed.

Before leaving EFA, we would like to examine SPSS syntax for one method of determining the number of factors, PA. The following syntax, developed by O'Connor (2000), was used to carry out PA for the SCAB data.

```
* Parallel Analysis Program For Raw Data and Data Permutations.
* This program conducts parallel analyses on data files in which
  the rows of the data matrix are cases/individuals and the
  columns are variables; Data are read/entered into the program
  using the GET command (see the GET command below); The GET
  command reads an SPSS systemfile, which can be either the
  current, active SPSS data file or a previously saved systemfile;
  A valid filename/location must be specified on the GET command;
  A subset of variables for the analyses can be specified by using
  the "/ VAR =" subcommand with the GET statement; There can be
  no missing values.
* You must also specify:
  -- the # of parallel data sets for the analyses;
  -- the desired percentile of the distribution and random
     data eigenvalues;
  -- whether principal components analyses or principal axis/common
     factor analysis are to be conducted, and
  -- whether normally distributed random data generation or
     permutations of the raw data set are to be used in the
     parallel analyses.
* WARNING: Permutations of the raw data set are time consuming;
  Each parallel data set is based on column-wise random shufflings
  of the values in the raw data matrix using Castellan's (1992,
  BRMIC, 24, 72-77) algorithm; The distributions of the original
  raw variables are exactly preserved in the shuffled versions used
  in the parallel analyses; Permutations of the raw data set are
  thus highly accurate and most relevant, especially in cases where
```

```
  the raw data are not normally distributed or when they do not meet
  the assumption of multivariate normality (see Longman & Holden,
  1992, BRMIC, 24, 493, for a Fortran version); If you would
  like to go this route, it is perhaps best to (1) first run a
  normally distributed random data generation parallel analysis to
  familiarize yourself with the program and to get a ballpark
  reference point for the number of factors/components;
  (2) then run a permutations of the raw data parallel analysis
  using a small number of datasets (e.g., 10), just to see how long
  the program takes to run; then (3) run a permutations of the raw
  data parallel analysis using the number of parallel data sets that
  you would like use for your final analyses; 1000 datasets are
  usually sufficient, although more datasets should be used if
  there are close calls.

* These next commands generate artificial raw data
  (50 cases) that can be used for a trial-run of
  the program, instead of using your own raw data;
  Just select and run this whole file; However, make sure to
  delete these commands before attempting to run your own data.

* Start of artificial data commands.
* End of artificial data commands.

set mxloops=9000 printback=off width=80 seed = 1953125.
matrix.

* Enter the name/location of the data file for analyses after
  "FILE ="; If you specify "FILE = *", then the program will read
  the current, active SPSS data file; You can alternatively enter
  the name/location of a previously saved SPSS systemfile instead
  of "*";
  you can use the "/ VAR =" subcommand after "/ missing=omit"
  subcommand to select variables for the analyses.
GET raw / FILE = * / missing=omit / VAR = V1 to V20.

* Enter the desired number of parallel data sets here.
compute ndatsets = 1000.

* Enter the desired percentile here.
compute percent = 95.

* Enter either
  1 for principal components analysis, or
  2 for principal axis/common factor analysis.
compute kind = 2 .

* Enter either
  1 for normally distributed random data generation parallel
  analysis, or
  2 for permutations of the raw data set.
compute randtype = 2.

* End of required user specifications.
```

```
compute ncases = nrow(raw).
compute nvars = ncol(raw).

* principal components analysis & random normal data generation.
do if (kind = 1 and randtype = 1).
compute nm1 = 1 / (ncases-1).
compute vcv = nm1 * (sscp(raw)-((t(csum(raw))*csum(raw))/ncases)).
compute d = inv(mdiag(sqrt(diag(vcv)))).
compute realeval = eval(d * vcv * d).
compute evals = make(nvars,ndatsets,-9999).
loop #nds = 1 to ndatsets.
compute x = sqrt(2 * (ln(uniform(ncases,nvars)) * -1) ) &*
        cos(6.283185 * uniform(ncases,nvars) ).
compute vcv = nm1 * (sscp(x)-((t(csum(x))*csum(x))/ncases)).
compute d = inv(mdiag(sqrt(diag(vcv)))).
compute evals(:,#nds) = eval(d * vcv * d).
end loop.
end if.

* principal components analysis & raw data permutation.
do if (kind = 1 and randtype = 2).
compute nm1 = 1 / (ncases-1).
compute vcv = nm1 * (sscp(raw)-((t(csum(raw))*csum(raw))/ncases)).
compute d = inv(mdiag(sqrt(diag(vcv)))).
compute realeval = eval(d * vcv * d).
compute evals = make(nvars,ndatsets,-9999).
loop #nds = 1 to ndatsets.
compute x = raw.
loop #c = 1 to nvars.
loop #r = 1 to (ncases -1).
compute k = trunc( (ncases-#r + 1) * uniform(1,1) + 1 ) + #r-1.
compute d = x(#r,#c).
compute x(#r,#c) = x(k,#c).
compute x(k,#c) = d.
end loop.
end loop.
compute vcv = nm1 * (sscp(x)-((t(csum(x))*csum(x))/ncases)).
compute d = inv(mdiag(sqrt(diag(vcv)))).
compute evals(:,#nds) = eval(d * vcv * d).
end loop.
end if.

* PAF/common factor analysis & random normal data generation.
do if (kind = 2 and randtype = 1).
compute nm1 = 1 / (ncases-1).
compute vcv = nm1 * (sscp(raw)-((t(csum(raw))*csum(raw))/ncases)).
compute d = inv(mdiag(sqrt(diag(vcv)))).
compute cr = (d * vcv * d).
compute smc = 1-(1 &/ diag(inv(cr)) ).
call setdiag(cr,smc).
compute realeval = eval(cr).
compute evals = make(nvars,ndatsets,-9999).
compute nm1 = 1 / (ncases-1).
```

```
loop #nds = 1 to ndatsets.
compute x = sqrt(2 * (ln(uniform(ncases,nvars)) * -1) ) &*
        cos(6.283185 * uniform(ncases,nvars) ).
compute vcv = nm1 * (sscp(x)-((t(csum(x))*csum(x))/ncases)).
compute d = inv(mdiag(sqrt(diag(vcv)))).
compute r = d * vcv * d.
compute smc = 1-(1 &/ diag(inv(r)) ).
call setdiag(r,smc).
compute evals(:,#nds) = eval(r).
end loop.
end if.

* PAF/common factor analysis & raw data permutation.
do if (kind = 2 and randtype = 2).
compute nm1 = 1 / (ncases-1).
compute vcv = nm1 * (sscp(raw)-((t(csum(raw))*csum(raw))/ncases)).
compute d = inv(mdiag(sqrt(diag(vcv)))).
compute cr = (d * vcv * d).
compute smc = 1-(1 &/ diag(inv(cr)) ).
call setdiag(cr,smc).
compute realeval = eval(cr).
compute evals = make(nvars,ndatsets,-9999).
compute nm1 = 1 / (ncases-1).
loop #nds = 1 to ndatsets.
compute x = raw.
loop #c = 1 to nvars.
loop #r = 1 to (ncases -1).
compute k = trunc( (ncases-#r + 1) * uniform(1,1) + 1 ) + #r-1.
compute d = x(#r,#c).
compute x(#r,#c) = x(k,#c).
compute x(k,#c) = d.
end loop.
end loop.
compute vcv = nm1 * (sscp(x)-((t(csum(x))*csum(x))/ncases)).
compute d = inv(mdiag(sqrt(diag(vcv)))).
compute r = d * vcv * d.
compute smc = 1-(1 &/ diag(inv(r)) ).
call setdiag(r,smc).
compute evals(:,#nds) = eval(r).
end loop.
end if.

* identifying the eigenvalues corresponding to the desired percentile.
compute num = rnd((percent*ndatsets)/100).
compute results = { t(1:nvars), realeval, t(1:nvars), t(1:nvars) }.
loop #root = 1 to nvars.
compute ranks = rnkorder(evals(#root,:)).
loop #col = 1 to ndatsets.
do if (ranks(1,#col) = num).
compute results(#root,4) = evals(#root,#col).
break.
end if.
end loop.
```

```
end loop.
compute results(:,3) = rsum(evals) / ndatsets.

print /title="PARALLEL ANALYSIS:".
do if (kind = 1 and randtype = 1).
print /title="Principal Components & Random Normal Data Genera-
tion".
else if (kind = 1 and randtype = 2).
print /title="Principal Components & Raw Data Permutation".
else if (kind = 2 and randtype = 1).
print /title="PAF/Common Factor Analysis & Random Normal Data Gen-
eration".
else if (kind = 2 and randtype = 2).
print /title="PAF/Common Factor Analysis & Raw Data Permutation".
end if.
compute specifs = {ncases; nvars; ndatsets; percent}.
print specifs /title="Specifications for this Run:"
/rlabels="Ncases" "Nvars" "Ndatsets" "Percent".
print results
/title="Raw Data Eigenvalues, & Mean & Percentile Random Data Ei-
genvalues"
/clabels="Root" "Raw Data" "Means" "Prcntyle" /format "f12.6".

compute root = results(:,1).
compute rawdata = results(:,2).
compute percntyl = results(:,4).

save results /outfile=* / var=root rawdata means percntyl .

end matrix.
```

To run the syntax, we must have the data set containing the items open, and indicate the variables to be included in the analysis (SCAB1–SCAB20). We indicate the number of random datasets that we would like to generate (1,000 in this case), and the percentile of interest (95th). In addition, we indicate the type of factor extraction (1 = principal components and 2 = principal axis), and the way in which the random data is to be generated (from the normal distribution or from permutations. The resulting output and graph appear below.

```
Run MATRIX procedure:

PARALLEL ANALYSIS:

PAF/Common Factor Analysis & Raw Data Permutation

Specifications for this Run:
Ncases      413
Nvars        20
Ndatsets   1000
Percent      95
```

Raw Data Eigenvalues, & Mean & Percentile Random Data Eigenvalues

Root	Raw Data	Means	Prcntyle
1.000000	4.895387	.463447	.547782
2.000000	1.888954	.385400	.440388
3.000000	1.646993	.328461	.379595
4.000000	1.379350	.278644	.322080
5.000000	1.087381	.232669	.270863
6.000000	.381248	.191289	.228211
7.000000	.201128	.152434	.187896
8.000000	.118100	.114925	.149626
9.000000	.078835	.078688	.109695
10.000000	-.026073	.044526	.074070
11.000000	-.049555	.010904	.039660
12.000000	-.069573	-.021539	.007586
13.000000	-.091872	-.053090	-.025036
14.000000	-.107669	-.084192	-.057068
15.000000	-.137411	-.115853	-.089293
16.000000	-.146233	-.147299	-.121721
17.000000	-.162005	-.179159	-.150825
18.000000	-.179658	-.213217	-.186561
19.000000	-.212114	-.250149	-.220550
20.000000	-.237911	-.295439	-.261071

----- END MATRIX -----

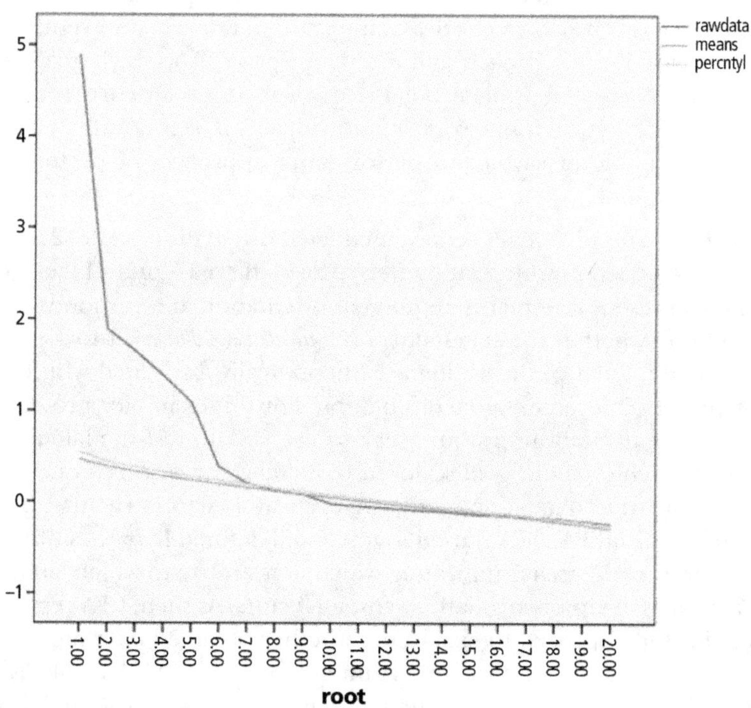

An examination of the output containing the eigenvalues reveals that the real eigenvalues are larger than the random ones through Factor 7, but for Factor 8 the 95th percentile of random eigenvalues (.149626) is larger than the real Factor 8 eigenvalue (0. 118100), thus supporting a 7-factor solution. Taking all of the results together, including the factor loading matrix, it appears that the 5-factor solution is very reasonable, thereby supporting the construct validity of the creativity scale.

Confirmatory Factor Analysis as a Tool for Investigating Construct Validity

Confirmatory factor analysis (CFA) is the preferred factor analytic approach to formally test a scale's dimensionality when existing theory and empirical evidence supports a particular latent structure of the data. For example, researchers in the area of achievement motivation have created a well-developed body of literature supporting the existence of two broad orientations to motivation: mastery and performance. Individuals favoring the mastery approach are primarily motivated by a desire to become more proficient in an area, whereas those favoring the performance approach are primarily motivated by a desire to manage their reputation with others. Within these two broad categories of motivation, it has been hypothesized that there are both approach and avoidance goals. Approach goals focus on a desire to succeed, while avoidance goals focus on a desire not to fail. Within this theoretical framework, an individual can be motivated by a mastery oriented, mastery avoidant, performance approach, or performance avoidance outlook.

To assess an individual's achievement goal orientation, say a 12-item instrument was used in which rating were provided on a 7-point Likert-scale. The items present statements about goal orientation and respondents are asked to rate whether the statement is *Not at all Like Them* = 1 to *Very Much Like Them* = 7. Each of the 12 items is theoretically associated with one of four types of achievement goal orientation. For this example, a researcher in achievement motivation would seek to use CFA to test the latent structure of this achievement goal scale. In particular, the research question is whether the scale data support the theoretical 4-factor structure. Therefore, unlike with EFA, CFA is used to test a well-defined hypothesis because it relies on the researcher indicating which items relate to which latent factors, as well as the inter-correlations among factors. As such, CFA represents a model-based approach to examining whether obtained data support the scale's theoretical factor structure. A unique feature of CFA results is that they can be used to judge the extent to which the theoretical model "fits" the actual data. To further clarify this, we can refer to Figure 5.1, which shows the hypothesized 4 factor model for achievement goal orientation that we outlined above.

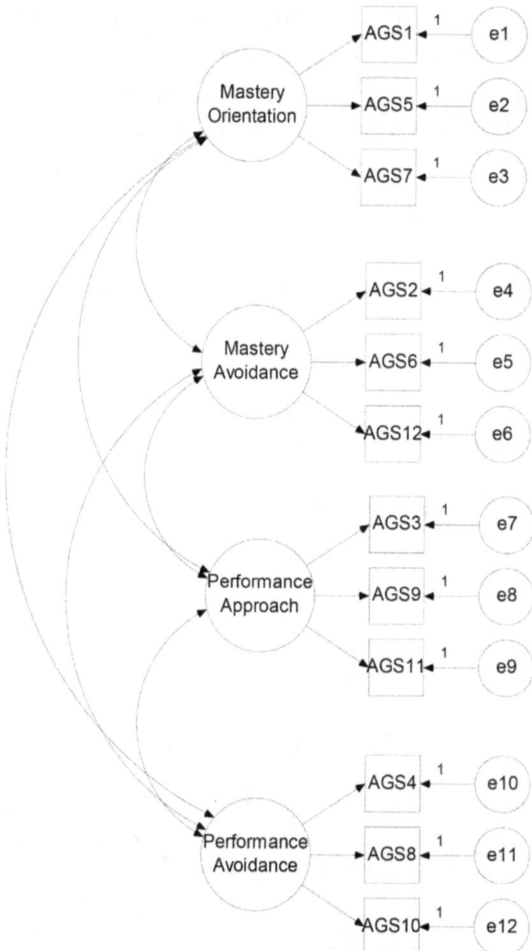

Figure 5.1 Proposed achievement goal orientation model.

This figure is referred to as a path diagram and provides a visual representation of the theoretical relationships between the observed and latent variables. Within path diagrams, squares are used to represent the observed variables (e.g., items), whereas circles represent the latent (or unobserved) variables. Single headed arrows from factors to observed variables are factor loadings, much as we saw in the context of EFA, and double-headed lines represent the covariances (or, correlations) between the latent traits. Each observed variable (e.g., item) is associated with both a factor and random error, represented by the circles, labeled e1, e2, e3, and so on. Finally, each factor must have a referent indicator whose loading is set to 1. The referent provides the latent variable with a measurable scale. Such scaling can also be established by setting the factor variance to 1.

Figure 5.1 provides an illustration of the path diagram displaying the instrument's hypothesized four-factor structure. Alternatively, Figure 5.2 shows another postulated theoretical model explaining the relationships between the items and two latent achievement motivation sub-domains,

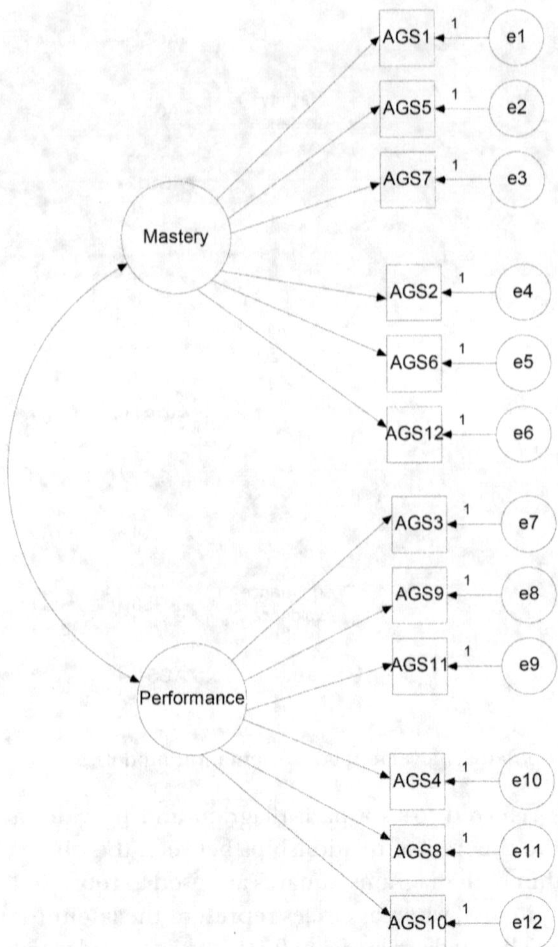

Figure 5.2 Alternative achievement goal orientation model.

namely: mastery and performance. This example serves to point out one of the primary goals of CFA: comparing competing models of the instrument's factor structure to see which provides a more parsimonious description of the data. The ability of CFA to compare the fit of alternative models of the data is one of its strengths versus EFA. Bollen (1989) identifies several advantages of the model-based approach of CFA compared to the data-driven approach associated with EFA (e.g., fixing factor loadings). It should also be noted, however, that use of CFA requires a great deal more in the way of pre-existing theory and empirical evidence to warrant its use. This is clearly evident in Figures 5.1 and 5.2 because there are a number of ways in which the relationships between the observed and latent variables could be described. Without consideration of theory, a CFA model may be fit to the data and be deemed acceptable due to chance alone, instead of based on theory. Indeed, while some theory plays an important role in EFA, it is at the heart of gathering construct validity evidence using CFA.

Fitting a CFA Model Using AMOS

Within SPSS, CFA can be conducted using AMOS, which is a separate software package that is frequently bundled with SPSS. CFA models are expressed in a purely graphical fashion, with rectangles used to identify observed variables and circles for latent variables. In order to create a latent variable with observed indicators, we will first click on the following icon in AMOS: and draw a circle. We then left click the mouse on , place the mouse over the circle that we created, and click once for each of the observed indicators and associated error terms. As an example, we see below the result of following these instructions for a single factor with three indicators.

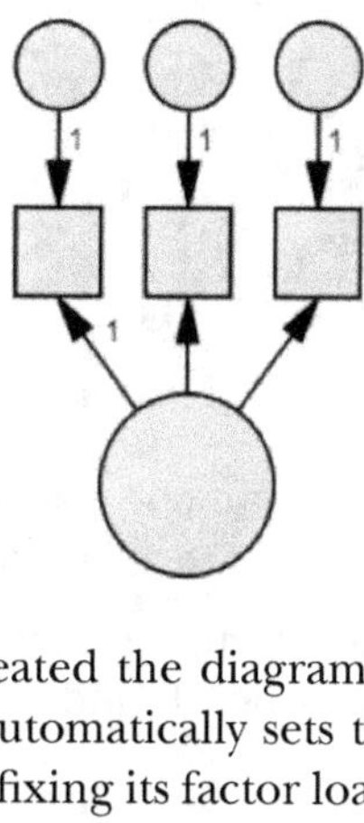

Using this approach, we created the diagrams that appear in Figures 5.1 and 5.2. Note that AMOS automatically sets the first observed variable to be the referent indicator by fixing its factor loading to 1.00. We can change this by right clicking on the line connecting the first indicator to the factor, and selecting **Object Properties**. Within this box we can delete the 1 from the **Regression Weights** box, and then click on another of the paths (e.g., the one linking the second indicator to the factor) and place a 1 in the **Regression Weights** box.

In order to name the latent variables (factors and errors), we right click the mouse over each in order to obtain a window from which we select the **Object Properties** window.

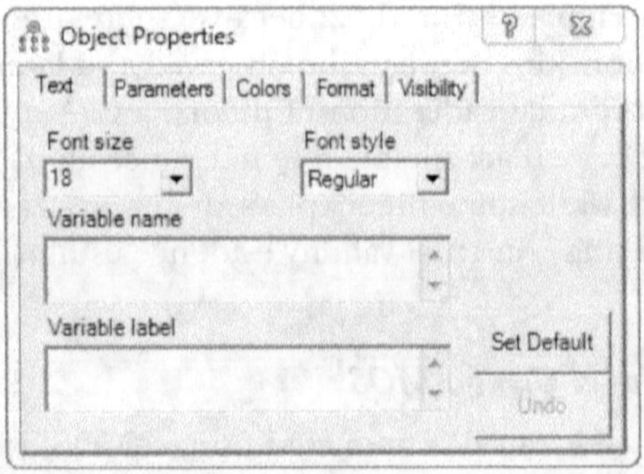

We can then type the name for the latent variable in the **Variable name** box. In order to name the observed variables, we use the following menu sequence **View ▶ Variables In Dataset** to obtain a window listing all of the observed variables available to us.

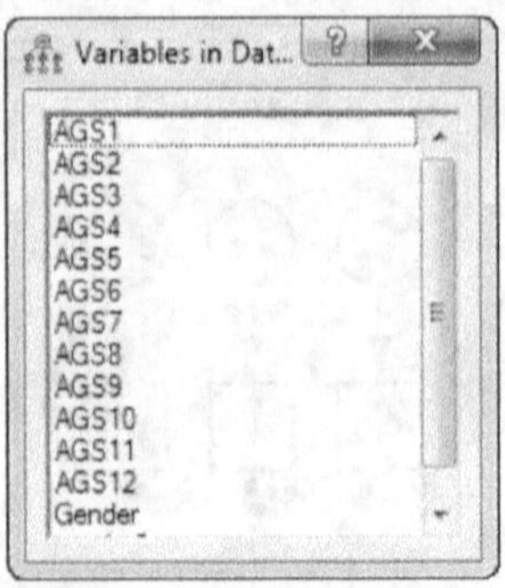

We can then drag each of the variable names to one of the rectangles, thereby specifying which variables are associated with each factor.

When we have finished creating the diagram for our CFA model, we are ready to specify how it will be fit, and what output we would like to see. To make these decisions, we use the menu command **View ► Analysis Properties**.

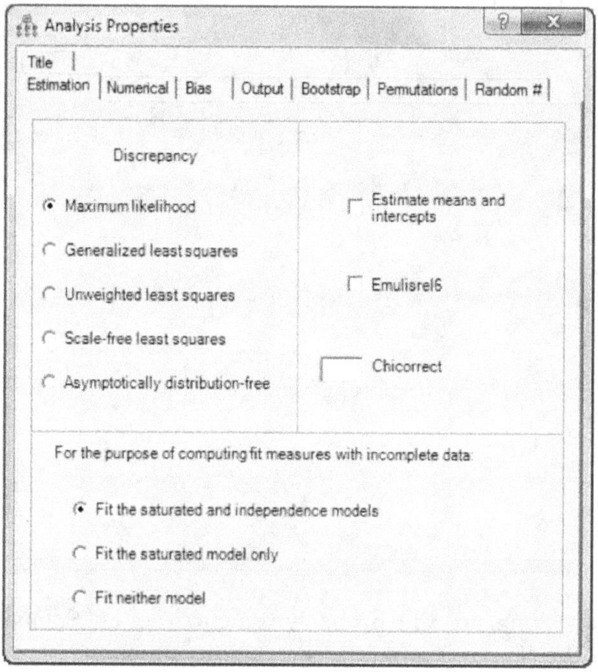

By default, **Maximum likelihood** estimation is selected, which is generally most appropriate, although other options are available and may prove most useful when the data are not multivariate normal (see Finney & DeStefano, 2013 for an excellent discussion of this issue). If we have any missing data then we will want to check the box titled **Estimate means and intercepts**. In order to control the output, we click on the **Output** tab.

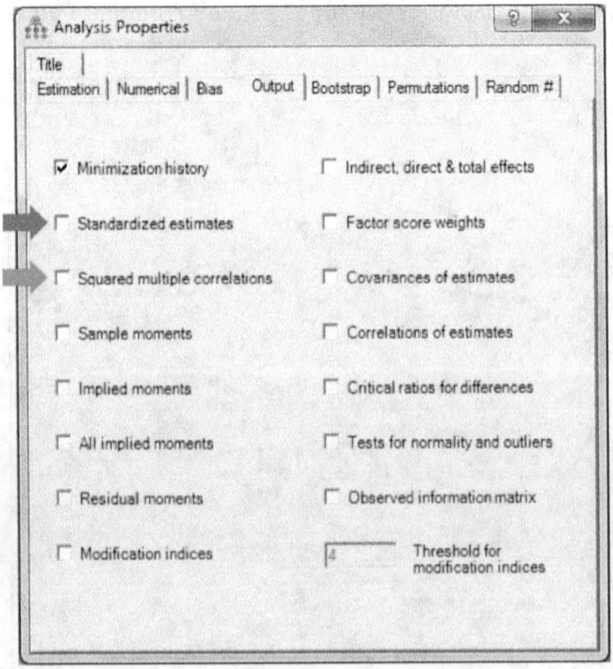

Generally speaking, we will probably want to request Standardized estimates, and the Squared multiple correlations for the observed indicator variables. When we have specified the analysis and output to our satisfaction, we can simply close the Analysis Properties window. At this point, we are ready to run the analysis, which we do using the menu command sequence: **Analyze ► Calculate Estimates.**

In order to view the output resulting from our analysis, we use the menu sequence **View ► Text Output** and obtain the following window.

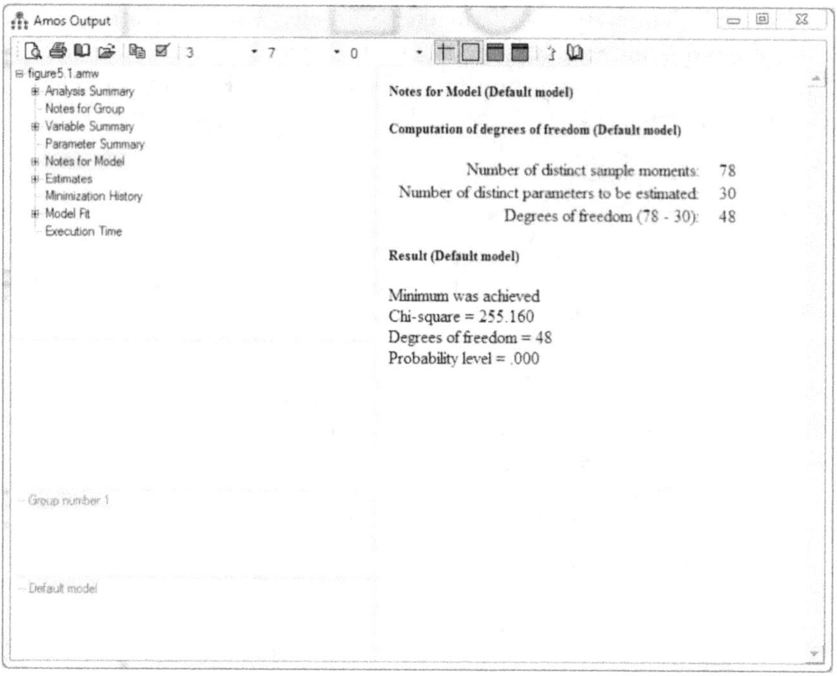

We will be particularly interested in some of the windows, and not in others.

The SPSS output begins by providing a table reporting the basic descriptive information about the model. Among others, this information includes the number of parameters in the model, degrees of freedom, and the results of the Chi-square goodness of fit test. As shown, the model has 78 variances and covariances (called sample moments) and 30 model parameters that we need to estimate, which results in 48 degrees of freedom (78 – 30 = 48). The fact that we have more moments than parameters means that our model is over-identified (i.e., we have more available information than we need). It is usually good for the model to be over-identified. An under-identified model will not yield estimates, and a just-identified model (equal number of informations and parameters) will provide estimates but not useful estimates of model fit. From this window we also see that the estimator converged, based on the message Minimum was achieved. A lack of convergence would mean that parameter estimates are suspect and cannot be trusted. We would then need to investigate the reason for a lack of convergence, which could include anything from a poorly defined model, to a small sample size, to variables that are highly skewed.

Next, we would click on the **Notes for Group** button to be sure that all 432 individuals in our sample were used in the analysis, which was the case.

The Variable Summary and Parmaeter Summary windows simply list the observed and latent variables, and the estimated parameters, respectively. The next table of primary interest is labeled Model Fit, and contains the indices of model-data fit.

Model Fit Summary

CMIN

Model	NPAR	CMIN	DF	P	CMIN/DF
Default model	30	255.160	48	.000	5.316
Saturated model	78	.000	0		
Independence model	12	2772.866	66	.000	42.013

RMR, GFI

Model	RMR	GFI	AGFI	PGFI
Default model	.019	.907	.849	.558
Saturated model	.000	1.000		
Independence model	.151	.379	.266	.321

Baseline Comparisons

Model	NFI Delta1	RFI rho1	IFI Delta2	TLI rho2	CFI
Default model	.908	.873	.924	.895	.923
Saturated model	1.000		1.000		1.000
Independence model	.000	.000	.000	.000	.000

Parsimony-Adjusted Measures

Model	PRATIO	PNFI	PCFI
Default model	.727	.660	.672
Saturated model	.000	.000	.000
Independence model	1.000	.000	.000

NCP

Model	NCP	LO 90	HI 90
Default model	207.160	160.851	260.990
Saturated model	.000	.000	.000
Independence model	2706.866	2538.272	2882.782

FMIN

Model	FMIN	F0	LO 90	HI 90
Default model	.592	.481	.373	.606
Saturated model	.000	.000	.000	.000
Independence model	6.434	6.280	5.889	6.689

RMSEA

Model	RMSEA	LO 90	HI 90	PCLOSE
Default model	.100	.088	.112	.000
Independence model	.308	.299	.318	.000

AIC

Model	AIC	BCC	BIC	CAIC
Default model	315.160	317.026	437.213	467.213
Saturated model	156.000	160.852	473.337	551.337
Independence model	2796.866	2797.612	2845.687	2857.687

ECVI

Model	ECVI	LO 90	HI 90	MECVI
Default model	.731	.624	.856	.736
Saturated model	.362	.362	.362	.373
Independence model	6.489	6.098	6.897	6.491

HOELTER

Model	HOELTER .05	HOELTER .01
Default model	111	125
Independence model	14	15

As evident, there are many statistics to which we can refer when making judgments about the degree to which a theorized model describes the actual data. Similar to determining the number of empirical factors using EFA, common practice is to use several indices to determine whether a CFA model provides acceptable fit. Notably, there is not a single fit statistic that is universally optimal for every analysis. We will highlight those that have been suggested as most useful in the literature (Brown, 2015; Kline, 2016). Perhaps first among these to examine is the chi-square statistic (CMIN), which tests model goodness of fit by comparing the model predicted and observed covariance matrices. The null hypothesis of this test is that the two covariance matrices are identical (i.e., the model predicted covariances are equal to those observed in the data itself). Thus, if we reject the null, we would conclude that the model does not fit well. This test must be used with some care however, as it has been shown to be both sensitive to sample size and not robust to departures from multivariate normality by the data (Kline, 2016). For this model, the chi-square is 255.160, with 48 degrees of freedom (the difference between informations and parameters), and a p-value<0.001. We would, therefore, reject the null hypothesis that the predicted and observed covariance matrices are identical, and conclude that model fit may be questionable.

A second fit index that we may consider in building the case for or against the performance of our model is the root means square error of approximation (RMSEA). This value is calculated as

$$\frac{\sqrt{\chi^2 - df}}{df(N-1)} \tag{5.9}$$

where N is the sample size, df is the degrees of freedom, and χ^2 is the goodness of fit statistic described above. Under the null hypothesis, $\chi^2 = df$, in which case the RMSEA would be 0. Of course, in practice such is rarely the case, so that a variety of cut-off values have been suggested for interpretation of RMSEA, with perhaps the most popular being 0.01 (Excellent fit), 0.05 (Good fit), and 0.08 (Mediocre fit), with values greater than 0.08 indicating poor fit (MacCallum, Browne, & Sugawara, 1996). Kenny, Kaniskan, and McCoach (2011) recommend that researchers use care when interpreting RMSEA for models with few degrees of freedom. AMOS also provides a confidence interval for RMSEA. In this example, the value of RMSEA itself is 0.100, with a 90% confidence interval of 0.088 to 0.112. Based on the standards suggested above, the RMSEA appears to be suggesting poor model fit as well.

Two other goodness of fit indices that are commonly used in assessing CFA solutions are the comparative fit index (CFI) and the Tucker Lewis index (TLI), which is also sometimes called the non-normed fit index (NNFI). These indices are part of a common family referred to as incremental fit indices, which compare the fit of the proposed model with that of the null model, which provides the worst possible fit. The logic of these indices, then, is that fit for the proposed model should be much better than that of the null model. Equations for the CFI and TLI appear below.

$$\text{CFI} = \frac{(\chi_0^2 - df_0) - (\chi_P^2 - df_P)}{(\chi_0^2 - df_0)} \tag{5.10}$$

$$\text{TLI} = \frac{(\chi_0^2 / df_0) - (\chi_P^2 / df_P)}{(\chi_0^2 / df_0) - 1} \tag{5.11}$$

In Equations 5.10 and 5.11, χ_0^2 and χ_P^2 are the chi-square goodness of fit statistics for the null and proposed models, respectively. Similarly, df_0 and df_P are the degrees of freedom for these models. A wide variety of recommendations for assessing model fit with these indices have been recommended with no absolute agreement. However, there is some consensus that at minimum, values greater than 0.90 and preferably greater than 0.95 be used to identify models exhibiting good fit (Kline, 2016). Based on these guidelines, it appears that the CFI (0.923) and TLI (0.895) indicate questionable fit. While the CFI does have a value greater than 0.90, TLI is below this cut-off, so collectively they do not support adequate model-data fit.

A final set of indices that we will examine are used not to assess whether a single model fits or not, but rather to compare the fit of two competing models with the same data. These relative fit indices include the Akaike Information Criterion (AIC; Akaike, 1987) and Schwarz's Bayesian Information Criterion (BIC; Schwarz, 1978). Both statistics are based on the chi-square goodness of fit statistic described above, with a penalty built in for model complexity. The notion here is that the goodness of fit statistic will always improve as more parameters are included in the model, even if these additional parameters are not substantively meaningful. Therefore, in order to ensure that the selected model provides the best fit *and* is as parsimonious as possible, model complexity is penalized. In practice this means that in order for additional parameters to be "helpful" to a model, they must meaningfully contribute to fit. The AIC, BIC, and CAIC are calculated as follows.

$$\text{AIC} = \chi_P^2 + 2p \tag{5.12}$$

$$\text{BIC} = \chi_P^2 + \ln(N)p \tag{5.13}$$

$$\text{CAIC} = \chi_P^2 + \ln(N+1)p \tag{5.14}$$

The terms are as defined above, with the addition that p is the number of parameters to be estimated. These indices will be used when we compare the relative fit of the proposed model (Figure 5.1) with the alternative (Figure 5.2), where smaller index values indicate better model fit. For the proposed model, AIC = 315.160, BIC = 427.213, and CAIC = 467.213.

To this point, we have devoted our discussion of CFA to the assessment of model-data fit based on the inspection of various fit statistics. Of equal importance are the factor loadings (also referred to as pattern coefficients) that report the relationships among the latent and observed variables. There are two types of factor loadings: unstandardized and standardized. Unstandardized pattern coefficients are expressed in the scale of the original observed data, while standardized coefficients are expressed in the standardized scale. AMOS first presents the unstandardized loadings along with the standard errors and a *t*-value (C.R.) that can be used to ascertain the relative significance of the loadings (P). *P*-values less than 0.001 are denoted by ***.

			Estimate	S.E.	C.R.	P	Label
AGS1	<---	Mastery_Orientation	1.000				
AGS5	<---	Mastery_Orientation	.703	.060	11.812	***	
AGS7	<---	Mastery_Orientation	1.095	.074	14.889	***	
AGS2	<---	Mastery_Avoidance	1.000				
AGS6	<---	Mastery_Avoidance	.917	.073	12.637	***	
AGS12	<---	Mastery_Avoidance	.988	.082	12.089	***	
AGS3	<---	Performance_Approach	1.000				
AGS9	<---	Performance_Approach	.911	.051	17.838	***	
AGS11	<---	Performance_Approach	1.158	.067	17.370	***	
AGS4	<---	Performance_Avoidance	1.000				
AGS8	<---	Performance_Avoidance	1.785	.121	14.752	***	
AGS10	<---	Performance_Avoidance	1.671	.110	15.260	***	

Standardized Regression Weights: (Group number 1 - Default model)

			Estimate
AGS1	<---	Mastery_Orientation	.723
AGS5	<---	Mastery_Orientation	.626
AGS7	<---	Mastery_Orientation	.849
AGS2	<---	Mastery_Avoidance	.695
AGS6	<---	Mastery_Avoidance	.728
AGS12	<---	Mastery_Avoidance	.687
AGS3	<---	Performance_Approach	.764
AGS9	<---	Performance_Approach	.831
AGS11	<---	Performance_Approach	.812
AGS4	<---	Performance_Avoidance	.649
AGS8	<---	Performance_Avoidance	.847
AGS10	<---	Performance_Avoidance	.891

Covariances: (Group number 1 - Default model)

			Estimate	S.E.	C.R.	P	Label
Mastery_Orientation	<-->	Mastery_Avoidance	.177	.019	9.125	***	
Mastery_Avoidance	<-->	Performance_Approach	.044	.016	2.846	.004	
Performance_Approach	<-->	Performance_Avoidance	.181	.018	9.812	***	
Mastery_Avoidance	<-->	Performance_Avoidance	.044	.011	3.997	***	
Mastery_Orientation	<-->	Performance_Avoidance	.021	.009	2.280	.023	
Mastery_Orientation	<-->	Performance_Approach	.028	.013	2.093	.036	

Correlations: (Group number 1 - Default model)

			Estimate
Mastery_Orientation	<-->	Mastery_Avoidance	.865
Mastery_Avoidance	<-->	Performance_Approach	.177
Performance_Approach	<-->	Performance_Avoidance	.953
Mastery_Avoidance	<-->	Performance_Avoidance	.254
Mastery_Orientation	<-->	Performance_Avoidance	.133
Mastery_Orientation	<-->	Performance_Approach	.123

Variances: (Group number 1 - Default model)

	Estimate	S.E.	C.R.	P	Label
Mastery_Orientation	.183	.023	8.032	***	
Mastery_Avoidance	.229	.031	7.507	***	
Performance_Approach	.274	.030	9.054	***	
Performance_Avoidance	.132	.018	7.311	***	
e1	.167	.014	11.552	***	
e2	.140	.011	12.906	***	
e3	.086	.011	7.493	***	
e4	.245	.021	11.605	***	
e5	.171	.016	10.940	***	
e6	.250	.021	11.743	***	
e7	.196	.016	12.425	***	
e8	.102	.009	10.965	***	
e9	.191	.017	11.510	***	
e10	.180	.013	13.664	***	
e11	.165	.015	10.952	***	
e12	.095	.011	8.915	***	

As discussed previously, items AGS1–AGS4 are indicators for the latent factors, and thus their loadings are not estimated. As an example of reading the output, let's consider item AGS5. The estimated loading value is 0.703, with a standard error of 0.060, and a *t*-value of 11.812 ($p < 0.001$). The fact that the *t*-value exceeds 2 indicates that the loading is significantly different from 0 (i.e., there is a relationship between factor f1 and AGS5). Indeed, we see that the *t*-values for each of the items are well in excess of 2, suggesting that the items are significantly related to the factors that we hypothesized they would be.

The standardized loadings appear next in the output. These values are comparable to the EFA loadings we discussed earlier in the chapter, and are in some ways more easily interpreted than these undstandardized values. Using the rule that we applied in the EFA case, stating that a variable was associated with a factor if the absolute value of the loading was greater than 0.32, we see that all of the items are clearly associated with their hypothesized factor. If we square the loadings, we obtain the R^2 value for the item, representing the total proportion of variance for the item that is explained by the factor. As an example, we can consider AGS1. The loading squared is $.723^2 = 0.523$, indicating that approximately 52% of the variation in Item 1 is explained by the Mastery_Orientation latent trait. The results in this table, then, can provide insights into which items are best explained by the factor model, and which are not. Specifically, in this example, items AGS7 and AGS10 have the highest proportion of their variance explained by the factor model, while AGS4 and AGS5 have the lowest proportions of explained variance. This information can be used by the researcher to determine which items should be most closely investigated as being potentially problematic in terms of the quality of their measurement of the latent traits. It must be noted that there are not guidelines for what proportion of variance would warrant the need for attention, but rather such decision are based on the relative performance of the items.

The next two tables produced by AMOS include the covariances and correlations of the latent variables. As shown, all of the covariances (and correlations) are positive and statistically significant at $\alpha = 0.05$. However, the correlations between Mastery_Avoidance and Performance_Approach, Mastery_Orientation and Performance_Avoidance, and Mastery_Orientation and Performance_Avoidance are all relatively small, with values less than 0.2 suggesting relatively weak relationships. The final table contains factor and error variances. In general, larger error variances indicate relatively lower reliability for an individual item. For this example, AGS12 had the largest error variance, suggesting that it was the least consistent, while AGS7 with the lowest error variance may be viewed as the most consistent.

This last result brings us to the alternative model displayed in Figure 5.2. Recall that here the 4 factor model has been reduced to 2 factors based on the mastery and performance domains. We can fit this model with the same sequence of commands in AMOS that we used for the model in Figure 5.1. The resultant goodness of fit indices appear below.

Model Fit Summary

CMIN

Model	NPAR	CMIN	DF	P	CMIN/DF
Default model	25	299.426	53	.000	5.650
Saturated model	78	.000	0		
Independence model	12	2772.866	66	.000	42.013

RMR, GFI

Model	RMR	GFI	AGFI	PGFI
Default model	.024	.895	.846	.608
Saturated model	.000	1.000		
Independence model	.151	.379	.266	.321

Baseline Comparisons

Model	NFI Delta1	RFI rho1	IFI Delta2	TLI rho2	CFI
Default model	.892	.866	.909	.887	.909
Saturated model	1.000		1.000		1.000
Independence model	.000	.000	.000	.000	.000

Parsimony-Adjusted Measures

Model	PRATIO	PNFI	PCFI
Default model	.803	.716	.730
Saturated model	.000	.000	.000
Independence model	1.000	.000	.000

NCP

Model	NCP	LO 90	HI 90
Default model	246.426	195.786	304.580
Saturated model	.000	.000	.000
Independence model	2706.866	2538.272	2882.782

FMIN

Model	FMIN	F0	LO 90	HI 90
Default model	.695	.572	.454	.707
Saturated model	.000	.000	.000	.000
Independence model	6.434	6.280	5.889	6.689

RMSEA

Model	RMSEA	LO 90	HI 90	PCLOSE
Default model	.104	.093	.115	.000
Independence model	.308	.299	.318	.000

AIC

Model	AIC	BCC	BIC	CAIC
Default model	349.426	350.981	451.137	476.137
Saturated model	156.000	160.852	473.337	551.337
Independence model	2796.866	2797.612	2845.687	2857.687

ECVI

Model	ECVI	LO 90	HI 90	MECVI
Default model	.811	.693	.946	.814
Saturated model	.362	.362	.362	.373
Independence model	6.489	6.098	6.897	6.491

HOELTER

Model	HOELTER .05	HOELTER .01
Default model	103	115
Independence model	14	15

When comparing two models, we can rely on the relative fit indices that we discussed previously, namely: AIC, BIC, and CAIC. Recall that they are model complexity penalized measures of unexplained variance so that larger values indicate worse fitting models. For the alternative model, AIC = 349.426 and

BIC = 451.137, while for the original model AIC = 315.160, BIC = 427.213, and CAIC = 467.213. Thus, the original four-factor model provides better model-data fit to the data than the alternative two-factor model. In addition, because the alternative model is a nested version of the primary model, we can compare their relative fit using a difference in the model chi-square values. The null hypothesis of this test is that the model fit provided by the two models is equivalent, so that a significant result means one model fits the data better than the other. The difference in chi-square values is itself distributed as a chi-square with degrees of freedom equal to the difference in model degrees of freedom. We calculate these values below, using results from the model fit statistics taken from the output for the two models.

$$\chi^2_{\Delta} = \chi^2_{Model\,2} - \chi^2_{Model\,1} = 299.426 - 255.160 = 44.266$$

$$df_{\Delta} = df_{Model\,2} - df_{Model\,1} = 53 - 48 = 5$$

We can obtain the *p*-value for this test using any reputable online *p*-value calculator for the chi-square distribution. In this case, $p < 0.00001$, meaning that models do not likely provide equivalent model-data fit. Therefore, given the AIC and BIC results discussed previously, as well as this chi-square result, we must conclude that the original four-factor model provides better fit compared to the alternative two-factor model. This said, given the not-so-excellent fit for either model, the researcher may want to dive into theoretical considerations about additional models that may be justified based on the consideration of modification indices and model parameter values.

Chapter Summary

It is not hyperbole to state that the topic of validity is truly a central component in educational and psychological measurement. Indeed, without evidence of validity, scores from an instrument cannot be deemed to be fully trustworthy. At the same time, the business of validation is extremely complex and not always easily defined. As we have seen, there are a number of ways that we can think about validity, and even more ways to investigate it. Indeed, the very notion of validity for a scale is probably nonexistent. Rather, we must think in terms of how the scale will be used, and whether that use can be thought of as valid, given the extant evidence. Thus, a college entrance exam score might be quite valid for an admissions officer determining who to let into the next freshman class, but totally not valid for an employer seeking to vet job applicants. Furthermore, the same exam might exhibit predictive validity for the purpose of admitting students to college, but not exhibit construct validity based on a CFA. In short, validity is a multifaceted construct that can be assessed in a number of ways.

Our goal in this chapter was to introduce you to the concept of validity and to methods by which it can be assessed using SPSS software. Given our emphasis on the computer, we focused on validation methods that are quantitative in nature. However, as we noted in the introduction, there are also extremely important approaches to validity assessment that do not rely on statistics at all, such as content validation (e.g., review of item content). The researcher truly interested in understanding when an instrument can be used with high validity and when it cannot will want to investigate as many of these pieces of evidence as possible. In addition to the type of use, researchers must also concern themselves with which populations the instrument might be validly used. A Physics graduate entrance exam is a potentially valid tool for advanced undergraduates who have taken a number of Physics courses, but not for students in their first year of the major.

Given both its central position in measurement, and the great complexity in understanding it, we strongly encourage the reader to use this chapter as a jumping off point for their own reading and investigation into the issue of validity. While it can certainly be difficult at times, the field is also immensely rewarding, both in terms of the intellectual challenge it presents and the potential for conducting truly meaningful work. We hope that the discussion and examples presented here will be helpful as you begin your own journey to understanding the meaning and importance of validity assessment.

6

Issues in Scoring

Introduction

The scoring of an instrument (e.g., survey, interim test) is central to the practice of psychometrics and assessment. It is the score that is typically of most interest to users of educational and psychological measures. Scores are used to aid in the determination of students' academic achievement; severity of client symptomology (e.g., depression, anxiety); program placement (e.g., designated program for gifted students); and, in the identification of students who may benefit from special education services. In short, scores are often the final destination of the assessment process. For this reason, it is crucial that they be calculated appropriately, and that their meaning be clearly understood by test users (e.g., researchers, clinicians) and examinees (e.g., students, patients). There are various types of scores, and careful consideration needs to be given to each to ensure that the optimal test score is being used for its intended purpose. With these issues in mind, the goals of this chapter include (a) introducing the most commonly used score types, and (b) describing how to estimate these scores using SPSS. Upon chapter completion, the reader will be familiar with using and interpreting different score types and how to derive these scores using SPSS.

Applied Psychometrics Using SPSS and AMOS, pages 169–194

This chapter is divided into four sections aligned with different score types that can be created using SPSS to guide decisions. The chapter begins with a brief description of the major types of scores available to characterize test performance. This is followed with a presentation on the mechanics of how these scores are calculated, including examples with SPSS. The chapter concludes with a brief review of scoring and a summary designed to promote the reader's ability to determine which score type(s) might be optimal for a given research scenario.

Types of Scores

Oftentimes when we think of a test score the total number of correct items or the proportion correct might come to mind. While these are routinely used score types, we will see that there are many other ways in which performance on an instrument can be reported, with some being more appropriate for certain instances. Therefore, it is important to match the intended use of the assessment with the most optimal score type so that the information we obtain is appropriate for our intended use. For example, the type of score we would use to compare individuals with one another might be very different from the score we would use to determine whether a student has met a particular performance standard (e.g., 80% correct an across item set aligned to a content standard). In the following section, we describe and contrast a number of the most common scores available to test users. This is followed by step-by-step instructions on how to calculate these scores using SPSS.

Raw Scores

Perhaps the most familiar score to test users is the simple summation of responses across an item set. As an example, let us focus on a 4th grade mathematics assessment comprised of 32 multiple-choice items scored as either correct (1) or incorrect (0). A raw score would be obtained by simply summing the number of correct responses across the entire set of items for each examinee, yielding the total number correct. We can also express this score as the proportion correct by dividing the total number correct by 32. Thus, if Student A answered 18 items correct, the raw sum score would be 18, and the proportion correct raw score would be 0.56 (or, 56% of items correctly answered). While the raw score has a primary advantage of being both easy to calculate and understand, there are potential problems with its use. Primarily, it is assessment specific meaning that it only communicates how many items a student answered correctly (or, 18 in the previous example) on a particular measure. However, in many instances, we may want to know how a student (or patient) performs relative to similar age/grade peers on an assessment. Alternatively, we may want to compare an individual's standing on a measure to the "typical" performance of all examinees. In short, raw scores provide no context against to compare individual test performance beyond the number correct, or the sum of responses. Another limitation of the raw score is that regardless of item complexity or the cognitive load required to answer the item, the raw score provides equal weight to all items used to report test performance.

Weighted Scores

A noted limitation of the simple raw score is that it assigns equal weights to each of the items used to report test performance. Thus, there is an assumption that the total score is equally impacted by each of the individual items and the trait or behavior that they are measuring. While this would certainly be a plausible assumption in some instances, it is not so in others. When we are unsure whether a simple sum score is appropriate, we may elect to use a weighted scoring system. Weighted scores are calculated as

$$Y = \Sigma w_i x_i, \tag{6.1}$$

where x_i is the response to item i, and w_i is the weight for item i. Thus, items with larger weights will contribute more to the total score, Y.

The primary issue with using weighted scores is the determination of the weights to apply to the items. In some cases, instrument developers will have determined the weights through some combination of expert judgment and statistical analysis (e.g., factor analysis). We examine an example shortly demonstrating the use of factor analysis to obtain weights to assign to items for scoring various instruments.

Percentile Scores

One commonly used alternative to the raw score is the percentile score. A loose definition of the percentile is that it is the proportion of all examinees whose score is equal to or less than that of a given examinee. More specifically, the percentile score is calculated as

$$p = \frac{(n_b + .5(n_e))}{n_t} \times 100 \tag{6.2}$$

where n_b is equal to the number of scores below the individual score of interest, n_e is the number of scores equal to the score of interest, and n_t is the total number of students taking the exam. Continuing with our mathematics test example, say 100 students took the exam, 38 of whom scored lower than Student A ($n_b = 38$), while 2 students obtained the same score as Student A ($n_e = 2$). Applying Equation 6.2, the percentile for Student A would be

$$p = \frac{(38+.5(2))}{100} \times 100 = \frac{(39)}{100} \times 100 = 0.39 \times 100 = 39.$$

Therefore, our student's score is in the 39th percentile of scores for all students who have completed the exam.

Percentiles are very frequently used with standardized assessments in which an individual's score is compared with similar age/grade peers. They are also routinely used on norm-referenced tests to report individual test performance relative to a norming (or, standardization) sample obtained to represent a cross-section of the larger population (e.g., United States college student population). For example, everyone who takes the Graduate Records Exam (GRE) receives both a standard score (to be discussed shortly) and a percentile score. The percentile is derived using the equation above, based on data obtained from a norm sample that was systematically selected to be representative of college students across the United States. A benefit of the percentile is that it is easy to interpret and provides test users key information regarding an individual's test performance relative to other test takers from the target population.

Despite its clear utility, the percentile score is not without its shortcomings. Perhaps first and foremost is the fact that equivalent differences in the percentile at different points in the score distribution do not correspond to equivalent differences in the raw or standard scores across the distribution. Take, for instance, a difference of 10 percentile points at the low end (e.g., 10th versus 20th percentile) and in the middle of the distribution (e.g., 40th versus 50th percentile). At the low end of the scale, there will typically be fewer examinees, meaning that a difference of 10 percentile points will likely suggest a fairly big difference in raw scores. On the other hand, in the middle of the distribution there will be many more examinees, such that a difference of 10 percentile points would be associated with a much smaller difference in raw scores than was true in the tails of the distribution. We can see an example of this in Figure 6.1. The difference in raw scores between the 10th and 20th percentiles is much smaller than that between the 40th and 50th percentiles.

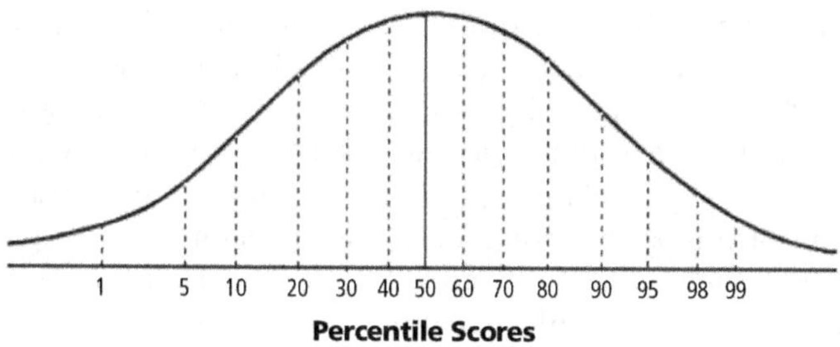

Figure 6.1 Percentile score distribution.

In addition, percentiles are not as amenable to further statistical analysis (e.g., regression) as are raw and standard scores. Nonetheless, these scores do represent an important way to communicate relative performance for individuals, and therefore should be used particularly when the relative position of individuals is of prime importance.

Standard Scores

As discussed previously, a problem with raw scores is that they are difficult to interpret outside the context of the assessment and sample with which they were obtained. Without knowing something about the number of items on the math test, and the average performance of the sample, our student's raw score of 18 doesn't tell us very much about the examinee's test performance. Knowing the proportion of items correct helps somewhat, but we still don't know how the student's score compares to others in the sample, nor can we easily compare it with performance on another assessment with a different number of items. The percentile score is helpful with the first part of this conundrum, in that it reflects student performance relative vis-à-vis to the rest of the test takers. However, as we noted, the percentile is limited in terms of comparisons across the distribution and with its inability to be used with other statistical analyses.

Standard scores are an alternative approach to estimating and reporting examinees' performance on an educational and/or psychological instrument. Standard scores involve the transformation of the raw scores to a scale with a set mean (e.g., 0, 50) and standard deviation (e.g., 1, 10). For example, intelligence (IQ) test scores are typically scaled to have a mean of 100 and a standard deviation of 15. Thus, an individual with an IQ score of 110 was measured at 2/3 of a standard deviation above the mean for the population. Similarly, if the individual is measured on two aspects of intelligence, such as verbal and spatial, and obtains scores of

115 and 105, respectively, we know that his/her verbal intelligence is 2/3 of a standard deviation higher than his spatial intelligence. Having known units and direct comparability of scores across assessments are the two primary advantages of standard scores. In addition, as with raw scores (but unlike percentiles), standard scores can be used in other statistical analyses, such as for comparing group means or calculating correlations among scores. Given their universality and flexibility, standard scores are very widely used throughout educational and psychological assessment. Standard scores considered in this chapter include: *z*-scores, IQ scores, and T scores. Although each of these types of standard scores have a unique mean and standard deviation, they can be interpreted the same way.

The use of standard scores requires a linear transformation of the raw score. The first step begins with the calculation of a *z* score:

$$z = \frac{x - \overline{x}}{s}. \tag{6.3}$$

In this equation, x is the raw score, $\overline{x}$ is the mean raw score for the sample, and s is the sample standard deviation. With a mean of 0 and standard deviation of 1, the z score transforms the raw score into a measure of the number of standard deviations the raw score is above or below the mean. So, a z of –2 indicates that the person's raw score is 2 standard deviations below the mean, while a value of 1 means that the raw score is 1 standard deviation above the mean. This transformation solves two problems with the raw score. First, it puts all raw scores on the same scale so that we can directly compare performance on one measure (e.g., verbal IQ) with that of another (e.g., spatial IQ). Second, it provides information about how an individual's performance compares to that of the entire sample of examinees. Specifically, we know that a z of 1 indicates that the examinee's raw score was 1 standard deviation above the average score for the entire sample of test takers, and we also know that a verbal IQ score of 1.5 is higher than a spatial IQ score of 0.5. Finally, the units of z are constant so that the difference in scores between –2.5 and –2.0 is exactly the same as the difference in scores between 0 and 0.5. In short, the z score overcomes a number of problems that were present with both raw and percentile scores. Nonetheless, the z is virtually never used in actual score reporting because of its scale. The fact that average performance is 0 and roughly half of the scores are negative renders z less than optimal for score reporting; that is, in practical educational assessment settings, a parent may have difficulty understanding what a z score of –1.5 means in terms of their child's mathematics performance, for example. Therefore, we routinely convert z itself into another standard scale that might be more useful for score reporting purposes. It should be noted, however, that these other scores are all based on first estimating the examinee's z-score, and are preferred due to their ease of communicating test performance to broad audiences (e.g., teachers, parents).

Collectively, standard scores are based on z and are all calculated in the same manner. Specifically, this is done by multiplying the z score by the standard deviation of the standard score, and then adding the mean:

$$\text{Standard score} = z * \sigma + \mu . \tag{6.4}$$

Here σ is the desired standard deviation for the score, and μ is the desired mean. As an example for IQ scores, which have a standard deviation of 15 and a mean of 100, we would first convert the raw score to z and then apply Equation 6.5:

$$\text{IQ} = z * 15 + 100 . \tag{6.5}$$

To demonstrate a complete example, let's consider a raw score of 19 from a sample with a standard deviation of 7 and a mean of 14. If we want to convert this raw score to the IQ scale, we would first need to calculate:

$$z = \frac{19-14}{7} = 0.43.$$

Thus, the raw score is 0.43 standard deviations above the sample's mean. Next, we transform this value into an IQ scale using the following Equation 6.5: $\text{IQ} = 0.43 * 15 + 100 = 106.45$. Thus the IQ score for this individual is 106.45, which anyone familiar with this scale knows would be above the average, but within 1 standard deviation of the overall mean (or, 100).

Another commonly used standard scale is the T score, not to be confused with the t distribution commonly used in statistics. T scores have a mean of 50 and a standard deviation of 10. Thus, converting the z obtained above to a T score would simply involve the following equation: $\text{T} = z * 10 + 50 = 0.43 * 10 + 50 = 54.3$. As with the IQ scale, the T is used very frequently, so that many users will already be familiar with it. Indeed, many standard scores that are used in practice are obtained in precisely this manner, and it is easy to see that one could develop a unique standard score with a desired mean and standard deviation, simply using the equations described above. The key, of course, is to first calculate the z score and then apply it to the desired scale equation (e.g., T score, IQ scale score).

Calculation of Raw Scores Using SPSS

In the previous section, the three major types of scores commonly used in educational and psychological assessment were presented. First, raw scores were described as the least optimal in many instances because of their lack of context. Nonetheless, raw scores do have a place in measurement as they are easy to calculate, and within the context in which the assessment is given (e.g., a classroom), raw scores do connote useful information. Therefore, we will first discuss the ways in which raw scores can be calculated using SPSS. Certainly the most common approach is the summation of item responses, typically referred to as the sum score or equal weighted score. Going back to our math test example, if correct responses are recorded as a value of 1 and incorrect responses a value of 0, then the following sequence of SPSS menu commands can be used to calculate the score on the 32-item exam, provided in the SPSS file math4.sav. To begin, we start by selecting **Transform** in the menu bar, and then clicking **Compute Variable** to obtain the following window:

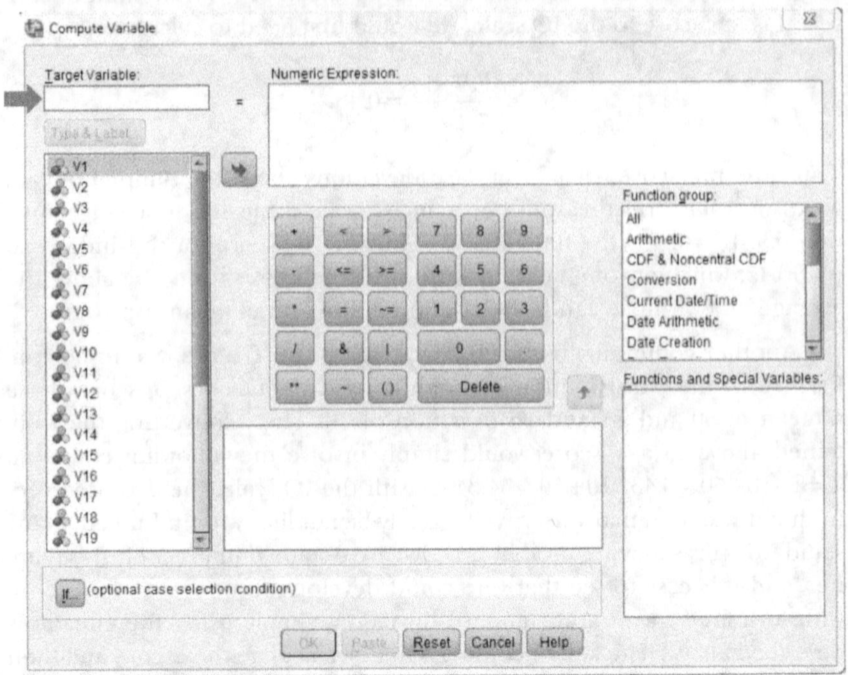

We must first put the name of the raw score in the **Target Variable** box, indicated by the red arrow. Subsequently, we have to select the items to be used in calculating the raw score, separated by +, in the **Numeric Expression** box. We do this by clicking on each variable individually, and then clicking on , and then clicking on . When we are done, the window will appear as below.

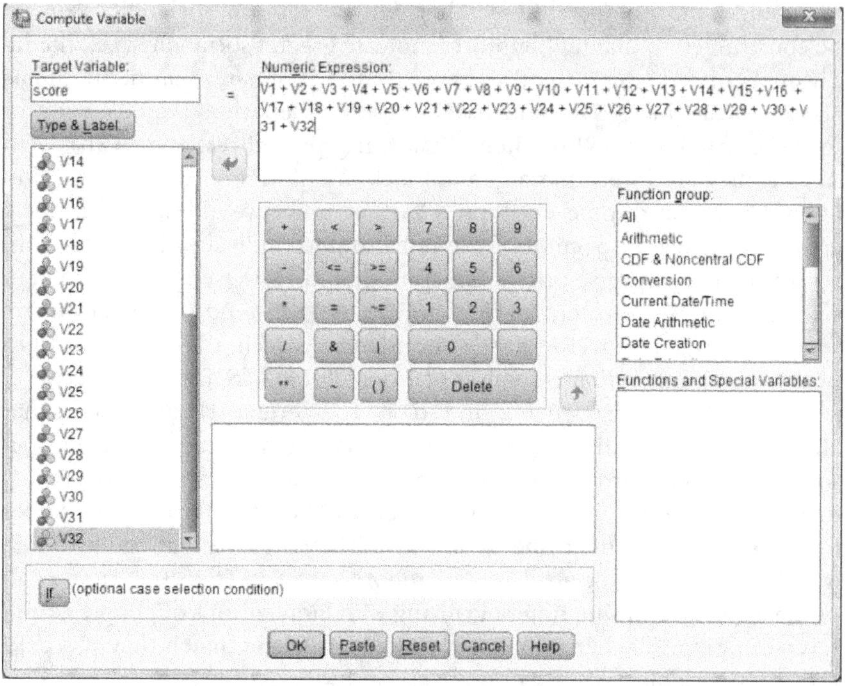

It is also possible to calculate the sum score for a set of ordinal (or Likert-type) items that may comprise an attitudinal survey in much the same way. For this example, we will use the sociability scale from a measure of adult temperament administered to 432 college students. The sociability scale consists of the following 5 items measured on the 7-point scale: 1 = *Extremely untrue of you*; 2 = *Quite untrue of you*; 3 = *Slightly untrue of you*; 4 = *Neither true nor false of you*; 5 = *Slightly true of you*; 6 = *Quite true of you*; and, 7 = *Extremely true of you.*

ATS14 = I would not enjoy a job that involves socializing with the public.
ATS19 = I usually like to talk a lot.
ATS37 = I like conversations that include several people.
ATS46 = I rarely enjoy socializing with large groups of people.
ATS67 = I usually like to spend my free time with people.

We would like for higher scores on the sociability scale to indicate that an individual enjoys interacting with other people on a regular basis.

We can use the same basic SPSS command sequence for these Likert scale items as we did for the dichotomously scored math test items. However, before doing this we first need to consider the issue of reverse scoring of certain item responses. Remember that we want the sociability score to be constructed so that higher scores indicate greater sociability (i.e., the individual enjoys being with other people). An examination of the five items above reveals that ATS14 and ATS46 describe behaviors that are counter to those in the other three items. Thus, if a person responds with a 7 to ATS14, they are indicating a general lack of enjoyment in a sociable situation, whereas a response of 7 on ATS19 is indicative of enjoyment in sociable situations. Inspection of the item content indicates that these item responses are in reverse order and, consequently, if we sum across the item set the responses on items ATS14 and ATS46 will tend to cancel out responses on other items for most respondents. As such, these items need to be reverse coded so that responses of 7 on ATS14/ATS46 are recoded as 1, responses of 6 are recoded as 2, and so on. This reverse scoring ensures that all of the items provide response patterns in the same general direction on sociability, so that a value of 7 for the recoded item response corresponds to a very positive attitude toward sociability for ATS14/ATS46, just as it does for the other items. If a response of 7 on ATS19 suggests that an individual who likes to talk a lot are likely to report a 1 for ATS46 (i.e., not at all positive about spending time socializing with large groups of people), then reverse coding will change the response for ATS46 to match that of ATS19 (i.e., very sociable people will now respond with a 7 for both items). This shows the importance of being familiar with the items and response options to assign accurate scores.

Recoding data in SPSS is a straight-forward process that facilitates the process of scoring instruments. One approach to reverse coding involves use of the recoding functions under the menu heading Transform. We have the choice of recoding the values into the same or different variables. If we choose the former, the original data will be overwritten by our reverse coded values. This is probably not usually desirable because we may want to use the original values at some point. Further, we typically want to retain original coding of the data to check our data manipulations for accuracy. For these reasons, we will use the Recode into Different Variables option. To do this, we use the menu sequence **Transform ► Recode Into Different Variables** to obtain the following window.

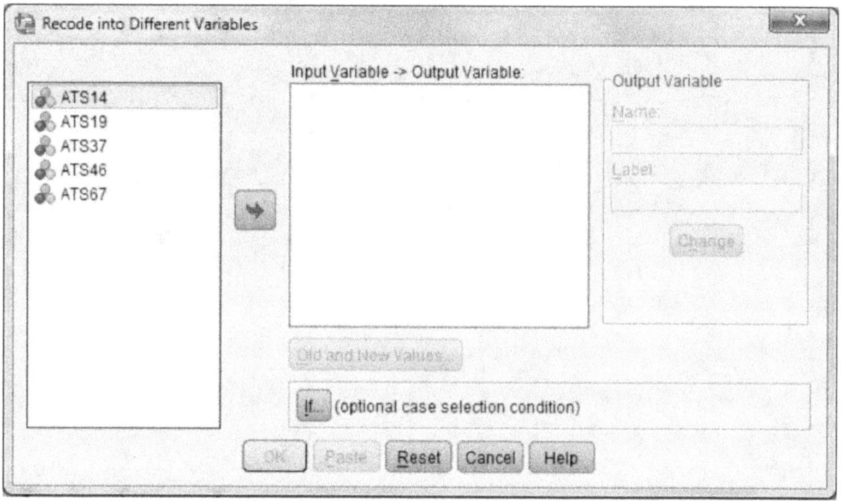

First, we move the two variables we seek to reverse code into the right-hand box, which includes variables ATS14 and ATS46.

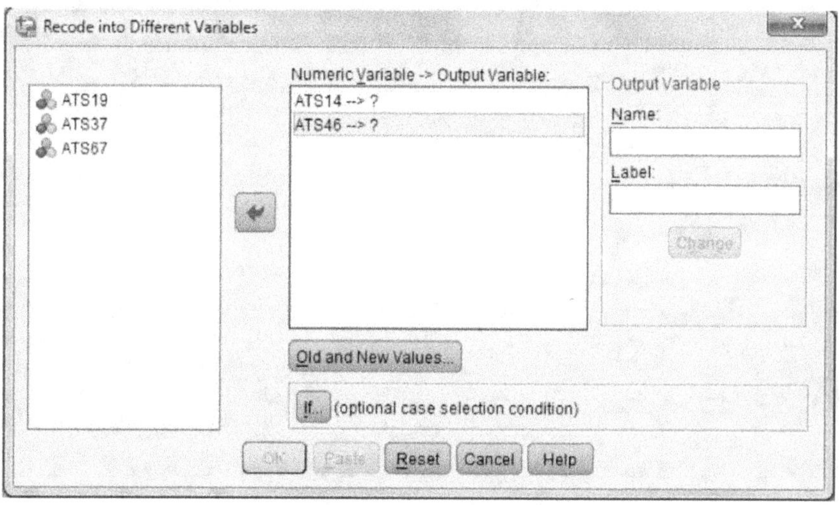

We then must name the new variable associated with each of the original variables. Notably, these are the variable names that will appear in the columns for these new variables in the SPSS dataset. We do this by clicking on the original variable (e.g., ATS14) and then type the name of the new variable (e.g., ATS14r) in the box under **Name**. We then click **Change**. The window will then appear as:

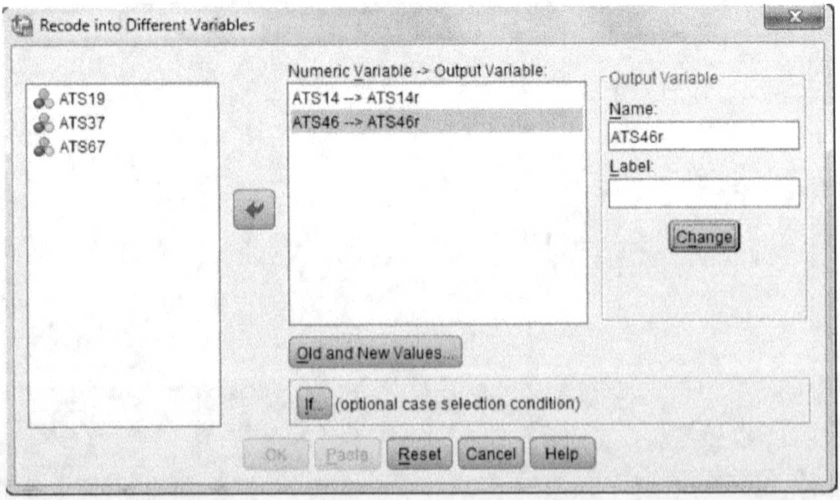

Next, we click **Old and New Values...** and the following window will appear.

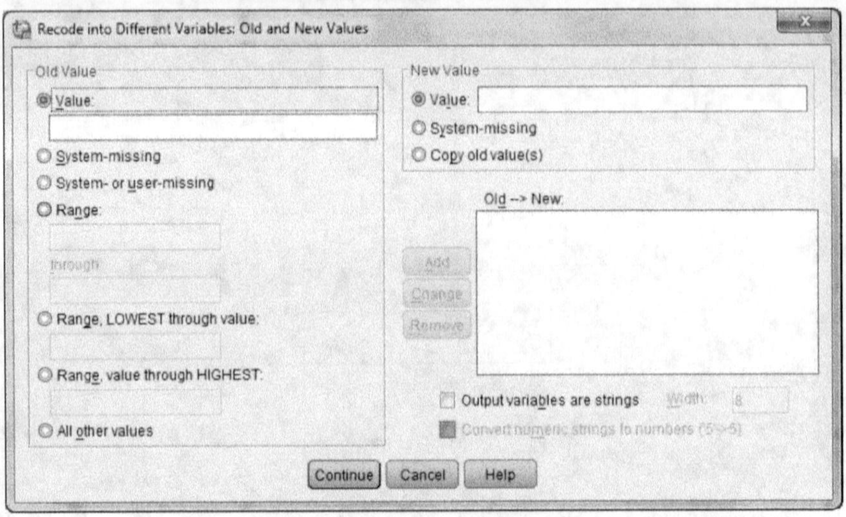

This box is where we specify the recoded values that will fall under the new variables in our dataset. We begin by identifying the original data value in the box under **Value** (located on the left-side of the window) and the new value in the box next to **Value** (right-hand side of the window). Once the old and new values have been identified, we then click **Add**, which places the values in the **Old –> New** box. As an example, to transform a 1 to a 7 in the recoded variable, the window would look like:

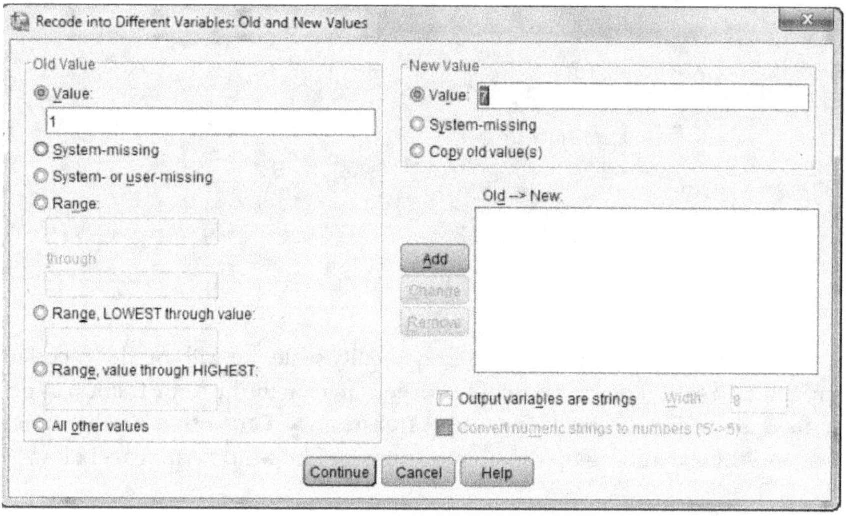

When all of the recoded values are entered, the table appears as below.

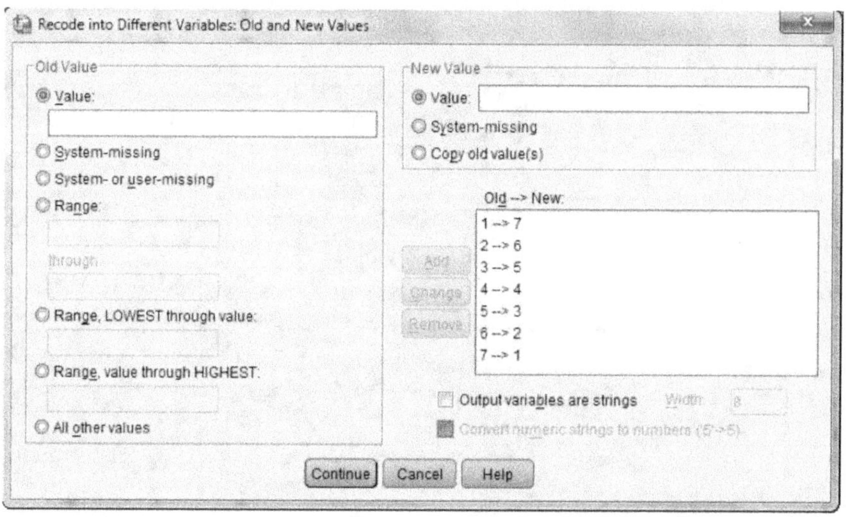

Because we are recoding both variables in the same fashion, we only need to go through this set of steps once. If we were recoding the variables differently, we would do this work separately for each of the variables. Once done, we click **Continue** and then **OK**. The data for the first 10 subjects appears below, with the recoded variables in the last 2 columns, labeled ATS14r and ATS6r.

ATS14	ATS19	ATS37	ATS46	ATS67	ATS14r	ATS46r
6	7		5	4	2.00	3.00
7	4	4	6	6	1.00	2.00
2	1	3	1	2	6.00	7.00
6	2	5	4	4	2.00	4.00
3	6	6	2	7	5.00	6.00
7	7	3	4	7	1.00	4.00
6	7	5	6	6	2.00	2.00
1	1	4	1	2	7.00	7.00
5	3	7	3	5	3.00	5.00
6	5	6	2		2.00	6.00

To create the raw scores for the sociability scale, we will use the recoded variables. Creation of the raw score proceeds in exactly the same fashion as described above for the math test, using **Transform ▶ Compute** from the menu bar, and then summing up the item responses. The window appears below.

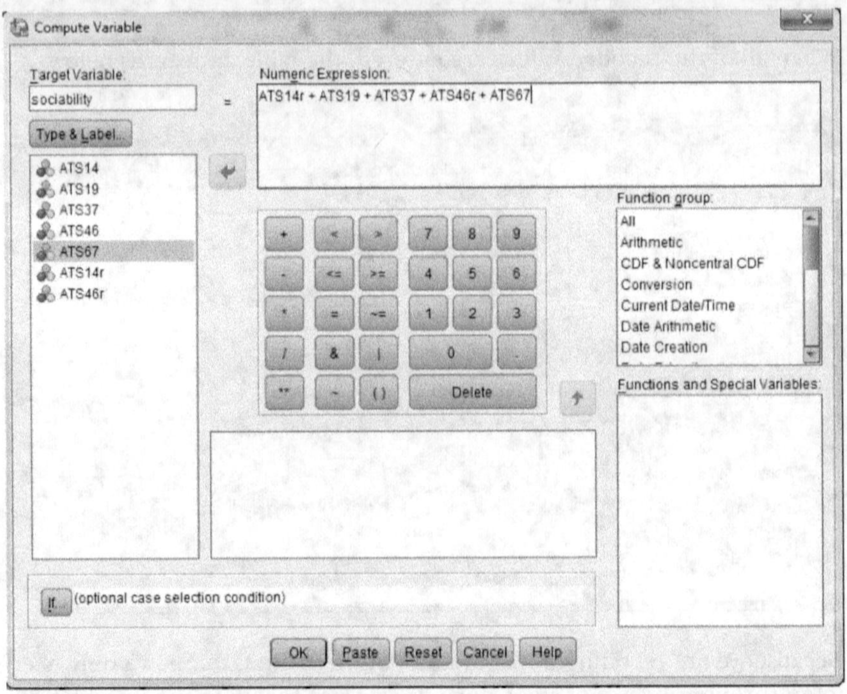

The data for the first 10 individuals in the sample appear below, including the sociability score in the last column of the dataset.

ATS14	ATS19	ATS37	ATS46	ATS67	ATS14r	ATS46r	sociability
6	7	.	5	4	2.00	3.00	.
7	4	4	6	6	1.00	2.00	17.00
2	1	3	1	2	6.00	7.00	19.00
6	2	5	4	4	2.00	4.00	17.00
3	6	6	2	7	5.00	6.00	30.00
7	7	3	4	7	1.00	4.00	22.00
6	7	5	6	6	2.00	2.00	22.00
1	1	4	1	2	7.00	7.00	21.00
5	3	7	3	5	3.00	5.00	23.00
6	5	6	2	.	2.00	6.00	

Perhaps the first thing we notice about these results is that for observations 1 and 10, the value of sociability is a "." (indicating that it is missing responses). The reason for this is that these individuals did not respond to one or more of the items that comprise the scale. If a respondent leaves an item missing, a score on the total scale will not be calculated for that individual.

Calculation of Weighted Scores Using SPSS

As discussed, the primary issue when considering the use of weighted scores is the source of the weights themselves. In some instances, scale developers will have already determined the weights, leaving us merely to apply them to our data. For example, imagine that the developer of the sociability scale assigned the following weights to the items:

ATS14 = 1.5
ATS19 = 1
ATS37 = 1.5
ATS46 = 0.5
ATS67 = 2

We can apply these weights and create the sociability scale using **Transform ► Compute** as below:

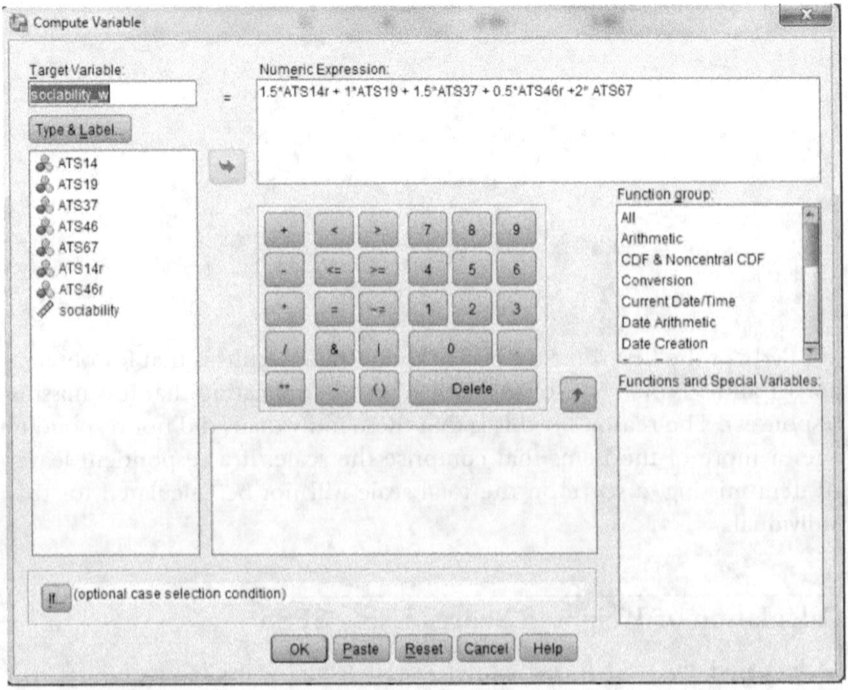

In many cases, however, we do not have the weights provided for us. Therefore, the question becomes, how do we determine what the weights should be if we do not have them predetermined? Perhaps the most common approach to addressing this issue is with the use of factor analysis. We discussed factor analysis in Chapter 5 in the context of scale validity, where we used factor analysis to assess the construct validity of a scale. Namely, do the items group together in a way that is consistent with what the theory underlying the measure would predict? Thus, we were primarily interested in determining the number of factors underlying the scale data. Another use of factor analysis, however, is in the determination of the relative relationship of the individual items to the factors. This relative importance is expressed in the form of weights that can be applied to the items to create a weighted sum score to report test performance.

An in-depth discussion of the theory underlying the estimation of factor analysis based weights is beyond the scope of this book. Rather, we will focus on using SPSS to obtain these weights, which can then be applied to a set of items. The general equation for obtaining these weights using factor analysis is

$$W_{ij} = R^{-1}\lambda \tag{6.6}$$

where

R = the correlation matrix for the items
λ = the factor loading matrix.

It is easiest to consider the use of factor analysis to obtain weights when we have only one trait being measured, though it is entirely possible to use it for multiple factors at once. In the case of a single factor, Equation 6.6 essentially says that the weights for the individual items are calculated as the factor loadings vector divided by the inter-item correlation matrix.

In order to demonstrate the use of factor scores, let's consider the sociability data. We can obtain the factor scores using the same command sequence that we described in Chapter 5 for fitting an exploratory factor analysis model to the data. Thus, from the menu we would use the following sequence: **Analyze ► Dimension Reduction ► Factor**, in order to get the following window.

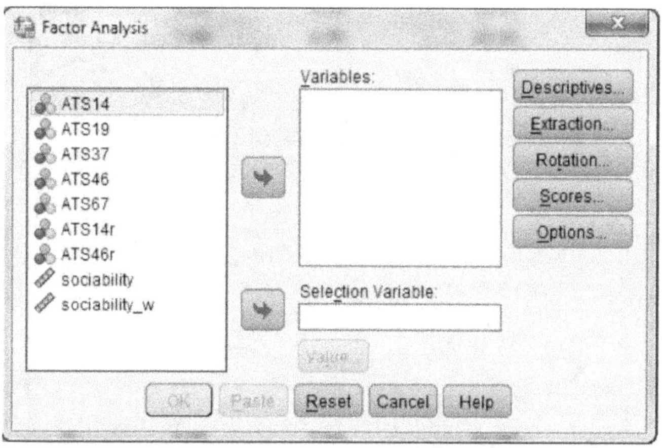

We will first move the variables belonging to the scale into the Variables window.

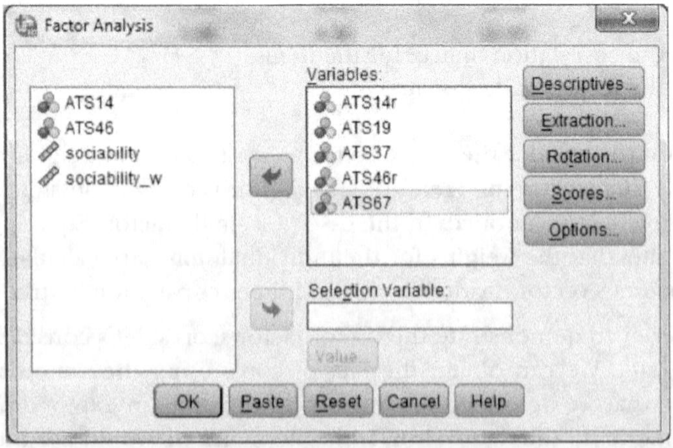

Next, we must select the method of extraction by clicking on **Extraction....**

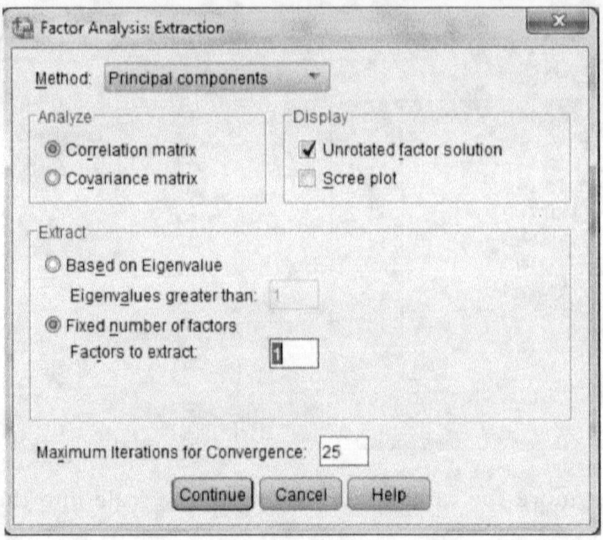

In this instance, we will use principal components analysis and request 1 factor. Next, we will click on **Scores....** In this window, we will click the box next to **Save as variables**, so that SPSS will create the factor scores for us and include them in the active dataset. If we would like to see the weights from Equation 6.6, we can do so by clicking on the box next to **Display factor score coefficient matrix**.

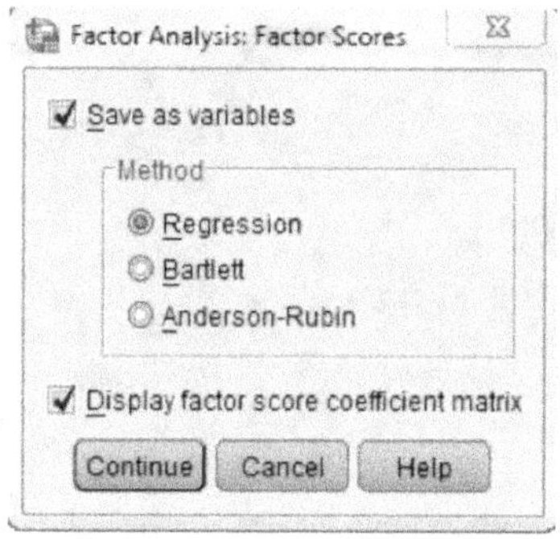

We then click **Continue**, and then **OK**. We are not concerned about the rotation in this case, as our primary interest is in the estimation of the weighted factor scores.

The factor analysis output will look much as it did in the example in Chapter 5. Again, because our primary interest here is in the estimation of scores, we will only focus on the weights and the scores themselves. We requested the weights from Equation 6.6, which appear in the following table.

Component Score Coefficient Matrix	
	Component
	1
ATS14r	–.306
ATS19	.276
ATS37	.292
ATS46r	–.309
ATS67	.338
Extraction Method: Principal Component Analysis. Component Scores.	

Notice that the largest weight was associated with ATS67, and the smallest weight with ATS19. However, in all cases, the weights are very close to one another in value. The scores themselves are placed in the dataset, the first 10 observations of which appear below.

FAC1_1
.
.71793
-2.31864
-.27922
.29004
.83966
1.17392
-2.29222
.11368
.

The weighted score from the factor analysis is called FAC1_1.

It is worth taking a moment to examine in more detail precisely what SPSS did to obtain the weighted scores contained in FAC1_1. Prior to applying the weights, each item was converted to a z score using Equation 6.3. Then, the weights obtained using principal components analysis, and displayed in the table above, were applied to the individual z scores as follows:

$$\text{Factor1} = -0.306 * z_{ats14r} + 0.276 * z_{ats19} + 0.292 * z_{ats37} + -0.309 * z_{ats46r} + 0.338 * z_{ats67}$$

Given that the data were first standardized prior to the application of the weights, the scale is obviously very different from that of either the raw sum scores or the weighted scores based on the raw data. Indeed, the score is put on the z scale so that a score of 0 is indicative of average performance. In addition, given that the data are standardized, it would be possible to turn these weighted values into standard scores such as the T or IQ.

Calculation of Percentiles Using SPSS

Using SPSS, it is possible to directly determine the percentile for each score in a sample, using the rank cases function under Transform. As noted in Equation 6.2, the percentile is essentially the percent of observations in the sample at or below a particular score in the distribution. To demonstrate calculating percentile scores in SPSS, let's return to the 4th grade math test data. Prior to obtaining percentile scores, we first need to calculate the raw test score, which we then submit to the following SPSS command sequence.

Transform ► Rank Cases. We will then see the following window.

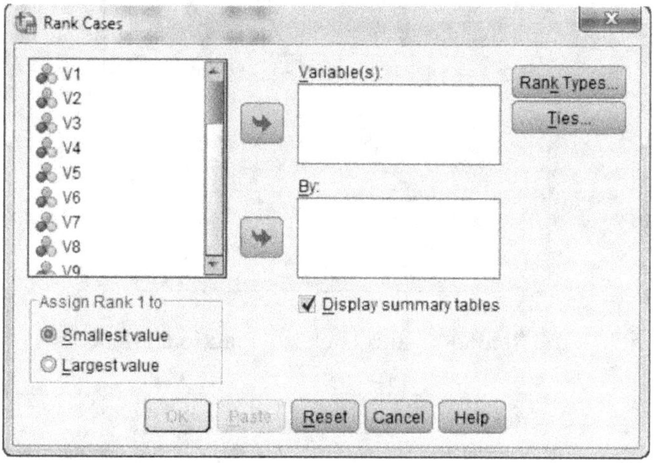

First, we put the variable (score in this case) for which we want percentiles in the **Variable(s)** box.

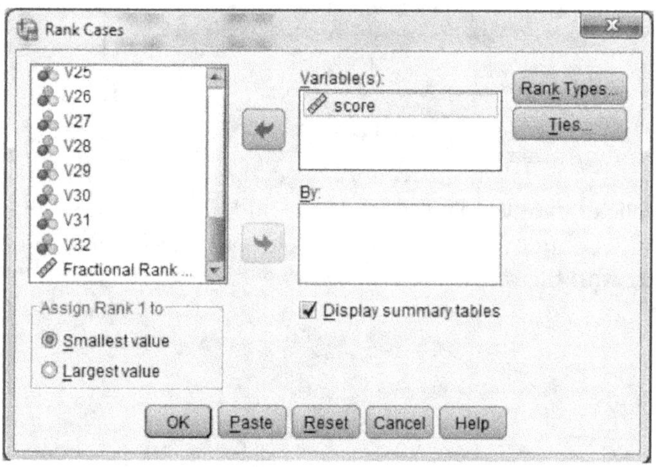

We must then click **Rank Types...** in order to obtain the following window.

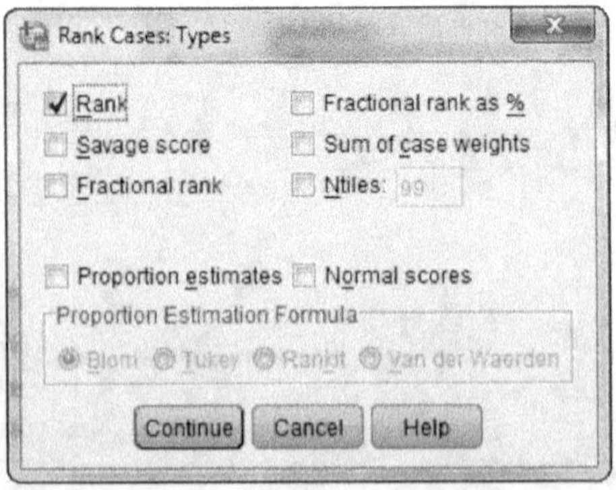

We will unclick the **Rank** box, and click the **Fractional rank as %** box.

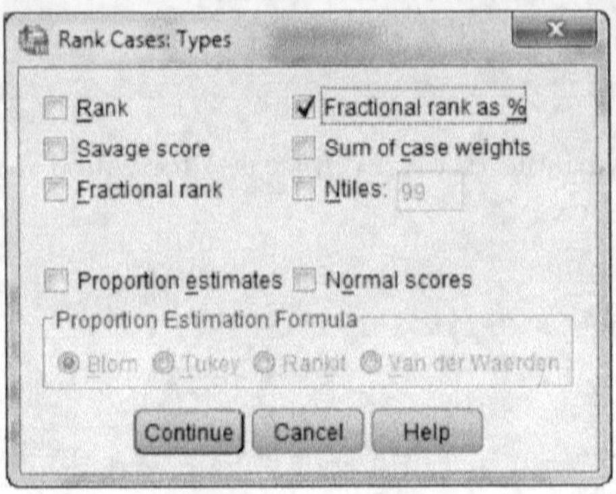

We then click **Continue**. The percentiles will be added to the final column of our dataset under the name Pscore. Below are the first 5 of these percentiles, along with the raw score.

score	Pscore
16.00	28.65
23.00	64.15
9.00	5.05
28.00	89.50
15.00	23.75

From these results, we see that an individual with a total score of 9 (out of 32) is in the 5th percentile, while someone with a score of 23 is in the 64th percentile.

Calculation of Standardized Scores Using SPSS

The standard score is the final type of score that we will consider in this chapter. There are a number of commonly used standard scores, as we discussed above, each characterized by a unique mean and standard deviation. Recall that all of these standard scores are based upon first converting the raw score to a z, and then applying Equation 6.4. SPSS will provide us with the z values that serve as the basis for the standardized scores described above. We can then create whichever standardized score we would like using the **Transform ► Compute Variable** sequence described above. As an example, let's calculate the T score values for the 4th grade testing data which, to recall, have a mean of 50 and a standard deviation of 10. First, we will obtain the z score using the following command sequence **Analyze ► Descriptive Statistics ► Descriptives** in order to obtain the following window.

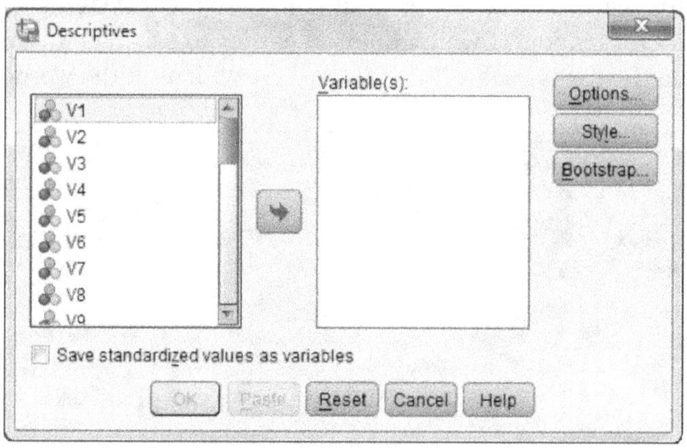

We would place the variable(s) that we would like to be standardized (score) into the **Variable(s)** box, and then click the **Save standardized values as variables** box.

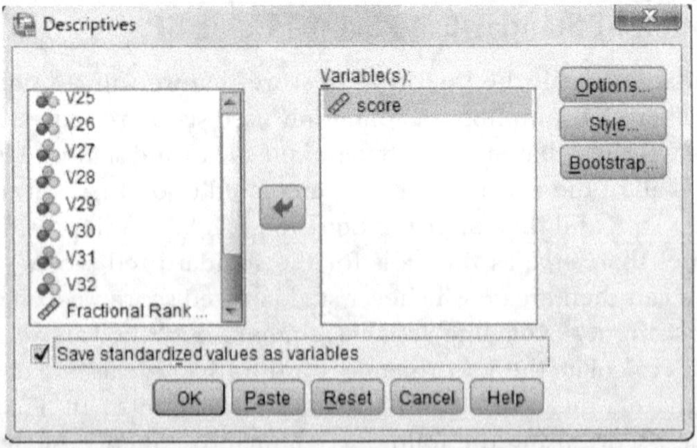

The *z* value for the raw score is saved under the name Zscore in the data file. In order to create the T score, we would then use the **Transform ▶ Compute Variable** menu sequence, which we used earlier to calculate the raw score. We will call the new variable T_score, and create it as in the window below:

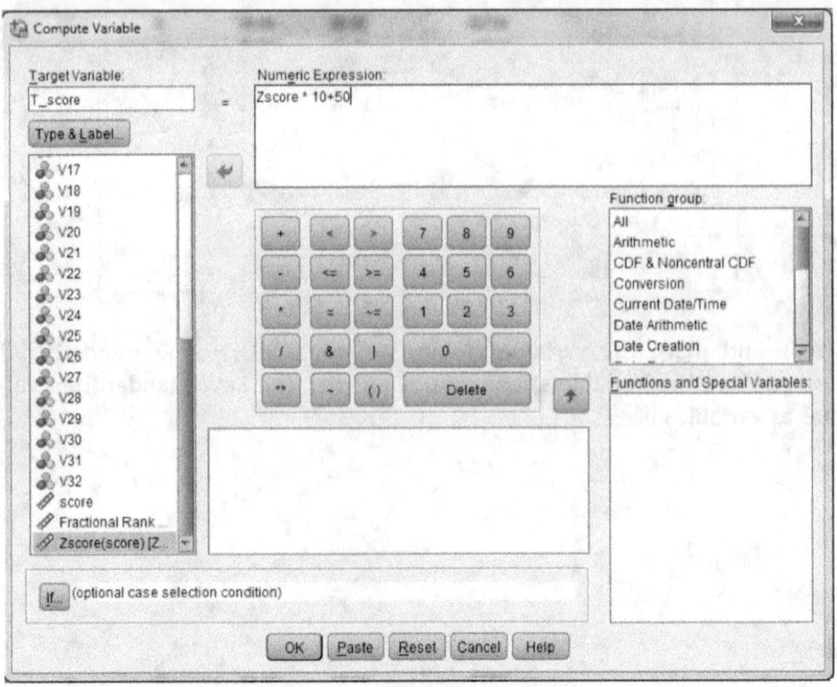

We then click **OK** and the *T* values will appear in the last column in the dataset.

The resulting standardized scores, along with the raw score, the percentile, and z appear below for the first 10 observations.

score	Pscore	Zscore	T_score
16.00	28.65	-.62724	43.73
23.00	64.15	.48743	54.87
9.00	5.05	-1.74192	32.58
28.00	89.50	1.28363	62.84
15.00	23.75	-.78648	42.14
20.00	48.55	.00971	50.10
16.00	28.65	-.62724	43.73
20.00	48.55	.00971	50.10
18.00	38.15	-.30876	46.91
26.00	80.75	.96515	59.65

Given that the mean of the T score is 50, we can see that examinees 1, 3, 5, 7, and 9 all had scores below average, while examinees 2, 4, 6, 8, and 10 had scores above the mean.

Chapter Summary

In this chapter, we have learned about a number of different methods for scoring performance on psychological and educational assessments, and how to obtain these scores using SPSS. The range of possible scores can be quite daunting, and each has its own particular strengths and weaknesses. For example, while raw scores are easy to calculate and familiar, they can be difficult to interpret out of the particular context in which the measurement was taken. Percentiles provide a more useful interpretation, particularly when primary interest is in determining how an individual score compares to those of the entire sample. On the other hand, percentiles are not easy to use with other statistical methods, and they do not have an equidistant scale. Standard scores have proven to be very useful and popular in a variety of contexts. In particular, they provide a ready context for interpretation because they have a known mean and standard deviation, which allows for comparison across time and instruments (as long as the mean and standard deviation are the same). Several standard scores (e.g., IQ, *T*), are routinely used in testing and assessment so that users are generally familiar with them. Finally, standard scores have the advantage of being useful in conjunction with other statistical analyses, unlike percentiles. In the final analysis, the decision regarding which type of score(s) are to be used depends in large part on the purpose behind the assessment. The test user must carefully consider how the scores will be used and then make a decision regarding which will provide the information that is called for in their application. If a response of 7 on ATS19 suggests that an individual who likes to talk a lot are likely to report a 1 for ATS46 (i.e., not at all positive about spending time socializing with large groups of people), then reverse coding will change the response for ATS46 to match that of ATS19 (i.e., very sociable people will now respond with a 7 for both items).

7

Differential Item Functioning

Introduction

The focus of this chapter is on the detection of differential item functioning (DIF), a key component in the process of instrument development and validation. Based on the implications of test score use across diverse settings (e.g., educational, vocational) and populations (e.g., students, patients), it is vital that the intended trait is measured correctly, and that the scale scores are not contaminated with undue bias (e.g., systematic error). Test scores, for example, are used in large-scale standardized testing programs to make decisions about individual students, as well as schools and school districts. For such scores to be appropriate and meaningful, they must be valid for the use in which they were designed (Linn, 2009). In turn, for such validity to exist, the employed assessment tools must produce comparable scores for individuals regardless of subgroup membership (e.g., sex, language spoken in the home). If this equivalence of measurement does not exist, the scores resulting from the instruments may carry different meaning for individuals from different groups, thereby compromising their validity, and introducing potential unfairness into decisions in which these scores play a role.

Applied Psychometrics Using SPSS and AMOS, pages 195–223

To ensure the equivalent meaning of test scores across diverse groups, researchers and instrument developers are encouraged to investigate the potential presence of DIF in scale items (Wu, Li, & Zumbo, 2007). DIF refers to the case where individuals from different population subgroups, who are matched on the trait being measured by the scale, have different probabilities of obtaining a particular item response (Camilli & Shepard, 1994). In the context of a mathematics achievement test, for example, DIF would occur if males and females who are matched on mathematics ability have different probabilities of getting a dichotomously scored (i.e., correct/incorrect) item correct. For an anxiety assessment comprised of items rated on a Likert Scale (e.g., 1 = *Strongly Disagree* to 5 = *Strongly Agree*), DIF would be present if males and females matched on anxiety had differing probabilities of providing a particular response category (e.g., 4 = *Agree*). While these two examples involve gender, DIF can result from such item response differences for any subgroups that exist in the population, including, among others: language spoken in the home, race/ethnicity, and opportunity to learn. Further, while such subgroups are often defined in terms of examinee demographics for DIF analysis, comparisons can be made across any salient features of a particular population, such as across teacher groups that differ in terms of students in their classroom, or treatment groups exposed to different interventions. Our presentation of DIF analysis will begin with the application of procedures to detect differential item performance on dichotomously scored items (e.g., multiple-choice). Subsequently, we present DIF detection procedures for polytomous, or Likert type, items, such as those designed to measure psychological traits (e.g., personality).

Traditionally, an item has been characterized as displaying two types of DIF: uniform and nonuniform. In the context of academic achievement testing, uniform DIF refers to the case where the probability of a correct item response between two matched groups differs consistently across the entire range of ability (e.g., reading ability). Figure 7.1 provides a visual representation of uniform DIF using the item characteristic curves (ICC) that report the probability of a correct item response on a dichotomously scored item across two distinct groups.

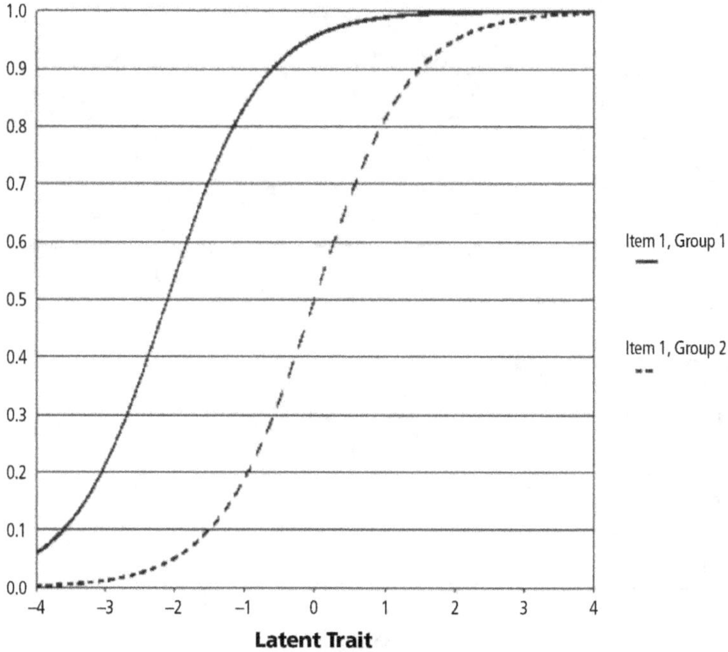

Figure 7.1 ICCs for uniform DIF between two groups.

As introduced in a previous chapter, the ICC serves to provide a graphical representation of the probability of an item endorsement (e.g., a correct response) as a function of the measured latent trait. This figure provides the ICCs reporting the probability of a correct response for two groups: Group 1 and Group 2. As shown, at any point along the latent trait axis (x), Group 1 has a higher probability of a correct item response than Group 2. Furthermore, this difference is consistent across the ability axis (i.e., Group 1 always has the higher likelihood of a correct response). Thus, we can conclude that this item displays uniform DIF.

Figure 7.2 illustrates the ICCs for an item displaying nonuniform DIF. As shown, the difference in the ICCs for two groups is not consistent across the latent trait continuum. Instead, as is the case of nonuniform DIF, the probability of a correct item response differs according to the groups' standing on the latent trait. Specifically, in this example, Group 1 has a lower probability of answering the item correctly for ability values below –1.0 and, alternatively, a higher probability of a correct item response than Group 2 when their trait standings is above –1.0.

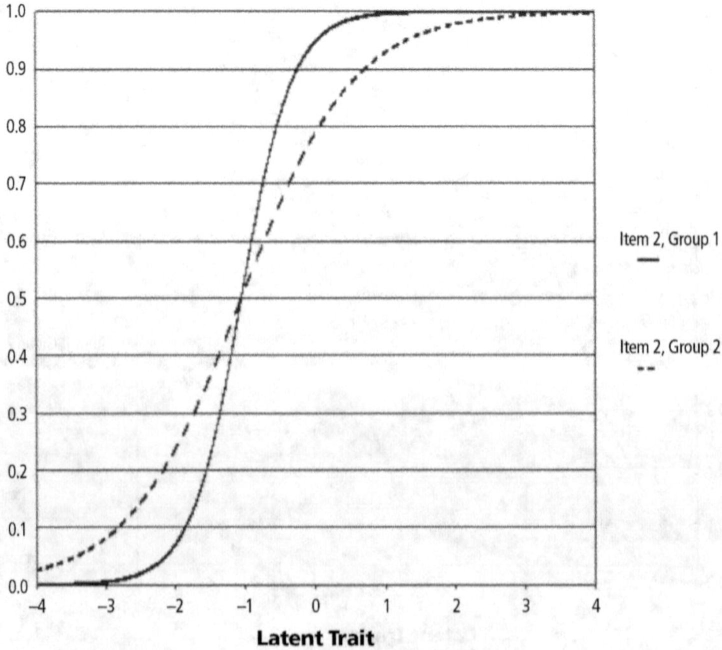

Figure 7.2 ICCs for nonuniform DIF between two groups.

While DIF is often described in terms of differences in item response probabilities, it can also be thought of as a difference in IRT model parameters between the groups (Raju, 1988). Recall from the previous chapter that we can represent the probability of a particular item response as a function of the latent trait of the individual being measured, in conjunction with the item properties of difficulty (*b*) and discrimination (*a*). In some cases, we can also consider the pseudo-chance (*c*) parameter when it is likely that a correct item response can be attributed to guessing, such as with multiple-choice items. Uniform DIF, then, can be thought of as a difference in item difficulty or *b*-DIF. In other words, if separate IRT models were estimated for each group, *b*-DIF would be present if there was a significant difference in the *b* parameter estimates between the groups. Similarly, nonuniform (*a*-DIF) occurs when the item discrimination parameter values (*a*) are significantly different between the groups. Although there has been some investigation of DIF with respect to the pseudo-chance parameter (*c*-DIF), results have heretofore not identified an effective tool for the identifying such. However, research has demonstrated that the presence of such DIF does create problems in terms of estimation of other item parameter values (Finch & French, 2011). Because there are not currently effective means for identifying the presence of *c*-DIF, it will not be discussed here further.

DIF Versus Impact

Prior to describing a number of the available statistical tools for DIF assessment and their realization using SPSS, we need to take just a moment to describe the concept of impact and its distinction from DIF in educational and psychological assessment. Impact refers to differences in item performance between two groups that can be attributed to a disparity in the amount of the latent trait being measured (Clauser & Mazor, 1998). For example, if we were interested in comparing performance on items measuring examinees' ability to correctly multiply fractions, we would expect different performances between a group of students who have received instruction in fraction multiplication to students who have received no instruction. In this instance, differential performance on items assessing fraction multiplication would be expected due to group differences on instructional exposure to multiplication of fractions. Thus, a difference in the probability of a correct response between the groups would be indicative of impact, not DIF. On the other hand, we would not expect to see any differences in the performance on the fraction multiplication item between members of different race/ethnic groups (matched on ability) who received instruction on fraction multiplication in the same classroom. If differential item performance was observed, after matching compared racial/ethnic groups on ability, we would say that the item displayed DIF. As such, the differentiating factor between item impact and DIF is the matching of individuals on the latent trait of interest. To state with some confidence that an item exhibits DIF, individuals in the sample must be matched on the latent trait (e.g., self-efficacy, mathematics ability). However, as shown, this matching of individuals is not a trivial matter.

Mantel–Haenszel Test

One of the more popular and enduring methods for DIF detection is the Mantel–Haenszel chi-square test (MH; Mantel & Haenszel, 1959). MH was first applied to the problem of investigating the presence of uniform DIF by Holland and Thayer (1988), and has subsequently been used in a wide variety of applications for DIF detection. When the MH procedure is applied to the case where there are two groups of interest, they are commonly referred to as the reference and focal groups. These designations are arbitrary, though quite often the focal group is taken to be the one of most interest, while the reference group represents the majority group (Camilli & Sheperd, 1994). Again, however, these group designations are arbitrary. The MHχ^2 is calculated as

$$\frac{\left\{\left|\sum_{j=1}^{S}\left[A_j - E(A_j)\right]\right| - .5\right\}^2}{\sum_{j=1}^{S} Var(A_j)}. \tag{7.1}$$

The value A_j is the number of individuals in the reference group with a test score of j who answer the item correctly. $E(A_j)$ is the expected number at score j who answer the item correctly, and is calculated as

$$E(A_j) = \frac{m_{1j} n_{Rj}}{n_{++j}} \tag{7.2}$$

where m_{1j} is the number of examinees answering the item correctly with test score j, n_{Rj} is the number of reference group examinees with test score j, and n_{++j} is the number of all examinees with test score j. The variance of A_j is calculated as

$$Var(A_j) = \frac{n_{Rj} n_{Fj} m_{1j} m_{0j}}{n_{++j}^2 (n_{++j} - 1)}, \tag{7.3}$$

where terms are as defined for Equation 7.2, n_{Fj} is the number of focal group examinees at score j, and m_{0j} represent the number of incorrect responses at score j. The score on the test, S, serves as the proxy for the latent trait being measured. The null hypothesis tested by the $MH\chi^2$ is

$$H_0: \frac{p_{R1j}}{1 - p_{R1j}} = \frac{p_{F1j}}{1 - p_{F1j}}$$

(i.e., the odds that a member of the reference group at score j will get the item correct is equal to the odds of a member of the focal group at score j also getting the item correct).

In addition to the hypothesis test for DIF, the MH procedure also yields a very useful measure of effect size, in the form of the odds ratio:

$$\alpha_{MH} = \frac{\sum A_j D_j / n_{++j}}{\sum B_j C_j / n_{++j}}. \tag{7.4}$$

The term A_j has already been defined as the number of reference group examinees answering the item correctly. In addition, D_j is the number in the reference group answering the item incorrectly, B_j is the number of focal group examinees answering the item incorrectly, and C_j is the number of focal group examinees answering the item correctly. Values of α_{MH} between 0 and 1 indicate that the item favors the focal group, whereas values exceeding 1 indicate that the item favors the reference group. While statistically this odds ratio is perfectly reasonable, Holland and Thayer (1988) suggested that the log of α_{MH} might be a more interpretable measure of the DIF effect, as it is symmetric about 0 so that negative values mean that the item favors the focal group and positive values mean that the item favors the reference group.

The Educational Testing Service (ETS) subsequently recommended an adjustment to this statistic that they referred to as Δ, or delta. This Δ_{ETS} is calculated as $-2.35\ln\alpha_{MH}$. Rescaling the odds ratio ensures that values between negative infinity and 0 indicate that the item favors the reference group, while values from 0 to positive infinity indicate the item favors the focal group. Furthermore, this statistic is on the ETS delta item difficulty scale. Thus, a Δ_{ETS} value of -0.5 means that the item is 0.5 delta scale units more difficult for the focal group than for the reference. ETS uses the Δ_{ETS} as an effect size measure which, in conjunction with hypothesis test results for $MH\chi^2$, serves to define when an item exhibits DIF, as well as the magnitude of DIF. Using this rubric, DIF is divided into 3 categories: A, B, and C. A DIF is defined as occurring when $MH\chi^2$ is not statistically significant ($\alpha = 0.05$), or when Δ_{ETS} is less than 1 in absolute value. An item has B DIF if $MH\chi^2$ is statistically significant, and Δ_{ETS} is greater than or equal to 1.0, but less than 1.5. Finally, an item exhibits C DIF when $MH\chi^2$ is statistically significant, and Δ_{ETS} is greater than 1.5. A more detailed discussion of these rules and their origination can be found in Zwick (2012).

The MH method can also be used to test for the presence of DIF with polytomous items using the Generalized $MH\chi^2$, which takes the form:

$$\chi^2 = \frac{\left(\Sigma_j \Sigma_T N_{RTJ} - \Sigma_J \dfrac{N_{2+j}}{N_{++j}} \Sigma_T N_{+TJ} Y_T\right)^2}{\Sigma_J Var(\Sigma_T N_{RTJ} Y_T)}. \tag{7.5}$$

Here, index J represents the score on the matching subtest, while T represents the response to the polytomous item, and R refers to the reference group. As with the MH procedure for dichotomous items, an effect size measure for the polytomous case, the standardized mean difference (SMD), has also been recommended for use when determining whether DIF is present. The SMD is calculated as

$$\text{SMD} = \Sigma_j \frac{N_{R+J}\Sigma_T N_{2TJ} Y_T}{N_{R++}N_{R+J}} - \Sigma_j \frac{N_{R+J}\Sigma_T N_{FTJ} Y_T}{N_{R++}N_{F+J}} \tag{7.6}$$

where all terms are as defined above, and F refers to the focal group. The MH effect size for polytomous items is the SMD divided by the pooled within-group standard deviation of the studied item. The National Center for Educational Statistics (NCES) has developed a heuristic for interpreting the degree of DIF present in a polytomous items that is analogous to the system used for dichotomous data (NCES, 2001). A polytomous item is classified as having the lowest level, or A DIF when $MH\chi^2$ is not statistically significant, and/or the absolute value of SMD is less than or equal to 0.17. The item exhibits BB DIF if $MH\chi^2$ is statistically significant, and SMD lies between 0.17 and 0.25. A designation of CC DIF corresponds to a statistically significant $MH\chi^2$ and SMD greater than 0.25 (Michaelides, 2008).

Clearly, a key component of correctly applying the $MH\chi^2$ to DIF detection is the calculation of the matching test score, S. As mentioned above, this score is used as the proxy for the latent trait being measured and serves as the metric upon which examinees in the reference and focal groups are matched with one another on ability. As such, the determination of what exactly constitutes the matching score is extremely important. There are two primary issues in this regard that the researcher must take into consideration when calculating S. First, the matching score should be free of the influences of DIF. Such a purified scale should consist only of items that are known not to contain DIF. Second is the issue of thick versus thin matching, or said another way, how wide should the score categories be? We address both concerns in this chapter.

Much research has been conducted investigating the impact of using a matching subtest score that includes items with DIF (Clauser, Mazor, & Hambleton, 1993; Colvin & Randall, 2011; French & Maller, 2007). In general, these studies all recommend the need to purify the scale by identifying items with DIF and removing them prior to calculating the final version of S to be used in calculating $MH\chi^2$. Some other results (Zwick, 2012) suggest that if, across items, there is equivalent DIF between the reference and focal groups (balanced DIF), then item purification may lead to slightly worse performance than would using the purified scale. On the other hand, if DIF consistently favors one group over the other (unbalanced DIF), item purification is necessary. In the final analysis, Zwick recommended that researchers use item purification in most instances, as it will not be known a priori whether DIF is balanced or unbalanced, and purification does not lead to serious degradation in performance, even in the balanced case. Item purification is a straightforward process in which the total test score,

S, is used as the matching criterion in the initial step. Each item is tested for DIF in turn, and those items identified as containing DIF are removed from calculation of S. This purified matching score is then used in a reanalysis of DIF using MHχ^2.

In addition to purification, a second important issue in the calculation of the matching score is whether it should be based on the total score of the instrument (i.e., thin matching, or whether it should involve the combination of several of these scores in a type of thick matching). Donoghue and Allen (1993) conducted a study comparing the performance of thin and several thick matching methods, and found that particularly for very short instruments (10 or fewer items), thick matching of some type provides more accurate DIF detection results compared to thin matching. On the other hand, with tests of 40 items thin matching provided more accurate results, particularly as sample size increased. With respect to the optimal type of thick matching to be used, overall the results of their study demonstrated that no one approach was uniformly best. However, they showed that an equal interval method, in which pairs of adjacent test scores are combined (e.g., 0 and 1, 2 and 3, etc.) often performed well. Therefore, given its relatively positive performance, coupled with its ease of use, it is the method that we would recommend. A final caveat regarding the use of thick matching must be made, however. Clauser, Mazor, and Hambleton (1993) reported that when the reference and focal groups have differing levels of the trait being measured, the use of thick matching will exacerbate an already problematic tendency of the MH procedure to identify the presence of DIF too often when it is not in fact present. It is therefore very important for researchers to first examine the data for the possibility of such group differences prior to conducting any DIF analysis.

Logistic Regression

While the MH technique for investigating DIF has been shown to be useful, particularly with small sample sizes (Roussos & Stout, 1996), its effectiveness is largely limited to the case of uniform DIF assessment (Rogers & Swaminathan, 1993). An alternative approach for assessing both uniform and nonuniform DIF involves the logistic regression (LR) model. Swaminathan and Rogers (1990) demonstrated the utility of LR for assessing uniform DIF, and Narayanan and Swaminathan (1996) showed that it was also an effective tool for nonuniform DIF testing. Zumbo (1999) expanded upon the discussion of employing LR for DIF assessment, and introduced the use of effect sizes in conjunction with significance testing in order to better describe the magnitude of DIF (Thomas & Zumbo, 1996). Finally, Jodoin and Gierl (2001) refined the effect size guidelines described by Zumbo and Thomas. Following is a summary of this methodology, combining the findings and recommendations provided by these authors.

The LR model for DIF detection as given by Swaminathan and Rogers is generally expressed as

$$p(y_i = 1 | g, \theta) = \frac{e^{\beta_0 + \beta_1\theta + \beta_2 g + \beta_3 \theta g}}{1 + e^{\beta_0 + \beta_1\theta + \beta_2 g + \beta_3 \theta g}}. \tag{7.7}$$

The probability of an individual correctly responding to the item, given the group (g) to which they belong (e.g., reference), and their ability (θ), is a function of the logistic equation where β_1 is the coefficient measuring the impact of ability level, β_2 is the coefficient associated with group membership, and β_3 is the coefficient associated with the interaction of group and ability. More specifically in the context of DIF, β_2 assesses uniform DIF, and β_3 assesses nonuniform DIF. Typically, as with MH, ability on the measured trait is represented by the total test score (excluding the target item). Group membership is usually identified as 0/1 or 1/2. If there are more than 2 groups, then rules for dummy coding these would need to be followed (see Agresti, 2002).

The examination of items for DIF with LR is a process of comparing three models for each item and testing the improvement in fit for these models as terms are eliminated in a stepwise fashion. The full model (Equation 7.7) is compared to a reduced model (*R1*) that lacks $\beta_3\theta g$. The second reduced model (*R*2) only contains $\beta_0 + \beta_1\theta$. These three models are compared through a loglikelihood ratio difference test, using the –2 (loglikelihood) statistics. For example, *R*1 is compared to the full model resulting in a 1 degree of freedom test of the interaction of group membership and ability, which is equivalent to testing for nonuniform DIF. Therefore, a significant difference in fit between the two models means that nonuniform DIF is present (i.e., the item discrimination parameters of the two groups are different from one another). To test for uniform DIF, *R*1 is compared to *R*2, also resulting in a 1 degree of freedom test. If this test is statistically significant, then we would conclude that there is uniform DIF, or that the item difficulty parameters of the two groups differ. If the researcher is interested only in determining whether DIF is present, and not in the type of DIF, the full model can be compared to *R*2 with a 2 degree of freedom test. The single degree-of-freedom change statistic evaluates the significance of the difference in two models, where the only difference in parameterization is the inclusion or exclusion of the term of interest. Thus, the hypothesis tests outlined above serve to test the significance of the excluded parameters (Camilli & Shepard, 1994; Zumbo, 1999). Collectively, the null hypotheses of these tests are that there are no significant differences in the fit of the compared statistical models with and without the term in the model. A significant result means that we reject the null, and conclude that inclusion of the term is important, thereby indicating the presence of DIF.

The effect size most commonly associated with LR is the R_Δ^2 statistic, which is calculated as

$$R_\Delta^2 = R_1^2 - R_2^2. \tag{7.8}$$

As in ordinary least squares (OLS) regression, R^2 in LR is a measure of the variation in the outcome variable (item response in this case) associated with the model. Thus, R_F^2 is the variance in an item response associated with the full model containing the estimate of the ability being measured, the group membership, and the interaction of the two variables. Similarly, R_1^2 measures the variance explained by the model containing only the trait being measured and the group membership. The difference in these two values is a measure of the improvement in model fit when the interaction of group and ability is included in the model.

Zumbo and Thomas (1996) recommend the following guidelines for interpreting R_Δ^2 in the context of DIF: values less than 0.13 constitute negligible DIF, values between 0.13 and 0.26 (with statistically significant hypothesis test) constitute moderate DIF, and values greater than 0.26 (with statistically significant hypothesis test) constitute large DIF. These values were based on earlier work by Cohen (1992) in the development of effect size interpretation guidelines. Subsequently, Jodoin and Gierl (2001) developed a separate set of recommendations for interpreting R_Δ^2 based upon an equating study, comparing it to the well-known SIBTEST effect size, $\hat{\beta}_U$. Their recommendations were: values less than 0.035 for negligible DIF, 0.035 to 0.07 for moderate DIF, and larger than 0.07 for large DIF. In addition, in order for moderate or large DIF to be present, the hypothesis test comparing the models must also be statistically significant. In the examples below, we will utilize both sets of effect size guidelines.

As was true with MH, LR can also be used with polytomous item response data. The most common approach for working with ordinal data in LR is the cumulative logits model, which appears in Equation 7.9. The cumulative logit is expressed as:

$$\text{logit}\left[P(Y \le j)\right] = \ln\left(\frac{P(Y \le j)}{1 - P(Y \le j)}\right). \tag{7.9}$$

More specifically, there are $J-1$ logits where J is the number of item response categories, and Y is the actual item response. Essentially this model compares the likelihood of the outcome variable taking a value of j or lower, versus outcomes larger than j. For example, if an item has 5 possible categories of response there would be 4 separate logits.

$$\begin{gathered}
\ln\left(\frac{p(Y=0)}{p(Y=1)+p(Y=2)+p(Y=3)+p(Y=4)}\right)=\beta_{01}+\beta_1\theta+\beta_1 g+\beta_1\theta g \\
\ln\left(\frac{p(Y=0)+p(Y=1)}{p(Y=2)+p(Y=3)+p(Y=4)}\right)=\beta_{02}+\beta_1\theta+\beta_1 g+\beta_1\theta g \\
\ln\left(\frac{p(Y=0)+p(Y=1)+p(Y=2)}{p(Y=3)+p(Y=4)}\right)=\beta_{03}+\beta_1\theta+\beta_1 g+\beta_1\theta g \\
\ln\left(\frac{p(Y=0)+p(Y=1)+p(Y=2)+p(Y=3)}{p(Y=4)}\right)=\beta_{04}+\beta_1\theta+\beta_1 g+\beta_1\theta g
\end{gathered} \tag{7.10}$$

In the cumulative logits model, there is a single slope relating the independent variable to the ordinal response, and each logit has a unique intercept. For a single slope to hold across all logits we must make the proportional odds assumption, which essentially states that this slope is identical across the logits. In other respects, using LR for DIF detection with ordinal items is essentially the same as LR for dichotomous DIF detection.

Examples

To demonstrate DIF analysis using SPSS, we will consider two examples, one focusing on DIF detection for dichotomous item responses (e.g., correct/incorrect), and the other on DIF detection for polytomous item responses (e.g., Likert Scale). The first example is based on the responses of Grade 5 students to 28 items on a language assessment. All of the items were scored as either correct (1) or incorrect (0), and gender was coded as 1 (Male) or 2 (Female). For this analysis, males will serve as the reference group. Prior to actually running the Mantel–Haenszel analysis, we will need to calculate a total test score. To do this, we will use the Compute window, which we have seen previously, and which can be obtained with the following menu command sequence: **Transform ► Compute Variable**.

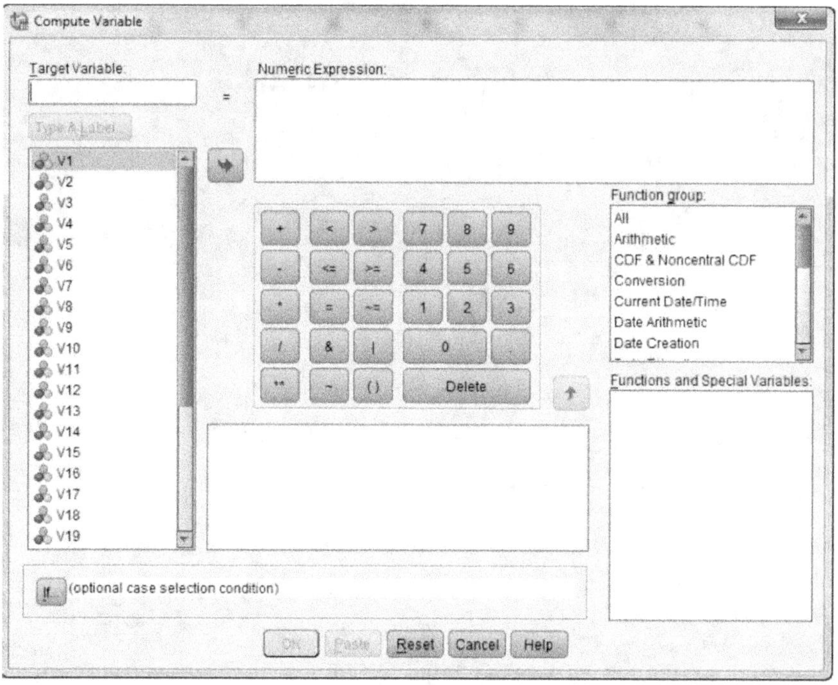

We will name the sum of item responses score, and then simply add the item responses, so that our window appears as below.

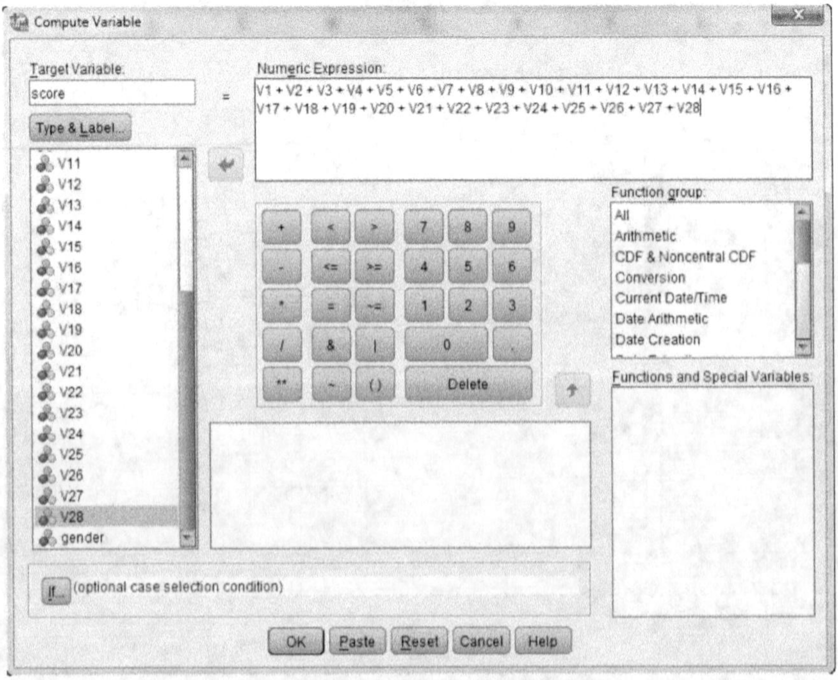

After clicking **OK**, the score variable will appear in the final column of our dataset.

We are now ready to conduct the Mantel–Haenszel test. We will need to do so for each of the items individually. The menu command sequence for this analysis is **Analyze ▶ Descriptive Statistics ▶ Crosstabs**.

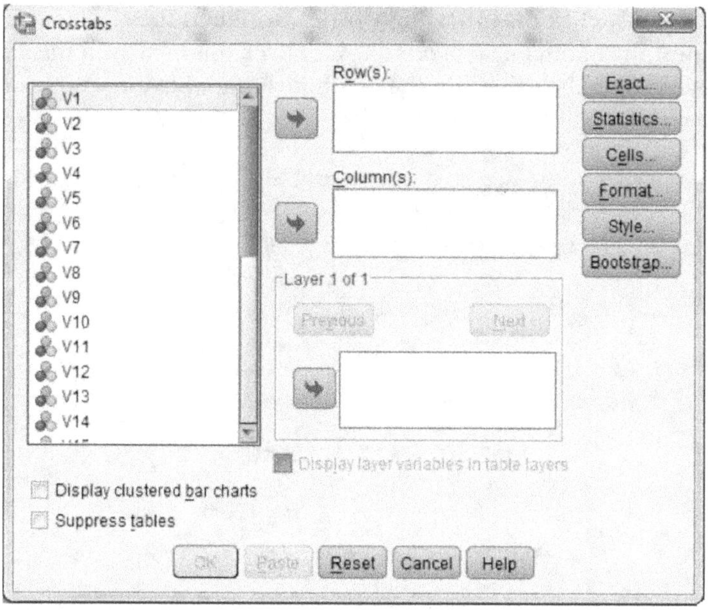

We can place the item of interest (V1 to begin) in the **Row(s)** box, and gender in the **Column(s)** box. This choice is arbitrary, so that we could just as easily put gender in Row(s) and the item in Column(s). Score goes in the box under **Layer 1 of 1**. The window then appears as follows:

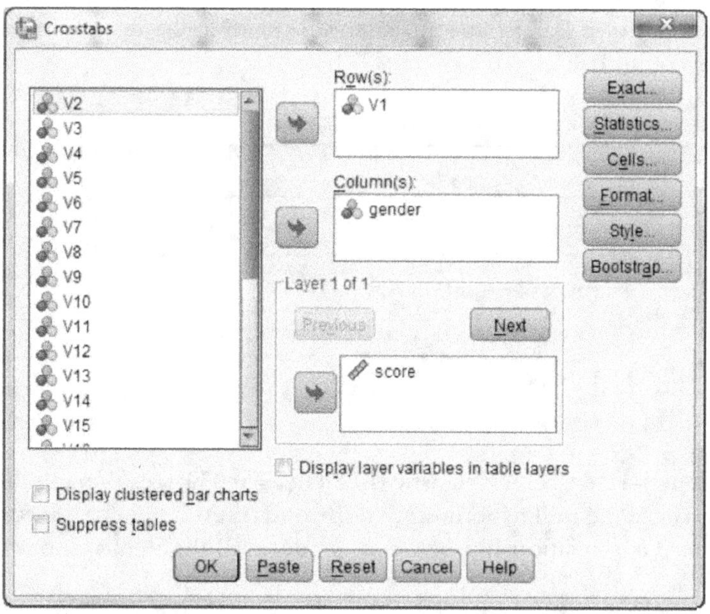

Next, we must click **Statistics...**, in order to obtain the window in which we request the Mantel–Haenszel test. We check this box, as in the example below, and leave the value 1 in the box indicating what our null hypothesis for the test will be.

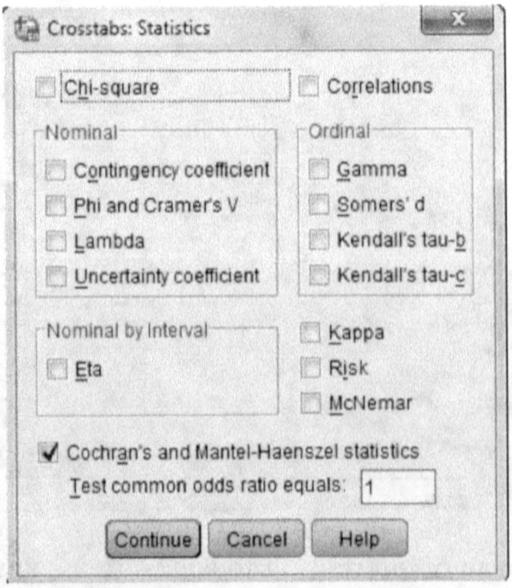

We can now click **Continue** and then **OK**, in order to run the analysis.

SPSS produces several tables when running the Mantel–Haenszel test, but we will only focus on those that are pertinent to the determination of whether uniform DIF is present. First, we examine the test of the null hypothesis of no DIF.

Tests of Conditional Independence

	Chi-Squared	df	Asymp. Sig. (2-sided)
Cochran's	4.398	1	.036
Mantel-Haenszel	4.241	1	.039

Under the conditional independence assumption, Cochran's statistic is asymptotically distributed as a 1 df chi-squared distribution, only if the number of strata is fixed, while the Mantel-Haenszel statistic is always asymptotically distributed as a 1 df chi-squared distribution. Note that the continuity correction is removed from the Mantel-Haenszel statistic when the sum of the differences between the observed and the expected is 0.

The Mantel–Haenszel test statistic is 4.241 ($p = 0.039$), resulting in the decision to reject the null hypothesis that the odds ratio is 1. Thus, we conclude that there is a relationship between gender and the item response, after matching on the total test score. Next, we will refer to the odds ratio and the log of the odds ratio.

Mantel-Haenszel Common Odds Ratio Estimate

Estimate			1.152
ln(Estimate)			.141
Std. Error of ln(Estimate)			.067
Asymp. Sig. (2-sided)			.036
Asymp. 95% Confidence Interval	Common Odds Ratio	Lower Bound	1.009
		Upper Bound	1.314
	ln(Common Odds Ratio)	Lower Bound	.009
		Upper Bound	.273

The Mantel-Haenszel common odds ratio estimate is asymptotically normally distributed under the common odds ratio of 1.000 assumption. So is the natural log of the estimate.

Here the odds ratio is 1.152, with a 95% confidence interval of 1.009 to 1.314. The log odds ratio is 0.141, with a 95% confidence interval of 0.009 to 0.273. We can calculate the ETS Δ as –2.35*0.141 = –0.331. Recall from our earlier discussion of Δ that a negative value indicates an item that is more difficult for the focal group (females in this case). In addition, based on the ETS guidelines for interpreting the value of Δ we would conclude that there is *a* DIF present, because although we have a statistically significant test, the value of ETS Δ is less than 1. In other words, we can conclude that DIF is not a problem for Item 1. Finally, we can calculate the 95% confidence interval for ETS Δ as –2.35 * 0.009 and –2.35 * 0.273, which yields an interval between –0.021 and –0.745.

It is important to consider two issues more closely before we move on to DIF assessment with logistic regression. First, the results presented above are based on the unpurified scale score. As noted above, there has been a great deal of research conducted to examine the impact and effectiveness of scale purification. In this case, the researcher would need to conduct a DIF analysis for each of the items initially using the total score, as we did here for Item 1. Then, a new total score would need to be calculated, removing items that were identified as containing DIF in this initial analysis. The Mantel–Haenszel would then be used again for all of the items, using this new matching score, and once again items that were identified as exhibiting DIF would be identified, and removed from yet another scale score value. This iterative process would continue until the matching score contained only items that were not identified with DIF. Items identified with DIF using this final matching score would then be those that are officially flagged.

The second issue to consider with respect to Mantel–Haenszel is the use of the thin or thick matching criterion. In this case, we used the thin criterion in the form of the original total test score containing 29 possible values (0 to 28). We could fairly easily create a thick matching score using the Recode command in SPSS. To do this, we would use the menu sequence **Transform ► Recode Into Different Variables**. We would then recode the original variables Score into a new one that we could name thickscore.

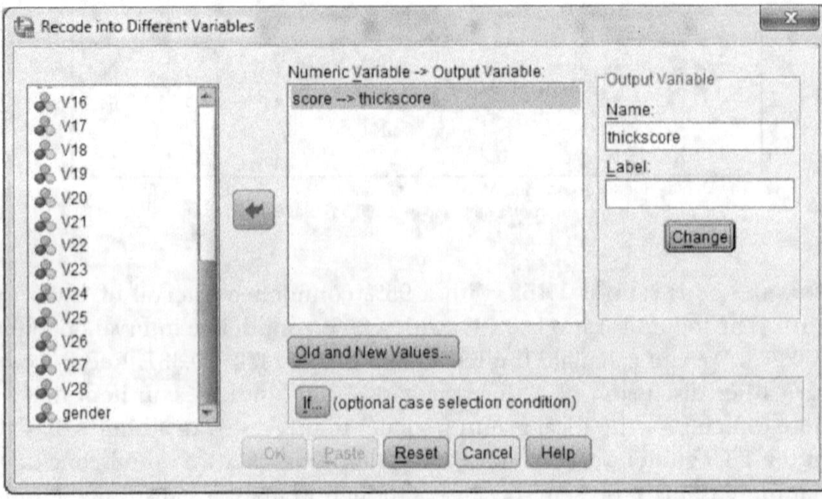

We would then click **Old and New Values...** and obtain the following window.

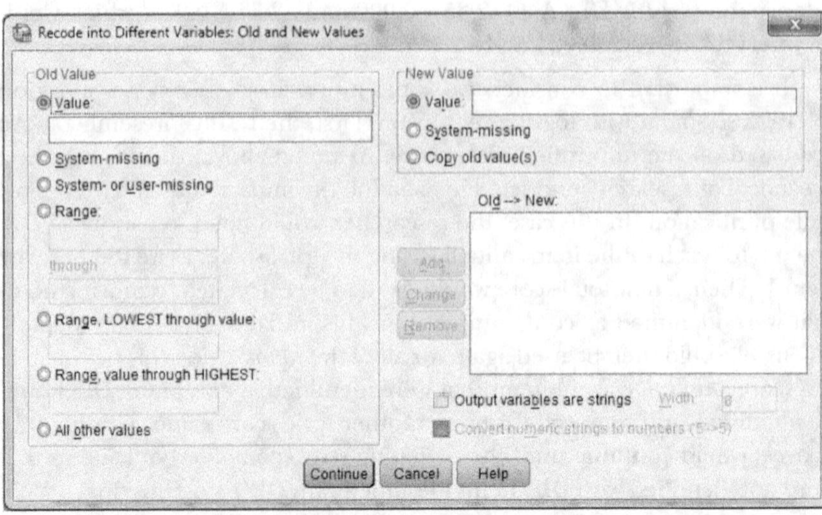

We can then use the Range option to combine adjacent scores (e.g., 0 and 1) and give them a new value (e.g., 1). For the first pair of adjacent scores, we would click the radio button next to **Range**, place **0** in the upper box and **1** in the lower box, and then type **1** in the box next to **Value** under **New Value**.

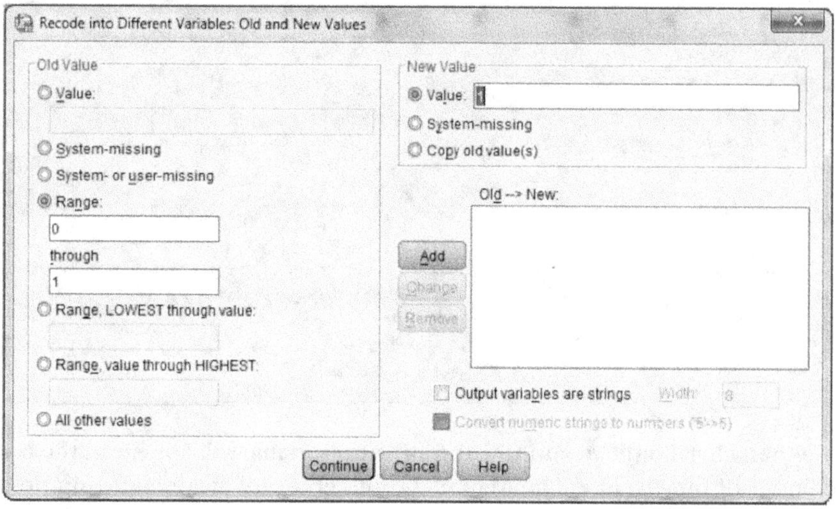

We would then click **Add**. And obtain the following:

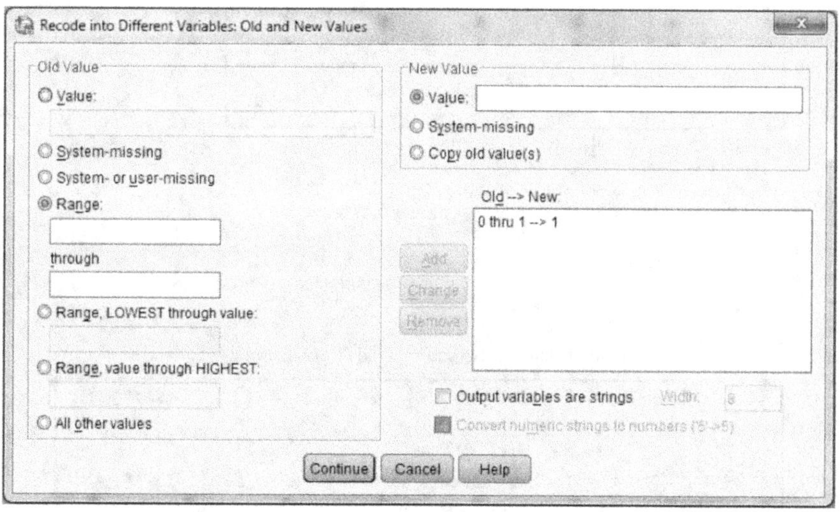

These steps would be repeated for all adjacent pairs of scores in order to obtain the following:

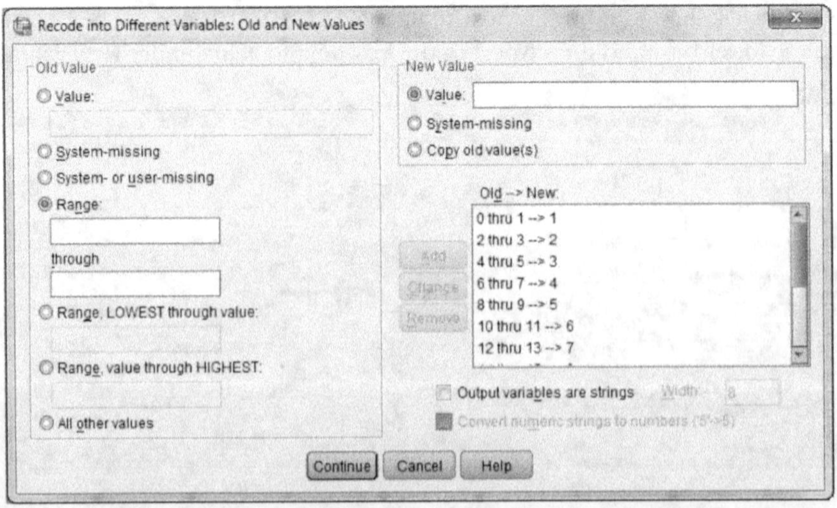

We then click **Continue** and **OK**, and the new variable will appear in the last column of our dataset. The Mantel–Haenszel results for Item 1 using the thick matching score appear below.

Tests of Conditional Independence

	Chi-Squared	df	Asymp. Sig. (2-sided)
Cochran's	4.762	1	.029
Mantel-Haenszel	4.608	1	.032

Under the conditional independence assumption, Cochran's statistic is asymptotically distributed as a 1 df chi-squared distribution, only if the number of strata is fixed, while the Mantel-Haenszel statistic is always asymptotically distributed as a 1 df chi-squared distribution. Note that the continuity correction is removed from the Mantel-Haenszel statistic when the sum of the differences between the observed and the expected is 0.

Mantel-Haenszel Common Odds Ratio Estimate

Estimate			1.158
ln(Estimate)			.147
Std. Error of ln(Estimate)			.067
Asymp. Sig. (2-sided)			.029
Asymp. 95% Confidence Interval	Common Odds Ratio	Lower Bound	1.015
		Upper Bound	1.321
	ln(Common Odds Ratio)	Lower Bound	.015
		Upper Bound	.279

The Mantel-Haenszel common odds ratio estimate is asymptotically normally distributed under the common odds ratio of 1.000 assumption. So is the natural log of the estimate.

The results are very similar to those obtained using the original total score. As pointed out earlier, however, this may not always be the case.

Logistic Regression Example

If we are interested in investigating both uniform and nonuniform DIF, we might consider using LR, which can be done with the following SPSS syntax. This syntax, which was provided in Zumbo (1999), provides all of the information that is required for testing both uniform and nonuniform DIF, as well as the 2 degree of freedom (*df*) test of overall DIF. In addition, it also provides the information needed to calculate the R^2_Δ effect size. The syntax for dichotomous data appears below. This would be typed directly into a SPSS syntax window, which can be obtained through **File ► New ► Syntax**.

```
* SPSS SYNTAX written by: .
* Bruno D. Zumbo, PhD .
* Professor of Psychology and Mathematics, .
* University of Northern British Columbia .
* e-mail: zumbob@unbc.ca .
* Instructions .
* Change the filename, currently 'binary.sav' to your file name .
* Change 'item', 'total', and 'grp', to the corresponding variables
* in your file.
* Run this entire syntax command file.

GET
FILE='lang5dif.sav'.
EXECUTE .
compute item= V1.
compute total= score.
compute grp= gender.
* 2 df Chi-squared test and R-squared for the DIF (note that this
* is a simultaneous test .
* of uniform and non-uniform DIF).
LOGISTIC REGRESSION VAR=item
/METHOD=ENTER total /METHOD=ENTER grp grp*total
/CONTRAST (grp)=Indicator
/CRITERIA PIN(.05) POUT(.10) ITERATE(20) CUT(.5) .
execute.

* 1 df Chi-squared test and R-squared for uniform DIF.
* This is particularly useful if one wants to determine the
* incremental R-squared .
* attributed to the uniform DIF.
LOGISTIC REGRESSION VAR=item
/METHOD=ENTER total /METHOD=ENTER grp
/CONTRAST (grp)=Indicator
/CRITERIA PIN(.05) POUT(.10) ITERATE(20) CUT(.5) .
execute.
```

Dr. Zumbo provides excellent comments embedded in the syntax regarding its use, so we will not repeat those here. We would note that we did include the name of the target item of interest (V1), the scale score (score), and the grouping variable (gender), along with the name of the data file containing these (`lang5dif.sav`), in the first 6 lines of the actual syntax. Lines beginning with * are commented out, and will not be run by SPSS, but instead are for the users of the code. In order to actually run this analysis, we simply select **Run ▶ All** from the top of the syntax window. The resulting output appears in the SPSS output window, and we will only refer to the portions of this output that are relevant for DIF assessment.

We first need to examine the Chi-square value for the model containing only the total score, which is contained in the first set of output to appear. The Chi-square value for the model with only score as a predictor of the item response is 1447.492.

Omnibus Tests of Model Coefficients

		Chi-square	df	Sig.
Step 1	Step	1447.492	1	.000
	Block	1447.492	1	.000
	Model	1447.492	1	.000

In order to test for any DIF at all, we would calculate the difference in Chi-square values for this model, with the model containing both the main effect for gender and the interaction of gender and score.

Omnibus Tests of Model Coefficients

		Chi-square	df	Sig.
Step 1	Step	4.683	2	.096
	Block	4.683	2	.096
	Model	1452.175	3	.000

This test is actually provided to us by SPSS in the line labeled Block, for which the 2 *df* Chi-square is 4.683. This is equivalent to the difference between the Chi-square for the full model, 1452.175, and the score only model. The *p*-value (0.096) is also provided here, and is not statistically significant at $\alpha = 0.05$. Thus, we would conclude that the model containing score, group, and the interaction of score by group does not yield statistically significantly better fit than the model containing only score. In other words, it would appear that no DIF is present for this item. We can also examine the effect size for DIF by calculating $R_{\Delta}^2 = R_{\text{Full Model}}^2 - R_{\text{Score Model}}^2$. These values appear in the tables displayed below.

Model Summary

Step	-2 Log likelihood	Cox & Snell R Square	Nagelkerke R Square
1	5723.709[a]	.186	.292

a. Estimation terminated at iteration number 6 because parameter estimates changed by less than .001.

Model Summary

Step	-2 Log likelihood	Cox & Snell R Square	Nagelkerke R Square
1	5728.393[a]	.186	.291

a. Estimation terminated at iteration number 5 because parameter estimates changed by less than .001.

In this case, $R_{\Delta}^2 = R_{\text{Full Model}}^2 - R_{\text{Score Model}}^2 = 0.292 - 0.291 = 0.001$. This value indicates negligible overall DIF, based on the commonly used guidelines discussed previously.

The set of LR results presented above tested for the presence of overall DIF. It is also possible to assess whether only uniform DIF is present. This was done using the second set of SPSS syntax in the code presented above. In that instance, the initial model contained only the total test score as an independent variable, whereas the second model included both score and group, but not the interaction. The resulting Chi-square tables produced by SPSS appear below.

Omnibus Tests of Model Coefficients

		Chi-square	df	Sig.
Step 1	Step	1447.492	1	.000
	Block	1447.492	1	.000
	Model	1447.492	1	.000

Omnibus Tests of Model Coefficients

		Chi-square	df	Sig.
Step 1	Step	4.656	1	.031
	Block	4.656	1	.031
	Model	1452.148	2	.000

The 1 *df* test comparing the models appears in the second table, with a value of 4.656, and $p = 0.031$. This result is statistically significant, indicating that after conditioning on the total score there was a significant relationship between gender and performance on the item. This result might seem counterintuitive given the non-significant result for the test of overall DIF. However, it is important to recall that this overall test has 2 *df*, and is assessing the combined effect of group and the interaction. Thus, if one of the model terms (e.g., the interaction) is not at all associated with performance on the item, then the reduction in model error obtained by including it may not outweigh the additional degree of freedom imposed when adding a second model term. That certainly seems to be the case here. Finally, we can calculate the R_Δ^2 value as before, using information from the following tables.

Model Summary

Step	-2 Log likelihood	Cox & Snell R Square	Nagelkerke R Square
1	5728.393[a]	.186	.291

a. Estimation terminated at iteration number 5 because parameter estimates changed by less than .001.

Model Summary

Step	-2 Log likelihood	Cox & Snell R Square	Nagelkerke R Square
1	5723.736[a]	.186	.292

a. Estimation terminated at iteration number 5 because parameter estimates changed by less than .001.

Thus, $R_\Delta^2 = R_{\text{Full Model}}^2 - R_{\text{Score Model}}^2 = 0.292 - 0.291 = 0.001$, indicating that though statistically significant, the actual effect size associated with uniform DIF was negligible, based on the previously described interpretive guidelines.

Finally, it is possible to directly test for uniform and nonuniform DIF separately using the SPSS code that appears below.

```
LOGISTIC REGRESSION VAR=item
/METHOD=ENTER total /METHOD=ENTER grp /METHOD=ENTER grp*total
/CONTRAST (grp)=Indicator
/CRITERIA PIN(.05) POUT(.10) ITERATE(20) CUT(.5) .
execute.
```

In this case, we have three `METHOD=ENTER` statements, one including only the (matching) score (total), the second including group (grp), and the third including the interaction (`grp*total`). The second `METHOD=ENTER` statement tests for uniform DIF only, and the third provides a test of nonuniform DIF. This is an alternative approach to the initial approach for assessing DIF that was presented above. In this instance, rather than assessing both types of DIF simultaneously, we test for each separately. The relevant tables from SPSS appear below.

Omnibus Tests of Model Coefficients

		Chi-square	df	Sig.
Step 1	Step	4.656	1	.031
	Block	4.656	1	.031
	Model	1452.148	2	.000

Omnibus Tests of Model Coefficients

		Chi-square	df	Sig.
Step 1	Step	.027	1	.869
	Block	.027	1	.869
	Model	1452.175	3	.000

Based on these tables, we would conclude that there is a statistically significant test for uniform DIF ($p = 0.031$), but not for nonuniform DIF ($p = 0.869$). Using the following tables, we can calculate the R^2_Δ values for each type of DIF.

Model Summary

Step	-2 Log likelihood	Cox & Snell R Square	Nagelkerke R Square
1	5728.393[a]	.186	.291

a. Estimation terminated at iteration number 5 because parameter estimates changed by less than .001.

Model Summary

Step	-2 Log likelihood	Cox & Snell R Square	Nagelkerke R Square
1	5723.736[a]	.186	.292

a. Estimation terminated at iteration number 5 because parameter estimates changed by less than .001.

Model Summary

Step	-2 Log likelihood	Cox & Snell R Square	Nagelkerke R Square
1	5723.709[a]	.186	.292

a. Estimation terminated at iteration number 6 because parameter estimates changed by less than .001.

As we determined before, R^2_Δ for uniform DIF was ($0.292 - 0.291 = 0.001$), and for nonuniform DIF it was ($0.292 - 0.292 = 0.000$). Thus, in both instances, we would conclude that the item displays only negligible uniform DIF. To assess DIF for the other items, we would simply repeat these steps. In addition, scale purification would be conducted just as was the case with Mantel–Haenszel, in which items would be tested and the matching scale score would be recalculated iteratively until it contained no items that exhibited DIF.

As discussed above, the MH and LR approaches can also be used to investigate the presence of DIF for polytomous items. At the time of this writing, SPSS does not allow for the calculation of the Mantel–Haenszel test statistic for variables that have more than two categories, except for the matching score. Therefore, we would recommend that the researcher interested in conducting DIF for an item with more than 2 categories (or a grouping variable with more than 2 groups), consider using an alternative to SPSS, such as SAS or R. It is possible, however, to investigate DIF for polytomous items in SPSS using LR. To demonstrate how this is done with SPSS, we will use a set of data including twelve items that constitute a scale measuring academic motivation (i.e., the motivation to succeed in academic endeavors). The items are coded as 1, 2, and 3, where lower values indicate lower motivation to succeed. For this example, we are interested in determining whether there exists any uniform DIF based on gender for any of the items, from a sample of 432 university students who completed the instrument. Prior to conducting LR, we will need to create a total score, which is the sum of the 12 motivation items, using **Transform ▶ Compute**, just as we did for the dichotomous items.

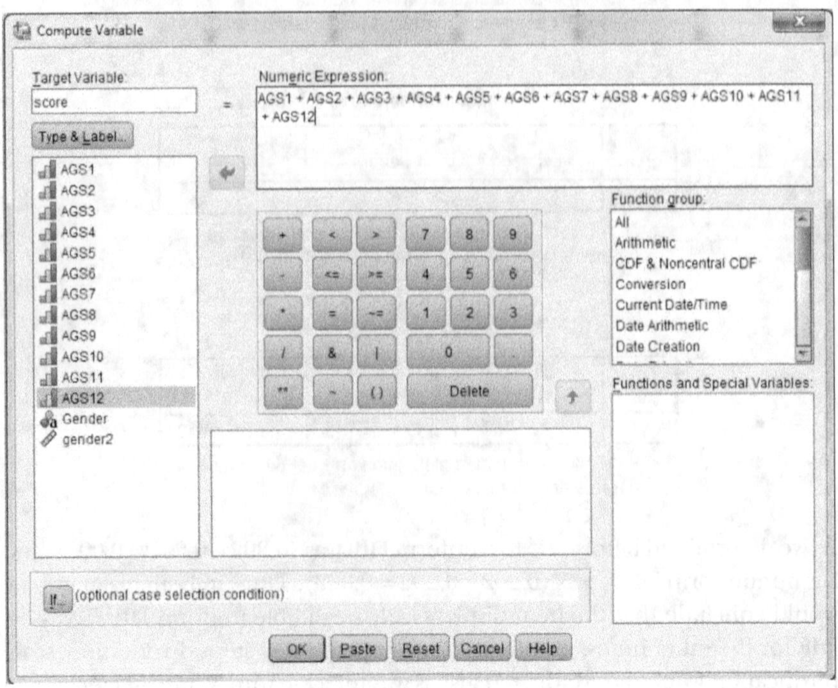

In order to use LR for identifying DIF with ordinal items, we can use the following SPSS macro, named DIFLRT, by opening it in the SPSS syntax editor. We can then run the macro by highlighting it and then selecting **Run ► Selection** from the menu.

```
DEFINE DIFLRT (!POSITIONAL !TOKENS(1)
/!POSITIONAL !TOKENS(1)
/!POSITIONAL !TOKENS(1)).
DATASET NAME original.
DATASET DECLARE temp.
OMS
/SELECT TABLES
/IF COMMANDS=['PLUM'] SUBTYPES=['Model Fitting Information']
/DESTINATION FORMAT=SAV NUMBERED=TableNumber_
OUTFILE='temp'.
OMS
/SELECT ALL
/IF COMMANDS=['PLUM']
/DESTINATION VIEWER=NO.
PLUM !1 BY !2 WITH !3
/LINK=LOGIT
/LOCATION=!3
/PRINT=FIT PARAMETER SUMMARY.
PLUM !1 BY !2 WITH !3
/LINK=LOGIT
/LOCATION=!3 !2
/PRINT=FIT PARAMETER SUMMARY.
PLUM !1 BY !2 WITH !3
/LINK=LOGIT
/LOCATION=!3 !2 !2*!3
/PRINT=FIT PARAMETER SUMMARY.
OMSEND.
DATASET ACTIVATE temp.
SELECT IF Var1='Final'.
COMPUTE LRT=ChiSquare-LAG(ChiSquare).
COMPUTE dof=df-LAG(df).
AGGREGATE
/OUTFILE=* MODE=ADDVARIABLES
/LRT_sum=SUM(LRT)
/dof_sum=SUM(dof).
COMPUTE ChiSquare=MIN(LRT,LRT_sum).
COMPUTE df=MIN(dof,dof_sum).
COMPUTE Sig=SIG.CHISQ(ChiSquare,df).
IF $CASENUM=1 Label_='Omnibus Test for Any DIF'.
IF $CASENUM=2 Label_='Test for Uniform DIF'.
IF $CASENUM=3 Label_='Test for Non-Uniform DIF'.
VARIABLE LABELS Label_ 'Effect'.
OMS
/SELECT TABLES TEXTS HEADINGS
/IF COMMANDS=['Summarize'] SUBTYPES=['Case Processing Summary']
/DESTINATION VIEWER=NO.
```

```
SUMMARIZE
/TABLES=Label_ ChiSquare df Sig
/FORMAT=LIST NOCASENUM NOTOTAL
/TITLE='Likelihood-Ratio Tests for Differential Item Functioning'
/MISSING=VARIABLE
/CELLS=NONE.
OMSEND.
DATASET ACTIVATE original WINDOW=ASIS.
DATASET CLOSE temp.
!ENDDEFINE.
```

We would then type the following line at the bottom of the syntax window, highlight it, and then choose **Run ► Selection** from the menu.

```
DIFLRT ags1 gender2 score.
```

Notice that we must provide the name of the item for which we want to assess DIF (ags1), the name of the grouping variable (gender2), and the name of the matching test (score).

The output produced by the DIFLRT macro appears below.

Likelihood-Ratio Tests for Differential Item Functioning

	Effect	Chi-Square	df	Sig.
1	Omnibus Test for Any DIF	3.296	2	.192
2	Test for Uniform DIF	.137	1	.712
3	Test for Non-Uniform DIF	3.159	1	.076

We are provided with three tests, one for either uniform or nonuniform DIF, one for uniform DIF only, and one for nonuniform DIF only. For this item, there was no type of DIF found to be present. As with the other examples in this chapter, we may want to engage in scale purification by iteratively testing items one at a time, and recalculating the matching test score until it includes only items that do not exhibit DIF.

Chapter Summary

The purpose of this chapter was to describe DIF, and to present two of the most common procedures approaches to DIF detection in the psychometric literature using SPSS: MH and LR. The aim of DIF detection is to identify items that show statistical evidence of functioning differently across diverse groups (e.g., sex, language spoken in the home) when individuals are matched on the latent trait being measured by the scale. DIF is an undesirable property of scale items that threatens test score validity. As described in this chapter and elsewhere (Camilli & Shepard, 1994; Holland & Wainer, 1993), there are two types of DIF to consider when considering the psychometric properties of items: uniform and nonuniform. Whereas the MH detection method is effective for screening items for uniform DIF, it is not so for identifying nonuniform DIF. Nonetheless, MH is widely used in large-scale testing programs to identify potentially biased items. On the other hand, LR has been found to be effective in the detection of both types of DIF and is widely used in practice. As shown, the methods can be used for DIF detection of dichotomous and polytomously scored items.

Importantly, these and other methods only provide statistical evidence of the presence of DIF in an item. Thus, they serve as a first step in the identification of potentially problematic items. Effect sizes further facilitate these statistics in identifying potentially biased items, which can be used to quantify the magnitude of DIF in the item parameter under investigation (i.e., difficulty, discrimination). Therefore, to aid in the identification of DIF, researchers and test developers are encouraged to consider the statistical significance of the test statistic (e.g., MH) and the corresponding effect size. Based on this information, the subsequent step is for the flagged item(s) to undergo content review by subject matter experts to determine the reasoning for DIF (e.g., language) to guide decisions regarding the elimination or modification of the item for applied assessment use. Thus, screening an item set for DIF is an important and multilayered process intended to promote an instrument's test score validity across diverse groups (e.g., sex, language spoken in the home). The desired method to use will depend on many factors (e.g., item type, sample size) and thus one should consult with the extant literature on DIF detection methods and inspection of the dataset.

8

Equating

Introduction

This chapter addresses test equating and demonstrates its application using SPSS. The aim of this chapter is to introduce the practice of equating and present procedures to conduct an equating study. Upon chapter completion, the reader should understand the purposes of equating, be familiar with common sampling designs, and apply basic statistical techniques to equate test scores. Notably, while a powerful and viable option for test score equating, we do not describe equating procedures using IRT, due to the fact that it is best carried out using specialized software (Du Toit, 2003). However, as we will see, SPSS affords a powerful and convenient platform for other types of equating. The chapter begins with an overview of the tenets of equating, followed by descriptions of commonly used sampling designs. Subsequently, three methods of equating that can be conducted using SPSS are presented with examples.

Equating is the process of establishing equivalent scores on different forms of instruments measuring the same construct (e.g., mathematics). For example, students taking the Graduate Records Exam (GRE) are not administered the same set of test items. Rather, each individual is

Applied Psychometrics Using SPSS and AMOS, pages 225–272

administered a different sample of items selected from a large pool of items maintained in a test bank. Despite taking what is essentially a different test, GRE scores for any two individuals are compared with one another by graduate programs making admissions decisions. A natural question is: How can these scores be compared when they are based on different sets of items? More specifically, despite attempts to ensure that test items are comparable in terms of content and difficulty, how can test developers be sure of comparable scores? The answer is that equating is used by test developers to place the scores from different tests on a common scale so that examinees' test performance on different tests can be compared. Simple raw scores on the tests are not comparable due to potential differences in item difficulty, including differences in the overall abilities of the test takers. This lack of equivalence is the reason that test equating is necessary. Indeed, in virtually every large-scale assessment program, some type of equating must occur to ensure the comparability of test scores obtained from diverse test forms and examinees.

In conducting an equating study there are two major considerations. First, the sampling design used for data collection must be determined; second, the statistical method used conduct the equating must be selected. We address these considerations by first describing the sampling methods commonly used in equating studies, and then discuss some of the more common statistical equating methods. For each method, we provide the relevant SPSS code for reading the data, equating, and producing usable results.

Equating Sampling Designs

When conducting an equating study, the first issue that must be decided is how the data will be sampled from examinees. To illustrate, let us assume that there are two test forms to be equated: Form 1 and Form 2. Perhaps the simplest approach to sampling would be to administer both forms to a single group of examinees. To mitigate the impact of fatigue and ensure that there is not an interaction between test placement and test performance, we could counterbalance the administration of the two test forms so that a random half of examinees receives Form 1 followed by Form 2, while the other half receives Form 2 followed by Form 1. This counterbalanced test administration should ensure that neither examinee fatigue nor increasing familiarity with the exam played a role in the relative performance of the sample on the forms. In practice, when exams are administered in hard copy format (as opposed to computer administration) examinees are administered the exam in a spiraled format, meaning that Examinee 1 receives the test booklet containing Form 1 followed by Form 2, Examinee 2 receives the test booklet containing Form 2 followed by Form 1, Examinee 3 receives the booklet containing Form 1 followed by Form 2, and so on.

This single group sampling method has several notable advantages. First, it is a simple and feasible approach to data collection because only a single examinee group is required. Second, there is no confounding of the examinee group and the test form. Third, it requires a smaller sample when compared to equating procedures based on the use of multiple examinee groups. As to the second point, when a single group of examinees completes both test forms in a counterbalanced fashion, any differences in performance on the two forms can be attributed to real differences in the difficulty of the test, not due to examinee differences.

Despite these advantages, this sampling approach has its own shortcomings. First, the time required to administer the two tests requires twice as much time as administering a single test. Correspondingly, it would be expected that examinees will experience fatigue, particularly in the presence of a long test (e.g., 75 items). While counterbalancing should ameliorate the impact of overall test fatigue, it may not be sufficient to overcome differential order effects that might be inherent in the two forms. Differential order effects essentially means that the impact of completing Form 2 after Form 1 is not the same as the impact of taking Form 1 after Form 2. In other words, there is an interaction between form and time so that the impact of fatigue or practice effects (or both) is different for different test forms. Thus, differential order effects can result in unstable equating results due to the fact that performance on the second test reflects factors beyond just abilities that the test seeks to measure.

A second popular sampling approach in equating studies is the random groups design. In this approach, a random sample of examinees from the population is selected and randomly divided evenly into two groups: Group 1, Group 2. Group 1 completes Form 1 and Group 2 completes Form 2. This design was suggested to solve the problems of testing fatigue and time associated with the single groups approach. Because the examinees are randomly selected from the population and assigned to take one of the test forms at random, any differences in test performance is inferred to reflect differential form difficulty and not due to group ability differences on the measured construct (e.g., intelligence, mathematics). While this approach has the advantage of not requiring as much time as the single group design, the trade-off is the need for a larger sample. Indeed, if the researcher has as a goal an examinee sample of 500 for each form, then in the random groups design would require a total sample size of 1,000 examinees. Contrary, only 500 examinees would be required for the single groups design described previously.

The third commonly used approach to sampling in equating studies is the common item nonequivalent groups design. In this approach, two groups are administered different test forms, with each form containing a set of common items. If these items count toward the total score obtained on the form, they are called internal items, and are generally interspersed throughout the test. On the other hand, when the items do not count toward the total score they are referred to as external items, and are typically administered as a separately timed section of the exam. Unlike with the random groups design, there is no assumption that the groups in this last sampling approach are equivalent in terms of ability. Most often, the groups are simply gathered based upon convenience. Therefore, differential performance of the groups on the forms cannot be attributed solely to differences in examinee ability or to differences in test difficulty. Thus, a prime goal of equating with this design is to use the common items to infer how much of any difference is due to the examinees and how much to the test itself. When using the nonequivalent group common items method, we must ensure that the common items cover the same content and have the same statistical properties (e.g., difficulty) as the items making up the entire test. The number of common items is recommended to be as large as possible in order to ensure accuracy of equating (e.g., 20% of total test), and that the common items be placed at the same location in both test forms (for the internal case), to ensure comparability.

The nonequivalent groups approach has some advantages over the previously described methods. First, it allows for the administration of only a single test form at any given time. This is most typical of testing programs. Contrary, the other approaches require that the two forms be administered at the same time to either one or two examinee groups. Second, the nonequivalent groups design allows for the items used in equating to be treated separately from those used in actually assigning examinees' scores. This issue is important when test developers need to make the actual items available to examinees or other stakeholders following the administration of the exam.

Despite these advantages, this approach also presents challenges to equating studies. First, as shown below, successfully using this sampling approach in conjunction with the statistical tools for equating requires that several assumptions about the data be tenable. When these do not hold, equating with this method may not be feasible. Second, when groups differ substantially in their ability, untangling performance differences due to examinee and due to form difficulty differences becomes a great challenge. Finally, the use of statistical equating methods with this approach can be difficult in some cases for a variety of reasons.

Each equating design offers its own practical advantages and disadvantages when used with these sampling approaches. In consideration of the interaction with the statistical equating methods, the single group design is probably the simplest to use. However, as noted above, it has some potentially severe drawbacks that are not shared by the other two methods. The random groups method may be the most straight-forward design approach to use when it is feasible to obtain two random samples of examinees, because it is not markedly more different to deal with analytically than the single group design (in some instances analysis of the two approaches is identical), and it overcomes some of the problems in the latter. However, from a practical perspective, this approach can sometimes be problematic to conduct in practice. In contrast, while generally the most difficult to use statistically, the nonequivalent groups common item design is the most practical in many situations. Specifically, relatively fewer examinees are required compared to the random group's design, testing at different times is allowed, and lengthy test administration is not required.

In the remaining chapter, we describe three statistical methods for equating scores from two test forms. These include: mean equating, linear equating, and equipercentile equating. As noted earlier in the chapter, there are other equating approaches such as those associated with IRT procedures. However, the techniques demonstrated in this chapter are proven to be effective (see Kolen & Brennan, 2004) and can be conducted using SPSS. We will begin with mean equating, the simplest of the designs. Subsequently, linear equating is presented, which is slightly more complex, followed by equipercentile equating. Each method is demonstrated to show how it can be employed with each of the previously described sampling designs.

Mean Equating

Mean equating represents perhaps the most straightforward approach to equating scores derived from two test forms. To use this approach, we must assume that the difficulty in the two test forms, Form A and Form B, is constant (or the same) across the entire score scale. For example, if Form B is more difficult than Form A by 3 points at a score of 15, it is also more difficult by 3 points at a score of 40. For both the single and random groups designs, mean equating starts with the equation:

$$x_A - \bar{x}_A = x_B - \bar{x}_B \tag{8.1}$$

In Equation 8.1, x_A and x_B are scores on Forms A and B, respectively, and $\bar{x}_A$ and $\bar{x}_B$ are means of test Form A and Form B. If we use the single group design, then one set of examinees takes both forms, while in the random groups case one group takes Form A and the other Form B. However, the statistical method is identical for both approaches. To carry out mean equating, we solve Equation 8.1 for the score for which we want to equate, in this case x_A:

$$x_A = x_B - \overline{x}_B + \overline{x}_A \tag{8.2}$$

As a simple numerical example of mean equating, let us assume that two random groups of examinees are administered a reading test with a maximum score of 50. Say that the mean, or average, score on Form A ($\overline{x}_A$) is 42, and on Form B it is ($\overline{x}_B$) 44. To obtain the mean equated score for Form A given a specific score on Form B, we would simply apply these means to Equation 8.2, and obtain: $x_A = x_B - 44 + 42 = x_B - 2$. Thus, for any score on Form B, we subtract 2 points to get the equated score on Form A.

To demonstrate mean equating with SPSS, we will refer to an example involving the random groups design, and a hypothetical mathematics test comprised of 20 items. Say two groups were created by randomly assigning 1,000 examinees to take test Form A and another 1,000 individuals to take test Form B. We are interested in using mean equating to obtain scores on Form A for those examinees who took Form B. Data are in a file called equating.sav, where each examinee appears on a single line, with their identification number (id), the form of the test that they were administered, and responses to the 20 items (i.e., 0 = Incorrect; 1 = Correct).

Within the dataset forms were coded as 1 (Form A) or 2 (Form B), and the total score on the instrument is the sum of these scores. We can calculate scores for each of these two test forms (e.g., Form A) using the menu sequence **Transform ► Compute Variable**. Next, we would click **If...** and then see the following window.

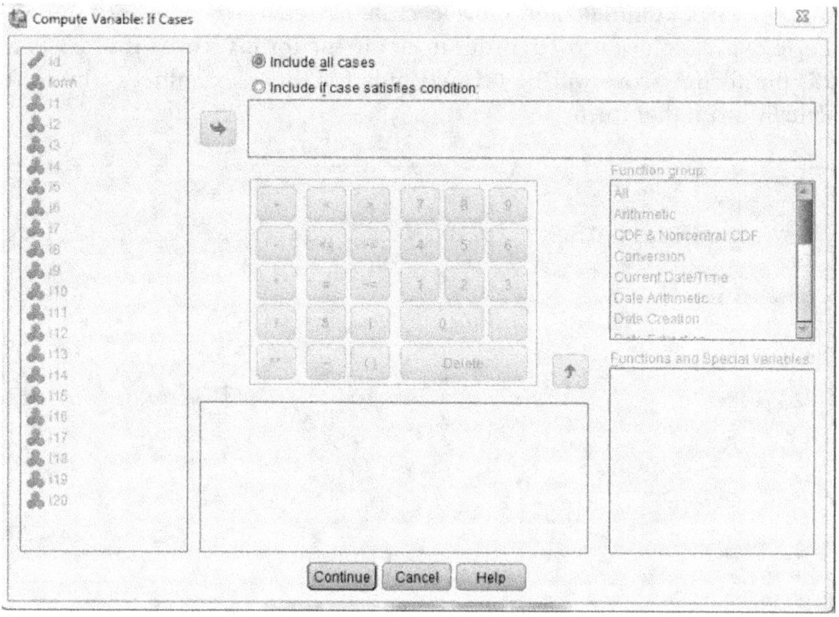

We would then click the radio button next to **Include if case satisfies condition**. We would then move the form variable into the window and indicate that it should equal 1 (the code for Form A) to be included in the calculation.

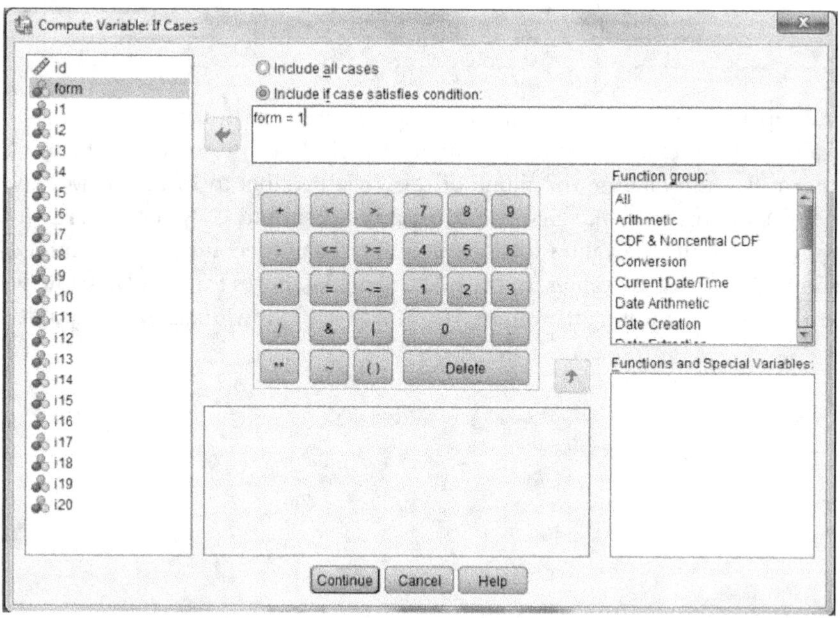

We then click **Continue**, and move each item, separated by +, into the Numeric Expression window in order to create the formA score. After clicking **OK**, the formA score will be created only for those examinees who were actually given that form.

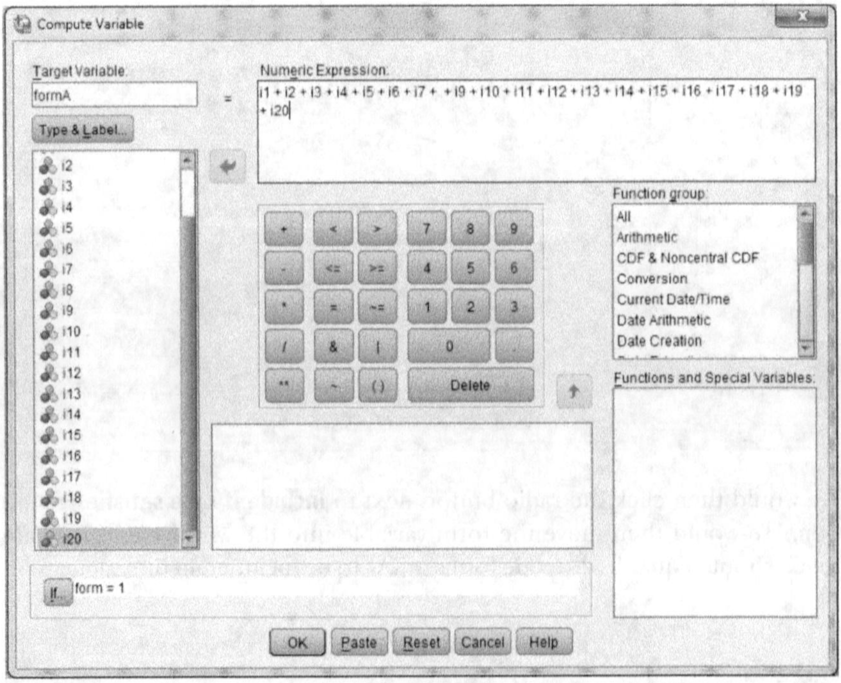

We repeat these steps to create a raw score on Form B, labeled: formB. To do so, we will change the if statement to include those for whom form = 2 (Form B), and change the name of the variable label to formB. If we have done this correctly, the first 1,000 examinees should only have scores for formA, and missing values for formB. Similarly, the second 1,000 examinees should have missing values for formA, and actual scores for formB. Below, we see the formA and formB columns for the first 10 individuals in the sample.

formA	formB
13.00	.
8.00	.
10.00	.
8.00	.
3.00	.
11.00	.
6.00	.
8.00	.
7.00	.
10.00	.

Now that we have the scores calculated for each individual in the sample, we will next request means for the two forms using the menu sequence: **Analyze ▶ Descriptive Statistics ▶ Descriptives**. We will then move the new variables formA and formB into the **Variable(s)** box, as below.

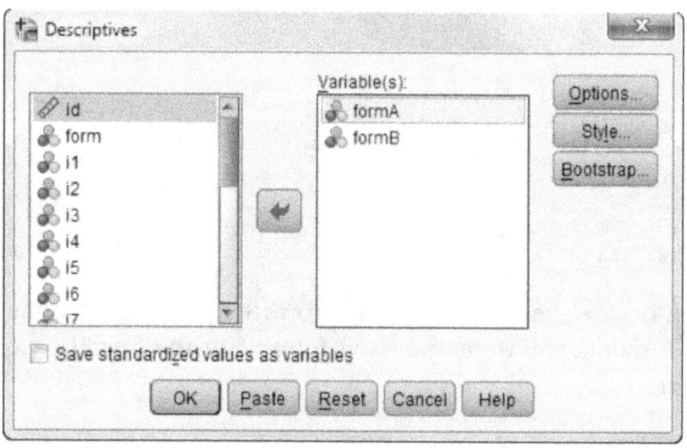

After clicking **OK**, we obtain the following output. As shown, Form B was slightly easier than Form A, given its higher mean score value. Variation in the scores was very comparable for the two forms.

Descriptive Statistics

	N	Minimum	Maximum	Mean	Std. Deviation
formA	1000	.00	19.00	8.2720	3.36621
formB	1000	.00	19.00	8.6140	3.44338
Valid N (listwise)	0				

Next, we will assign the mean values for each form to each examine, using **Transform ▶ Compute**. As an example, we see how this window will look for the assignment of formA_mean. Note that we have turned off the If option by clicking **If...**, and then clicking the radio button next to **Include all cases**.

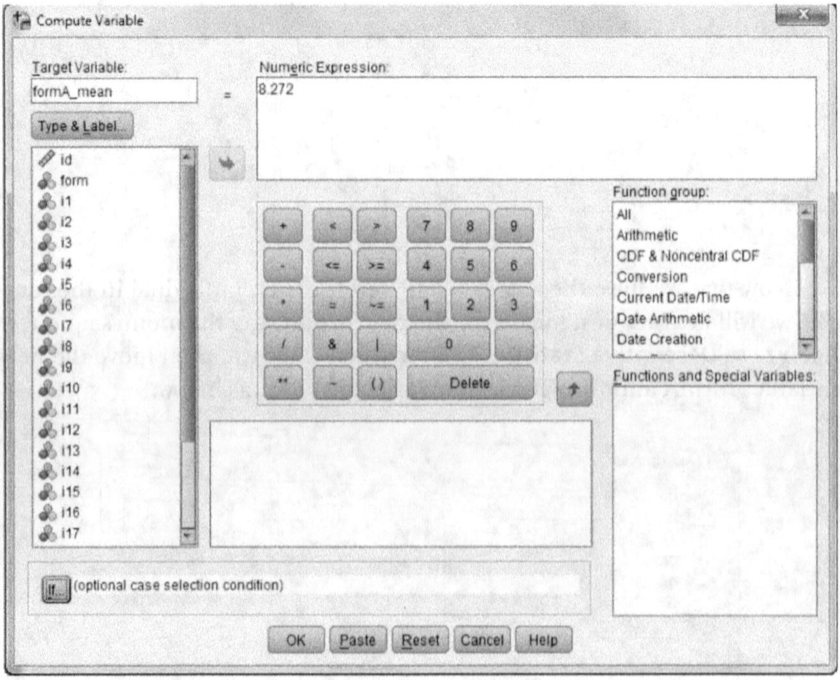

We will follow the same set of steps for formB, assigning it a value of 8.614. The new variables will then appear as follows for the first 10 examinees in the dataset.

formA	formB	formA_mean	formB_mean
13.00	.	8.27	8.61
8.00	.	8.27	8.61
10.00	.	8.27	8.61
8.00	.	8.27	8.61
3.00	.	8.27	8.61
11.00	.	8.27	8.61
6.00	.	8.27	8.61
8.00	.	8.27	8.61
7.00	.	8.27	8.61
10.00	.	8.27	8.61

The actual mean equating of form B to form A is carried out by creating the equated FormA for examinees who were administered FormB. This is done by first using the menu sequence **Transform ► Compute**. We then need to click **If...** and indicate that we will only conduct the calculation for those who were given Form 2 (Form B).

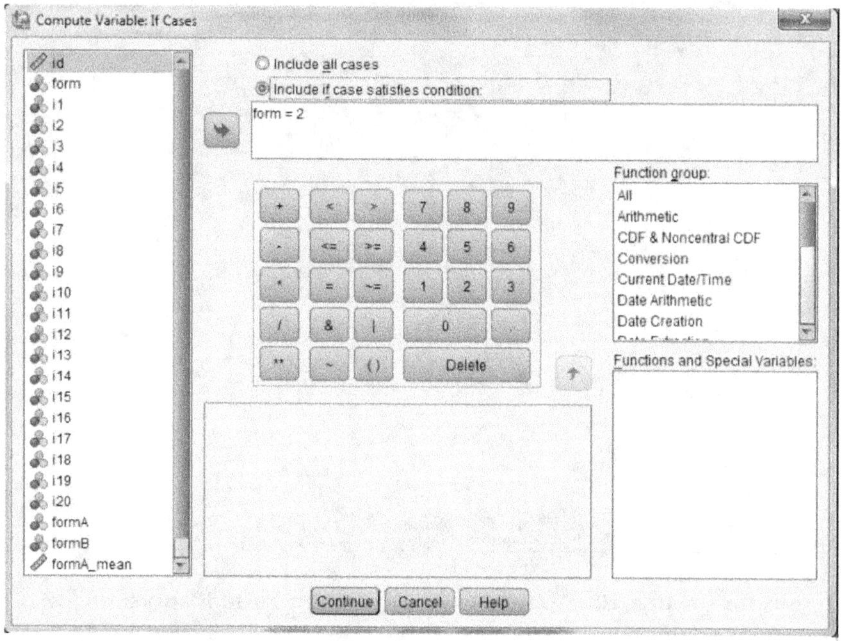

After clicking **Continue**, we compute the equated version of Form A for examinees administered Form B using Equation 8.2.

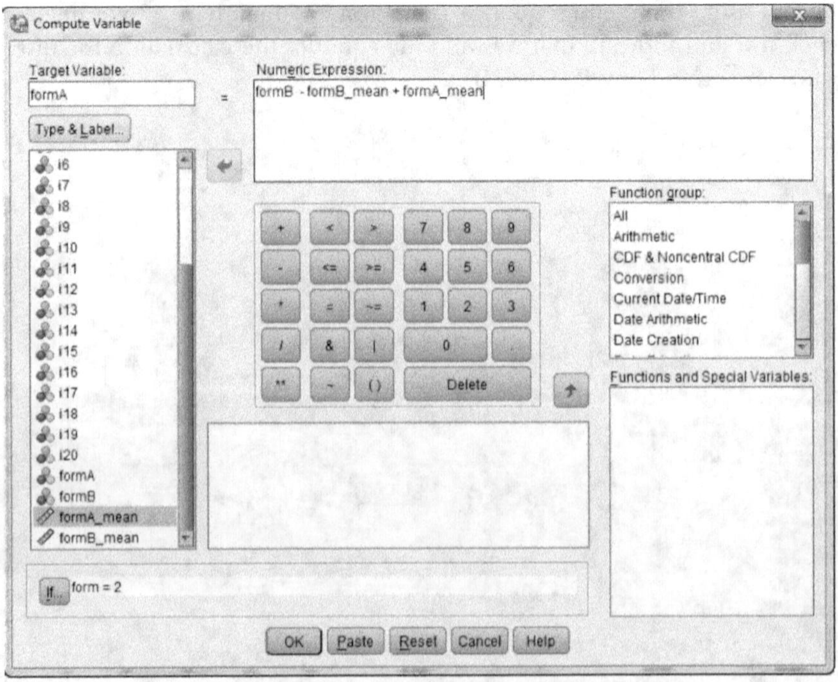

Results for the first 10 examinees who were given Form B appear below.

formA	formB
5.66	6.00
3.66	4.00
5.66	6.00
5.66	6.00
10.66	11.00
9.66	10.00
9.66	10.00
8.66	9.00
3.66	4.00
7.66	8.00

From these results, we can see that the two examinees obtaining a score of 6 on Form B have an equated score of 5.66 on Form A, whereas the examinee obtaining a score of 4 on Form B had an equated score of 3.66 on Form A. These lower results for the equated Form A as compared to Form B reflect that the former test is slightly more difficult than the latter.

Linear Equating

Linear equating is an alternative to mean equating that does not assume the differences between forms is constant. In the previous example, we found that the mean score for Form A was 0.342 points lower than the mean for Form B. As such, when using mean equating, we must implicitly assume that this difference holds across all scores. However, this assumption may not be tenable. For example, it is possible that Form A is more difficult for low and middle achieving examinees but not for high achievers. In that case, mean equating would not be optimal because it would not take account of this differential level of form difficulty. Linear equating solves this problem by including not only form means but also form standard deviations in calculating an equated score. In this case, we set the deviations of individual scores and means on the two forms, divided by their standard deviations equal to one another. The reader will notice that in reality, we are simply setting equal the standard (z) scores of the two forms equal to one another in Equation 8.3:

$$\frac{x_A - \overline{x}_A}{s_A} = \frac{x_B - \overline{x}_B}{s_B} \tag{8.3}$$

where all terms are as defined for Equation 8.2, with the addition that s_A and s_B are the sample standard deviations for the two forms. Once again, we proceed under the framework of the random groups equating design. To conduct linear equating, we must solve Equation 8.3 for the score for which we would like to obtain an equated value, in this case x_A in terms of x_B:

$$x_A = \frac{s_A}{s_B} x_B + \left[\overline{x}_A - \frac{s_A}{s_B} \overline{x}_B \right] \tag{8.4}$$

We will need to include the standard deviations of the forms, along with the means. To do this, we simply use the **Transform ► Compute** menu sequence and then input the standard deviations for each form, as we do for Form A below. Be sure that you have turned off the selection condition in the **If...** button.

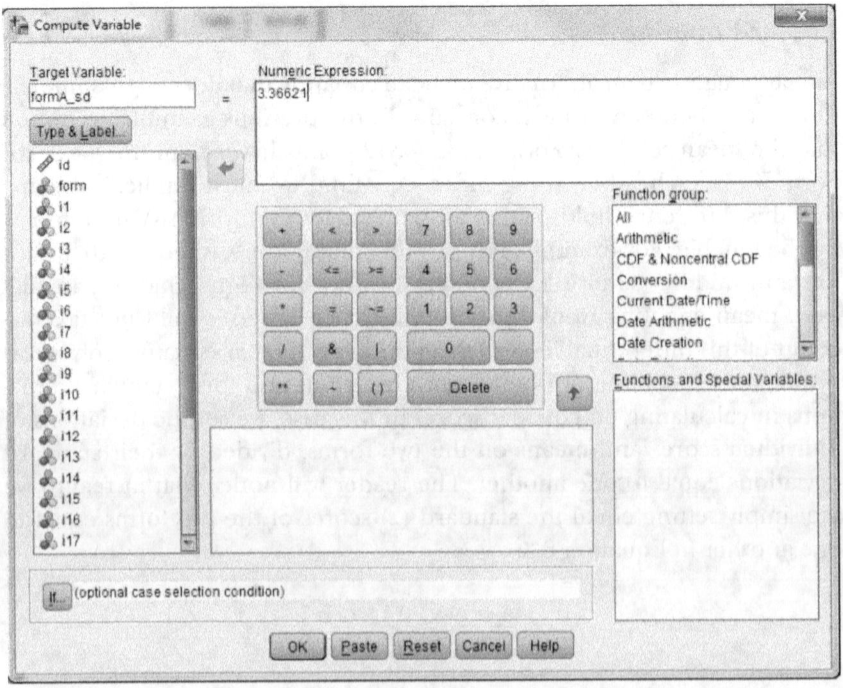

The final several columns for the first 10 subjects, including the standard deviations for the forms, appear below.

formA_mean	formB_mean	formA_sd	formB_sd
8.27	8.61	3.37	3.44
8.27	8.61	3.37	3.44
8.27	8.61	3.37	3.44
8.27	8.61	3.37	3.44
8.27	8.61	3.37	3.44
8.27	8.61	3.37	3.44
8.27	8.61	3.37	3.44
8.27	8.61	3.37	3.44
8.27	8.61	3.37	3.44
8.27	8.61	3.37	3.44

The SPSS steps needed to conduct linear equating in the random groups design is very similar to that used for the mean equating that was demonstrated above, and appears below for equating Form B to Form A. Much of the method is identical to that for conducting mean equating. The primary difference is that we now use the standard deviations of the forms, as well as their means.

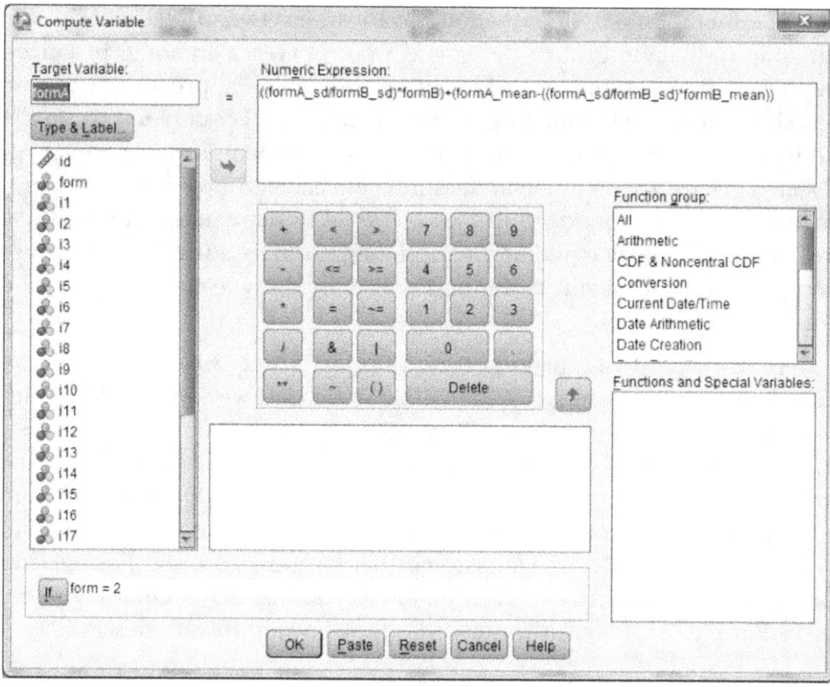

Equated results for the first 10 individual cases appears below.

formA	formB
5.72	6.00
3.76	4.00
5.72	6.00
5.72	6.00
10.60	11.00
9.63	10.00
9.63	10.00
8.65	9.00
3.76	4.00
7.67	8.00

Inspection of these results shows that the equated values for Form A (fA) are very similar to those obtained previously using mean equating procedures. The reason for the very similar results is that the standard deviations of the two forms are nearly identical. Indeed, when the standard deviations are identical, the results from mean equating will exactly equal those from linear equating.

The methodology described above for linear equating applies to the random and single groups designs as well. However, in some instances, neither of these sampling designs presents a viable approach for the researcher interested in equating. In such cases, it is necessary to rely on the nonequivalent groups common items design, in which two non-randomly selected groups are included in the study, and each group provides responses to a set of common items that can be used in the equating process. We can apply the linear equating methodology to the nonequivalent groups design in order to obtain scores on Form A for those examinees who were administered Form B.

As an example of linear equating with the nonequivalent groups common items design, let us consider the dataset that we were working with previously. Now, however, we will consider the first 5 items to represent the individual forms, and Items 6 through 20 are the common items. Each form was administered to independent samples of 1,000 individuals and all respondents were also administered the 15 common items. For the purposes of this example, we will assume that Group 1 received Form A and Group 2 received Form B. The equation to conduct linear equating to obtain a Form A score for individuals who took Form B for this design is:

$$x_A = a((x_B - c)) + d \tag{8.5}$$

where

$$a = \sqrt{\frac{s_A^2 + b_{AZ1}^2(s_z^2 - s_{z1}^2)}{s_B^2 + b_{BZ2}^2(s_z^2 - s_{z2}^2)}}$$

$$c = \bar{x}_B + b_{BZ2}(\bar{x}_z - \bar{x}_{z2})$$

$$d = \bar{x}_A + b_{AZ1}(\bar{x}_z - \bar{x}_{z1})$$

s_A^2 = variance of form A

s_B^2 = variance of form B

s_z^2 = variance of common items score for both groups combined

s_{z1}^2 = variance of common items for group 1

s_{z2}^2 = variance of common items for group 2

$\bar{x}_A$ = mean of form A

$\bar{x}_B$ = mean of form B

$\bar{x}_z$ = mean of common items score for both groups combined

$\bar{x}_{z1}$ = mean of common items score for group 1

$\bar{x}_{z2}$ = mean of common items score for group 2

b_{AZ1} = regression slope relating form A score to common items score for group 1

b_{AZ2} = regression slope relating form A score to common items score for group 2

The steps using SPSS to conduct the equating demonstrated in Equation 8.5 appear below. First, we must calculate the common items (Items 6 through 20) sum score.

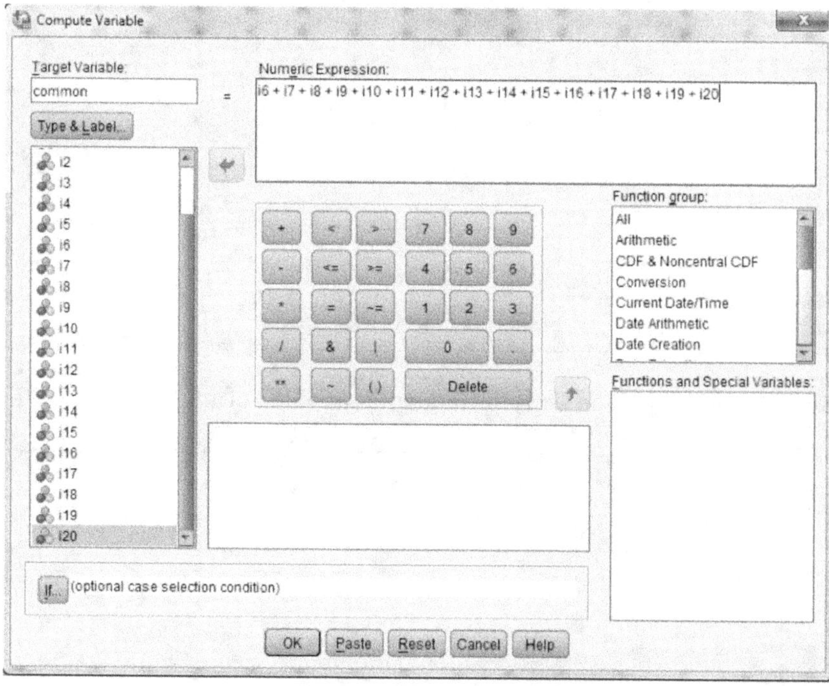

Next, we must calculate scores for Forms A and B (the first 5 items), which is done just as in the examples above. Below, we see the computation for Form A.

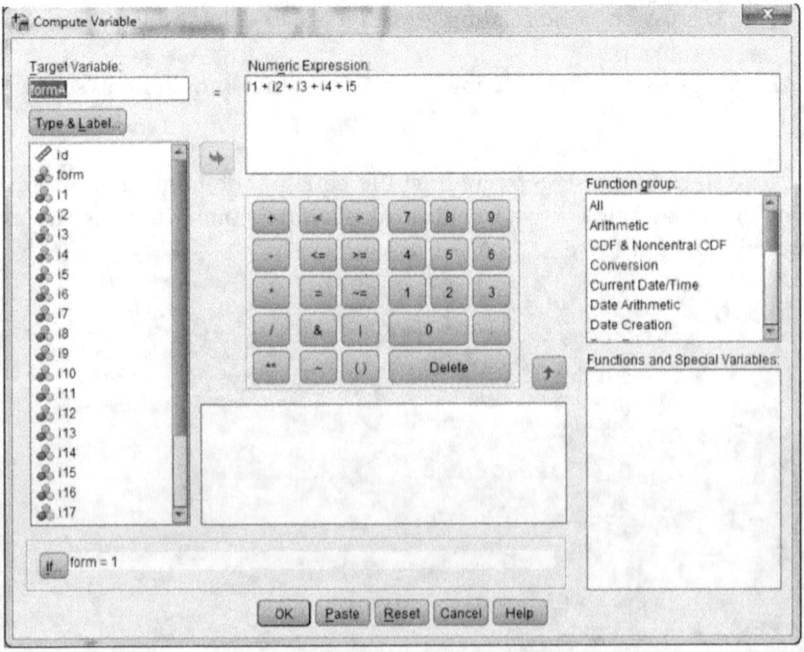

We will follow the same steps to create the variable FormB.

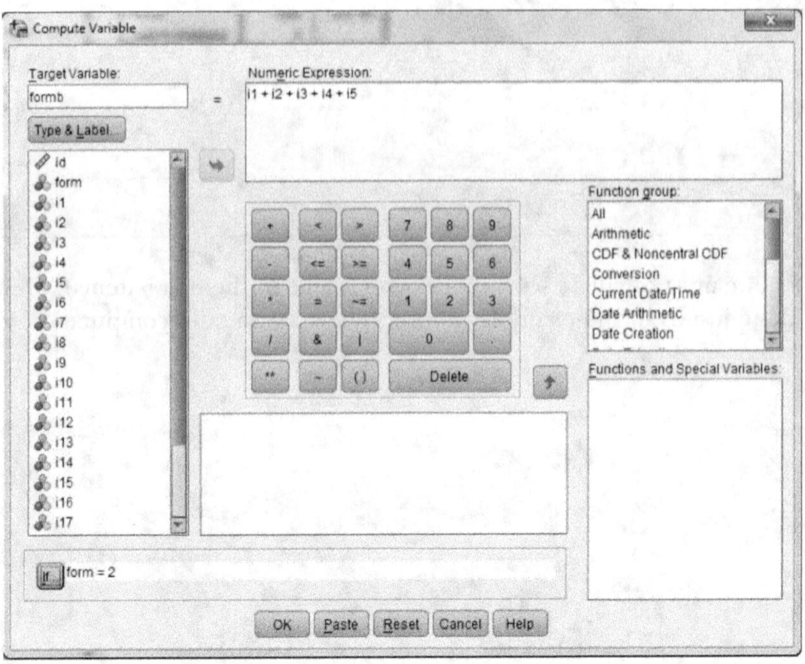

Make sure to change the If statement so that it includes only those who were given Form B. We will now need to create common items sum scores for those who were administered Form A. Note that we use the same commands as we did for the overall common score, but that we only include those who were administered Form A (form = 1 in the **If...** section of the window).

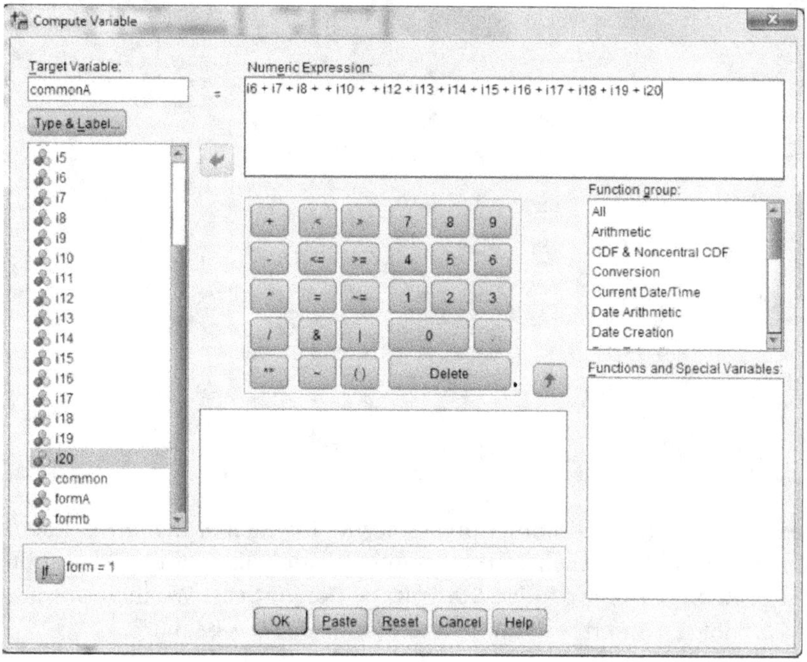

We will also calculate a common score for those given Form B.

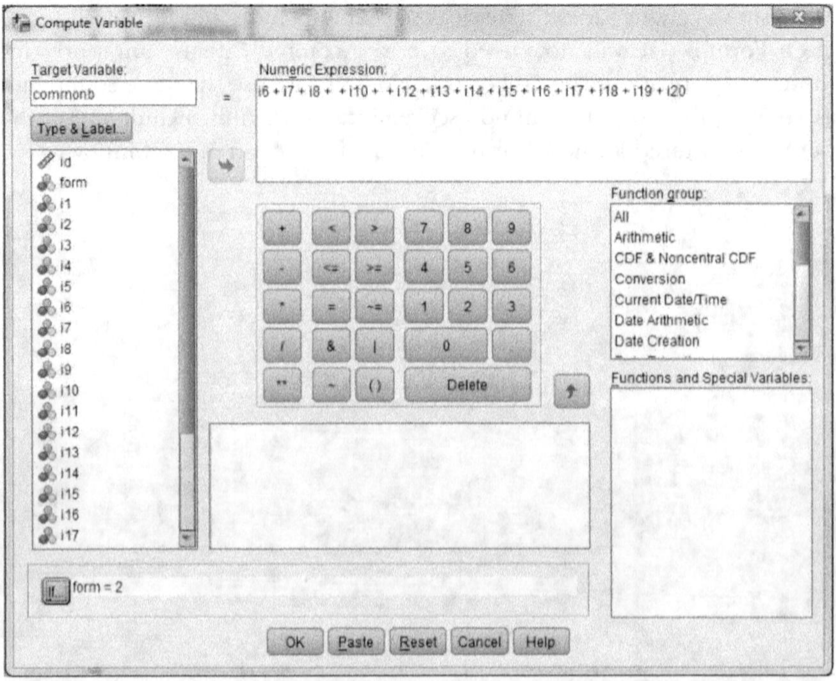

Next, we need to obtain descriptive statistics for each of the forms, and the common scores for each of the groups. We do this as was demonstrated above, **Analyze ► Descriptive Statistics ► Descriptives**. We then put all of the variables of interest in the Variable(s) window, as below.

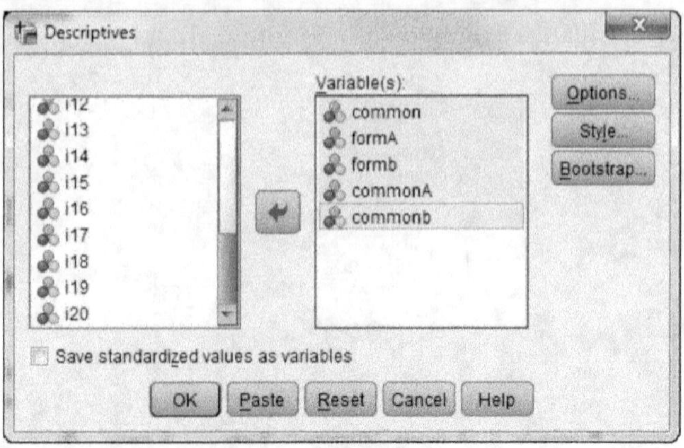

The resulting output appears below.

Descriptive Statistics

	N	Minimum	Maximum	Mean	Std. Deviation
common	2000	.00	13.00	5.8370	1.87515
formA	1000	.00	5.00	2.0530	1.22216
formb	1000	.00	5.00	2.2820	1.30544
commonA	1000	.00	13.00	5.7870	1.88446
commonb	1000	.00	13.00	5.8870	1.86540
Valid N (listwise)	0				

Next, we must conduct regression analyses relating each form score (as the dependent variable) to the common item score for individuals who were administered that form. Thus, we will first conduct a regression analysis for Form A. This is done using the menu sequence **Analyze ► Regression ► Linear** to obtain the following window.

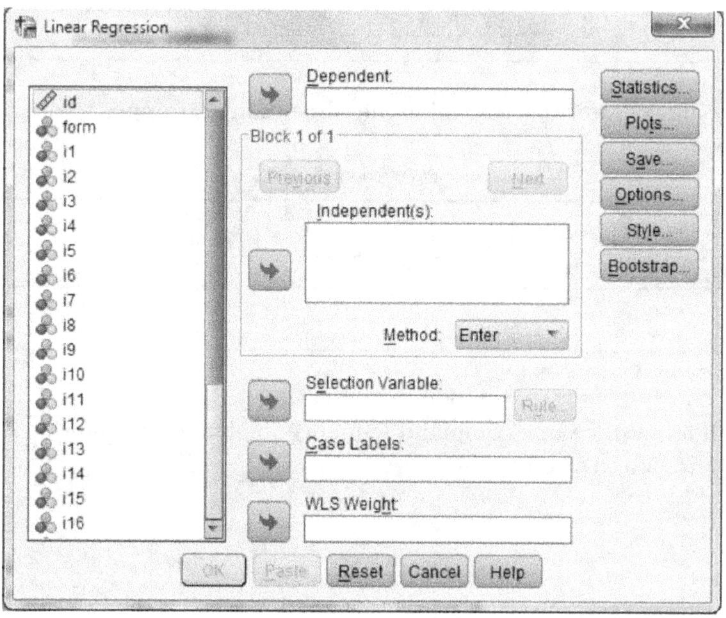

We will then move the FormA score into the Dependent window, and commonA score into the Independent(s) window.

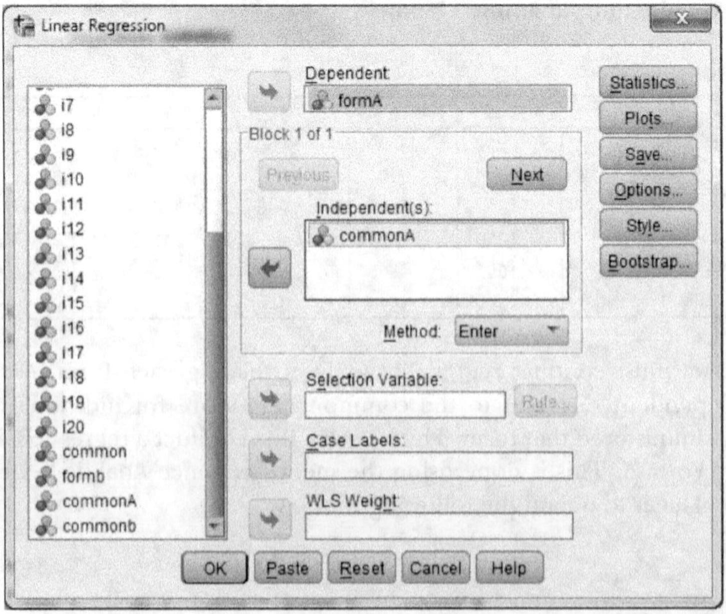

The results of interest, containing the slope estimates, appear below.

Coefficients[a]

Model		Unstandardized Coefficients B	Unstandardized Coefficients Std. Error	Standardized Coefficients Beta	t	Sig.
1	(Constant)	-.773	.082		-9.398	.000
	commonA	.488	.014	.753	36.140	.000

a. Dependent Variable: formA

We will follow the same command sequence to obtain the following regression window and output.

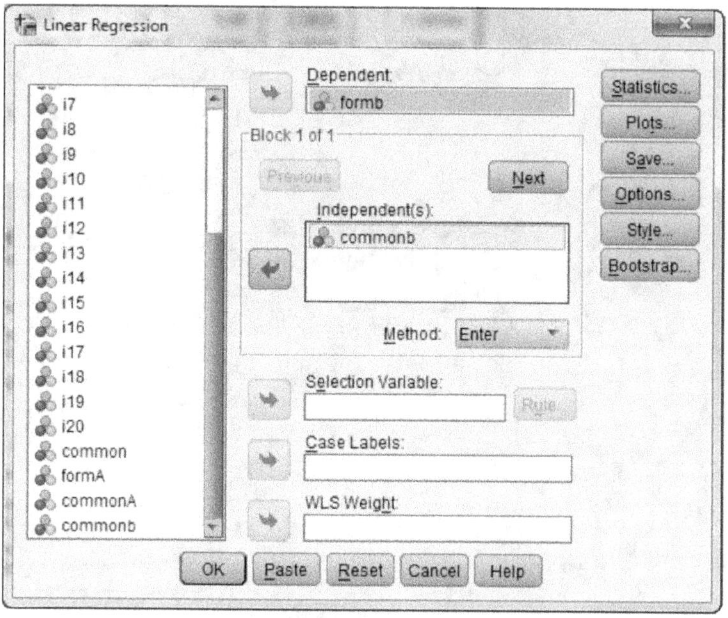

Coefficients[a]

Model		Unstandardized Coefficients		Standardized Coefficients	t	Sig.
		B	Std. Error	Beta		
1	(Constant)	-.822	.090		-9.138	.000
	commonb	.527	.015	.753	36.197	.000

a. Dependent Variable: formb

Next, we will need to add the descriptive statistics and slope estimates to the dataset, much as we did above in the random groups equating example. Following is an example for including the mean for FormA. The same steps will be followed for the other means, standard deviations, and regression slopes, which appear in the calculations of the terms in Equation 8.5.

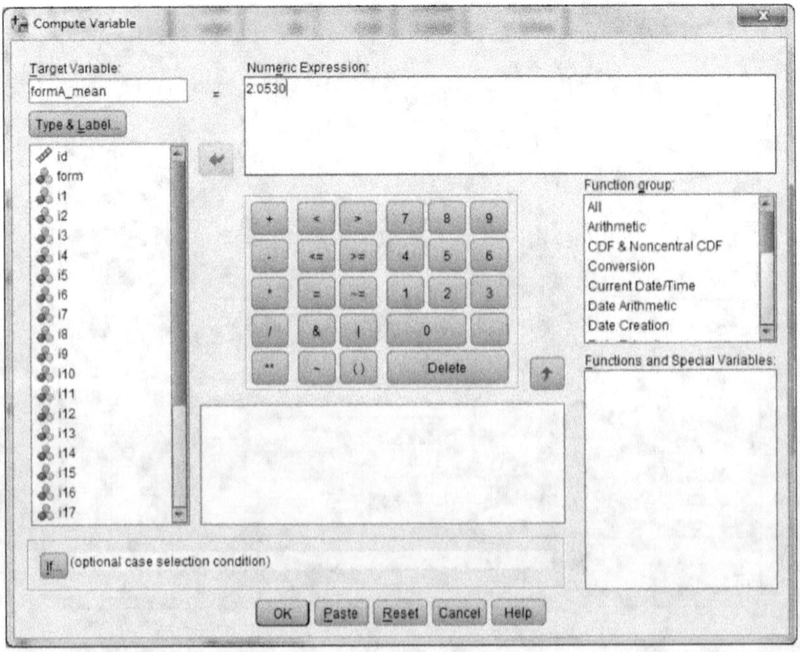

Next, we need to calculate the terms *a*, *c*, and *d* from Equation 8.5 above. The computation for *a* appears below.

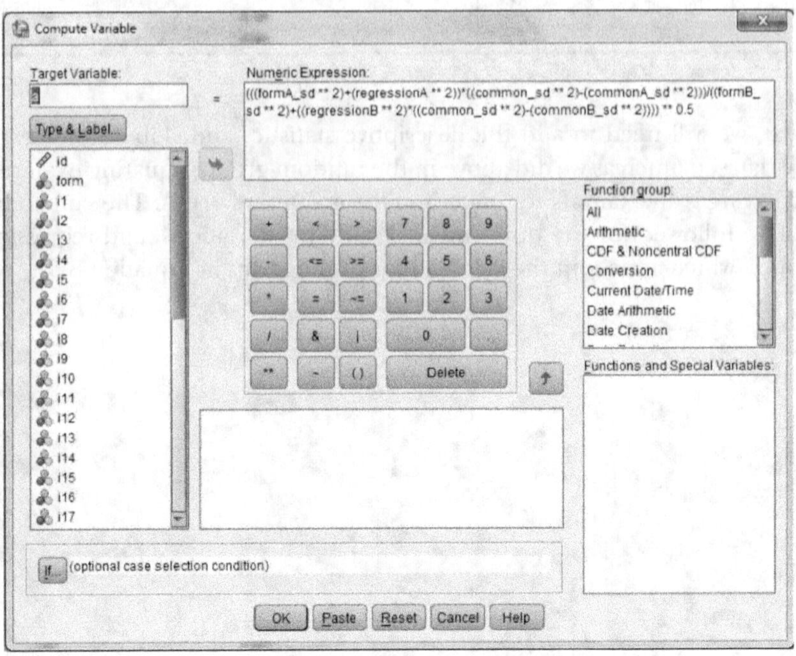

Similarly, *c* is calculated as:

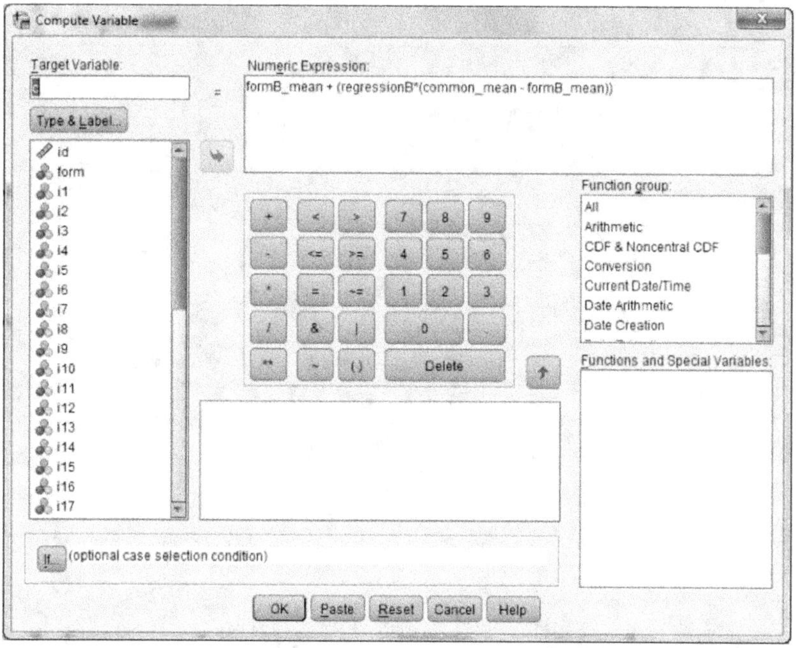

The quantity *d* is calculated as:

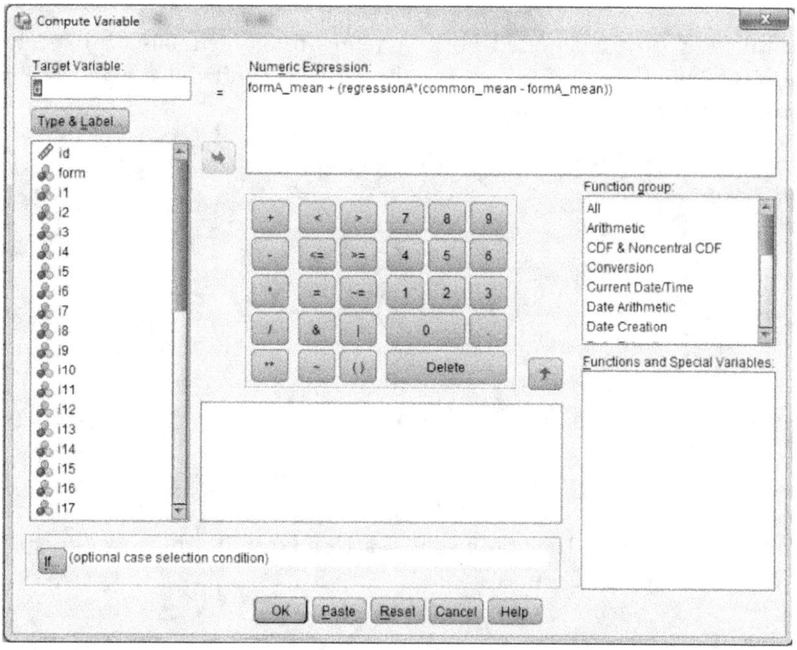

Finally, the equated value of Form A for those who were administered Form B is calculated as below.

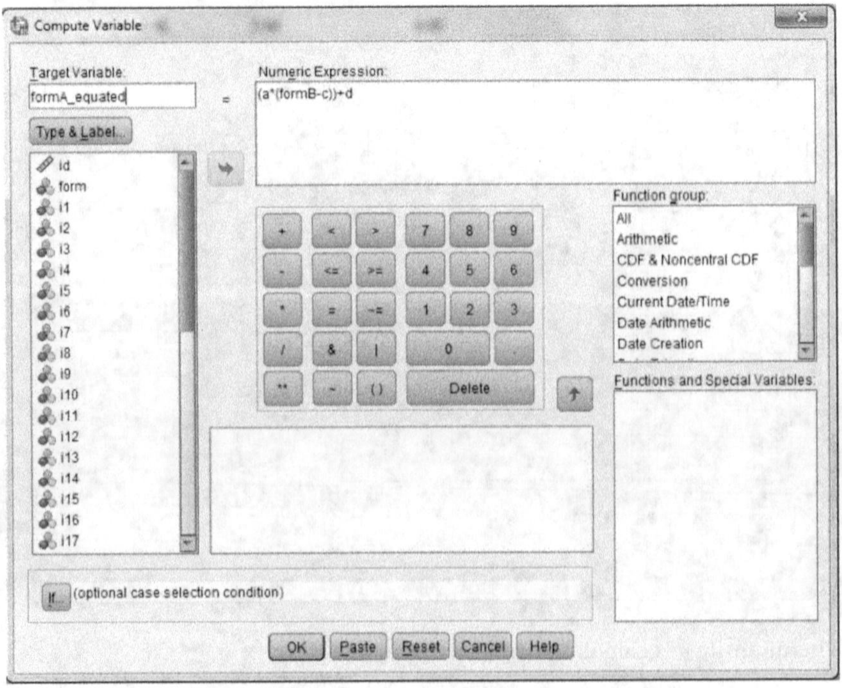

We will only obtain equated Form A values for individuals who received Form B. Below are the values for the first 10 individuals who received Form B, along with the values of *a*, *c*, and *d*.

	a	c	d	formA_equated
1001	-.05	4.16	3.90	4.05
1002	-.05	4.16	3.90	4.05
1003	-.05	4.16	3.90	4.00
1004	-.05	4.16	3.90	4.05
1005	-.05	4.16	3.90	3.91
1006	-.05	4.16	3.90	3.95
1007	-.05	4.16	3.90	3.95
1008	-.05	4.16	3.90	4.05
1009	-.05	4.16	3.90	4.05
1010	-.05	4.16	3.90	4.00

Examinees 1001 and 1002 both scored a 1 on Form B, which would equate to a score of 4.05 on Form A.

Equipercentile Equating

Equipercentile equating is the most complex method of equating considered in this chapter and requires the fewest assumptions about the data. Whereas mean equating assumes that only the mean performance on two forms differ, and linear equating assumes that only the mean and standard deviation of performance differ, equipercentile equating allows for both of these population parameters to differ, as well as the skewness and kurtosis of the two forms. In other words, using equipercentile equating, we are implicitly allowing the distributions of two forms to differ from one another. This added flexibility does come at a cost, however, as equipercentile equating is not only more complex than the other two methods, but also typically requires a larger sample size in order to work properly (Kolen & Brennan, 2004). If a sufficiently large sample is available, though, this third approach to equating may provide the most accurate results.

Conceptually, equipercentile equating involves finding the percentile that a particular score is on one form and equating that score to the score on the other form that is at the same percentile. For example, if a score of 18 on Form B is at the 80th percentile, then to equate this to Form A, we simply find the score on this latter form that is also at the 80th percentile. If the Form A 80th percentile score is 16, then we conclude that the equated value for a Form B score of 18 is 16 on Form A. Equipercentile equating can be done in two ways: graphically and analytically. We will first examine the graphical approach, and then move to the analytic.

To conduct equipercentile equating graphically, we must first define the percentile rank (PR) for each score on each instrument. The PR is the percentage of examinees below a particular score, plus ½ of the percentage of examinees at that score, which is given in Equation 8.5:

$$PR(x) = 100\left[F(x-1) + \frac{f(x)}{2}\right]. \tag{8.6}$$

Here, $F(x-1)$ is the cumulative proportion of the test score 1 point below the score of interest. Thus, if our score of interest is 5, then $F(x-1)$ is the cumulative proportion for a test score of 4 (i.e., the proportion of individuals scoring at or below 4). The term $f(x)$ is the proportion of examinees with a score of x, our target, so that in the current example $f(x)$ would be the proportion of examinees with a score of 5. To conduct equipercentile equating using the graphical approach, we would create a scatterplot with PR on the y-axis, test score on the x-axis, and a separate line for each test form.

An example of the SPSS commands necessary to conduct graphical equipercentile equating appears below for the 20 item data that we have been working with, heretofore. Note that we first must calculate total scores for the forms, as has been the case previously. In this example, we will use all 20 items, and calculate the Form A scores as below. Form B scores are calculated in exactly the same manner. Be sure that you have selected the appropriate group (form = 1 for Form A and form = 2 for Form B) using the **If** button in the **Compute Variable** window.

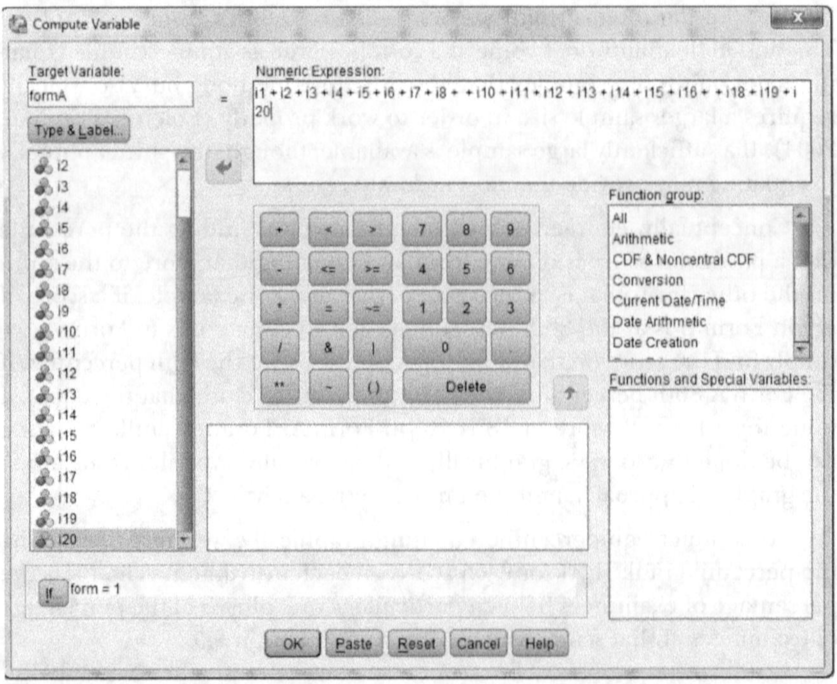

Next, we must calculate the percentile ranks for each of the forms. This can be done easily in SPSS using the menu command sequence **Transform ▶ Rank Cases**, which yields the following window.

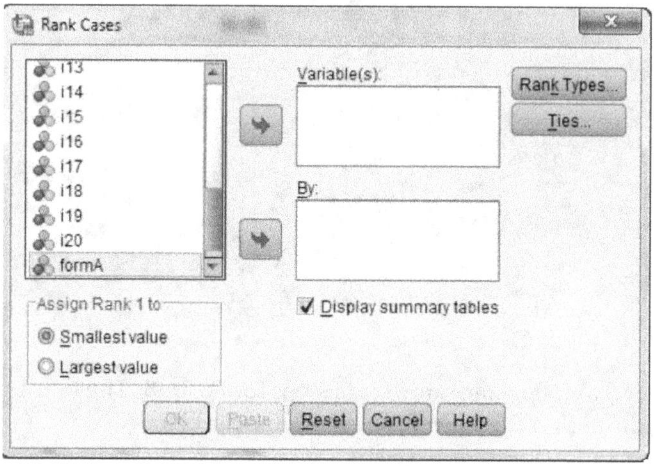

We will want to include Form A in the **Variable(s)** window, and then click **Rank Types....** Within this window, we will unclick the box next to **Rank**, and click the box next to **Fractional rank as %** in order to obtain the percentiles.

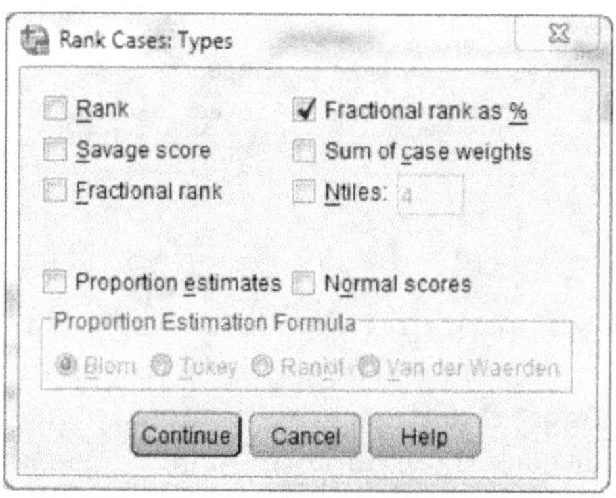

Next, we click **Continue** and then **OK**. This will yield percentiles as in Equation 8.6. The first 10 lines of the data will now appear as below.

	formA	formB	PformA
1	12.00	.	88.90
2	8.00	.	50.45
3	10.00	.	70.30
4	8.00	.	50.45
5	3.00	.	4.25
6	11.00	.	80.35
7	6.00	.	28.90
8	8.00	.	50.45
9	7.00	.	40.55
10	10.00	.	70.30

We will need to follow the same set of steps for Form B. The first 10 observations for those who were given this form appear below.

	formA	formB	PformA	PformB
1001	.	6.00	.	25.00
1002	.	4.00	.	6.80
1003	.	6.00	.	25.00
1004	.	6.00	.	25.00
1005	.	11.00	.	76.30
1006	.	10.00	.	67.85
1007	.	10.00	.	67.85
1008	.	8.00	.	49.10
1009	.	4.00	.	6.80
1010	.	8.00	.	49.10

Next, we need to summarize the data in terms of how the scores correspond to the percentile values. This can be accomplished using the menu sequence **Data ► Aggregate**. Using this window, we need to calculate the mean percentile for each score on Form A. Of course, the same scores on Form A will have the same percentile values, so that what we are really doing in this step is to reduce the data to include only the scores and their corresponding percentile values. We will save the results in a data set called formA_percentiles.

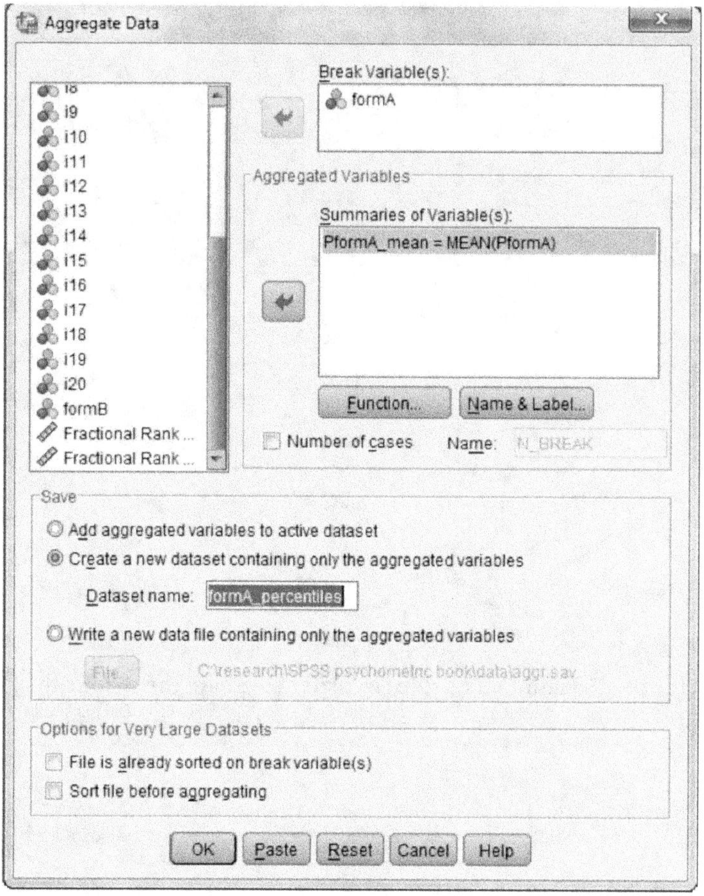

The results are opened in a new SPSS data file, which appears as below.

	formA	PformA_mean
1	.	.
2	.00	.25
3	1.00	.70
4	2.00	1.65
5	3.00	4.25
6	4.00	9.00
7	5.00	17.15
8	6.00	28.90
9	7.00	40.55
10	8.00	50.45
11	9.00	60.30
12	10.00	70.30
13	11.00	80.35
14	12.00	88.90
15	13.00	93.75
16	14.00	96.10
17	15.00	97.65
18	16.00	98.85
19	17.00	99.65
20	18.00	100.00

We will follow the same set of steps in order to create the results for Form B, as below.

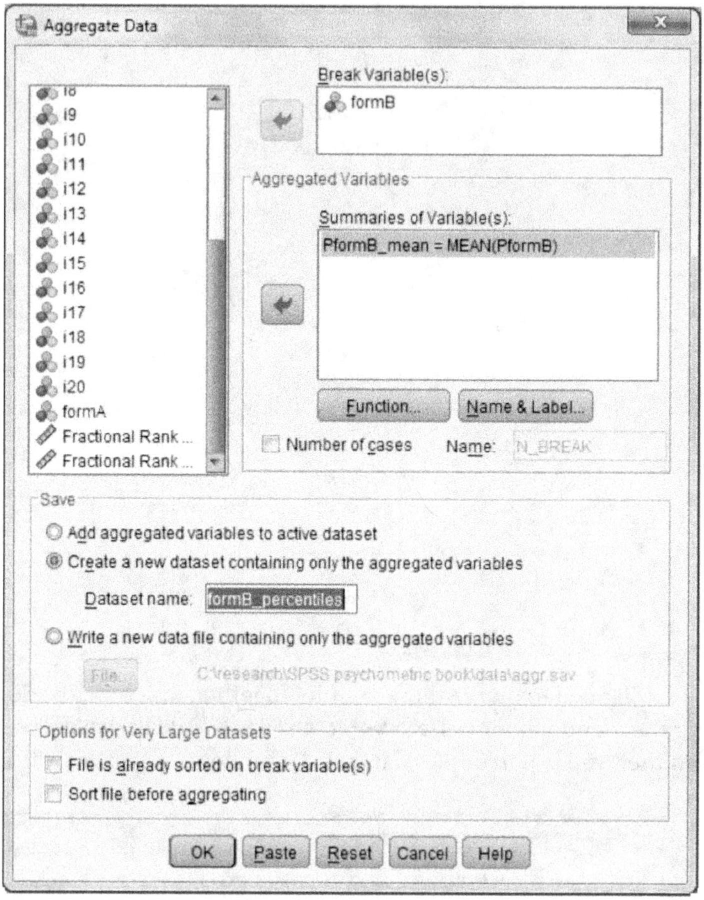
Aggregate Data
Break Variable(s):
formB
i9
i10
i11
i12
i13
i14
i15
i16
i17
i18
i19
i20
formA
Fractional Rank ...
Fractional Rank ...
Aggregated Variables
Summaries of Variable(s):
PformB_mean = MEAN(PformB)
Function...
Name & Label...
Number of cases
Name:
N_BREAK
Save
Add aggregated variables to active dataset
Create a new dataset containing only the aggregated variables
Dataset name:
formB_percentiles
Write a new data file containing only the aggregated variables
File...
C:\research\SPSS psychometric book\data\aggr.sav
Options for Very Large Datasets
File is already sorted on break variable(s)
Sort file before aggregating
OK
Paste
Reset
Cancel
Help

	formB	PformB_mean
1	.	.
2	.00	.10
3	1.00	.50
4	2.00	1.40
5	3.00	3.15
6	4.00	6.80
7	5.00	13.60
8	6.00	25.00
9	7.00	37.85
10	8.00	49.10
11	9.00	59.00
12	10.00	67.85
13	11.00	76.30
14	12.00	83.70
15	13.00	89.80
16	14.00	94.40
17	15.00	97.15
18	16.00	98.60
19	17.00	99.45
20	18.00	99.90

Finally, we will need to merge these two files together, which can be done simply using the menu sequence **Data ► Merge Files ► Add Variables**. We will do this from the formA_percentiles data set. The following window will appear:

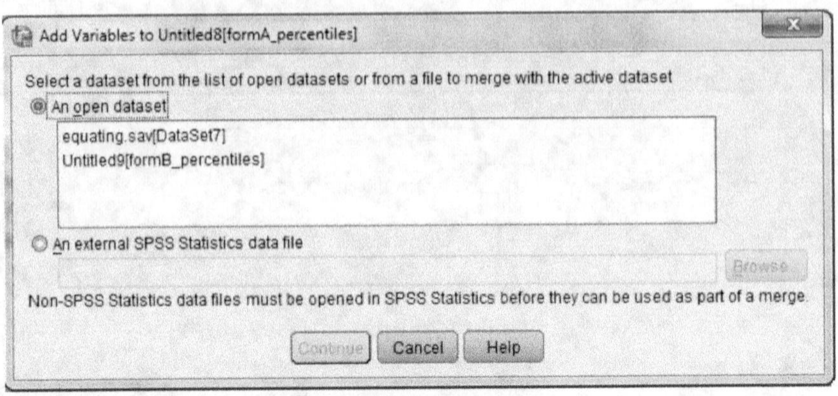

We will select the file called `Untitled9[formB_percentiles]` and click **Continue**. When the following window appears, we can simply click **OK**.

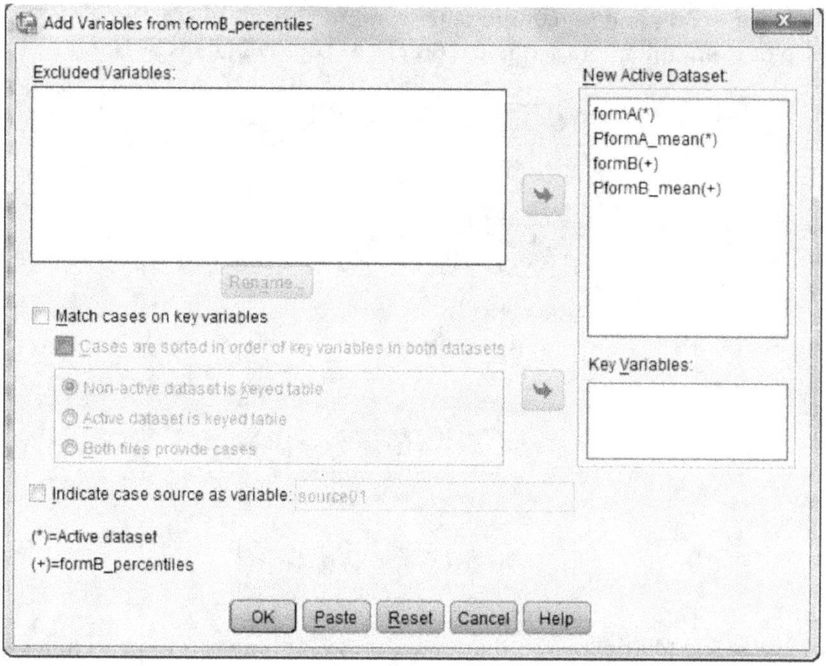

The resulting dataset appears below.

	formA	PformA_mean	formB	PformB_mean
1	.	.	.	.
2	.00	.25	.00	.10
3	1.00	.70	1.00	.50
4	2.00	1.65	2.00	1.40
5	3.00	4.25	3.00	3.15
6	4.00	9.00	4.00	6.80
7	5.00	17.15	5.00	13.60
8	6.00	28.90	6.00	25.00
9	7.00	40.55	7.00	37.85
10	8.00	50.45	8.00	49.10
11	9.00	60.30	9.00	59.00
12	10.00	70.30	10.00	67.85
13	11.00	80.35	11.00	76.30
14	12.00	88.90	12.00	83.70
15	13.00	93.75	13.00	89.80
16	14.00	96.10	14.00	94.40
17	15.00	97.65	15.00	97.15
18	16.00	98.85	16.00	98.60
19	17.00	99.65	17.00	99.45
20	18.00	100.00	18.00	99.90

The form scores and percentile ranks can then be plotted on the same scatter plot using the menu sequence **Graphs ► Legacy Dialogs ► Line**.

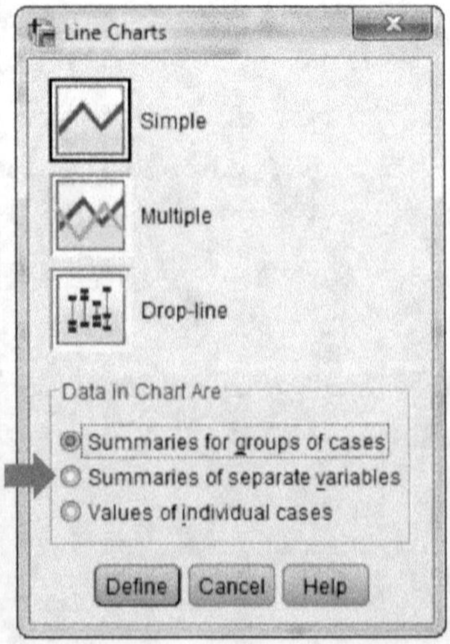

We will select **Multiple** given that we want to plot both sets of percentiles in the same graph. We will also click the radio button next to **Summaries of separate variables** (marked with the red arrow) because the two variables to be plotted appear in different columns. We then click **Define**.

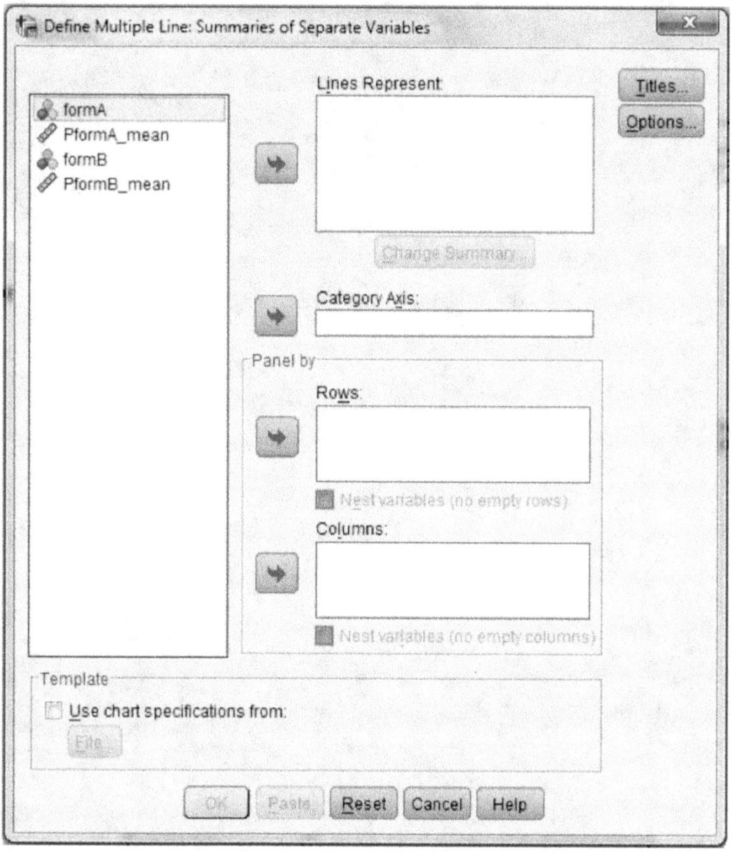

The separate lines are represented by the percentile scores for Forms A (PformA_mean) and B (PformB_mean). The category axis should contain the scores for the test. Thus, either formA or formB can be placed there. Once we have made our selections, we can click **OK**.

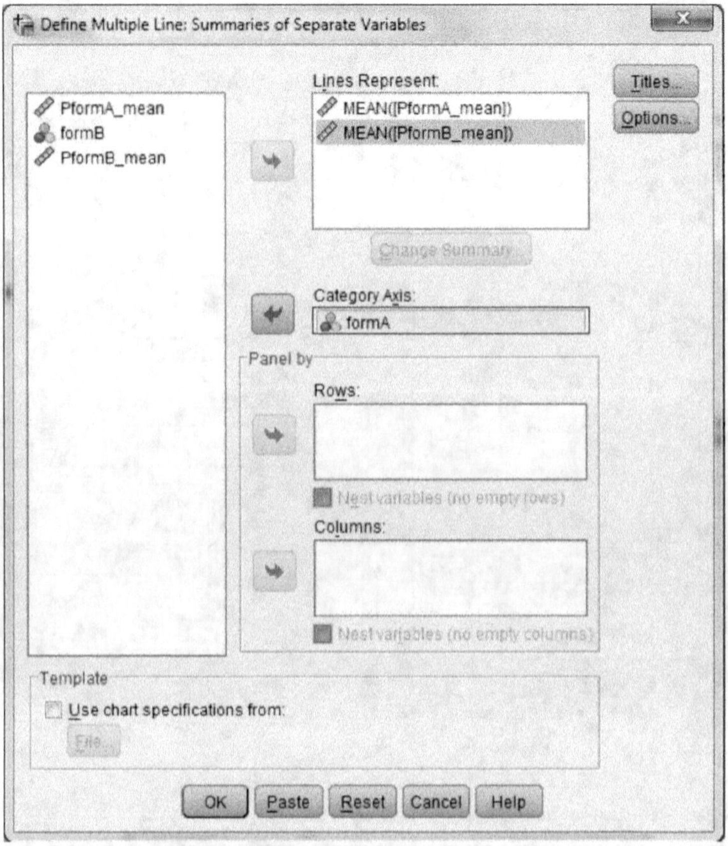

The resulting graph appears below.

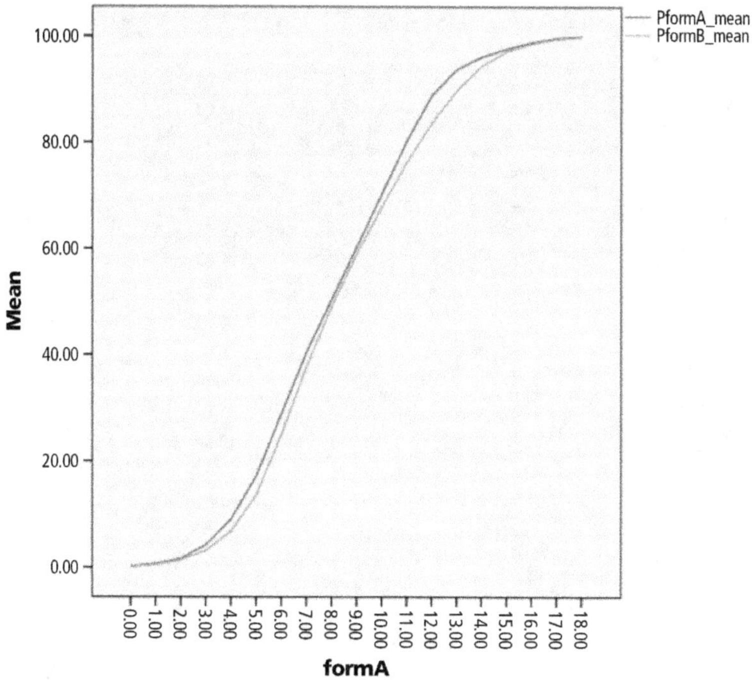

Form A is represented by the blue line and Form B is represented by the green line. To conduct equipercentile equating graphically, we first select a point on the *x*-axis, which represents the raw scores on Form A. Let's equate a Form B score of 13 to Form A. We go up from 13 on *x* to the Form B line, which corresponds to a PR of approximately 0.90. We then move horizontally left to the Form A line, and then move vertically back down to the *x*-axis, landing on a score of approximately 12. Thus, we would conclude that a Form B score of 13 corresponds to a Form A score of approximately 12. Using the graphical approach to equate a Form B score of 9, we see that the corresponding Form A score is also 9.

In addition to using the graphical approach to equipercentile equating, we can also simply examine the percentile values in the data along with their corresponding scores for Forms A and B.

	formA	PformA_mean	formB	PformB_mean
1	.	.	.	.
2	.00	.25	.00	.10
3	1.00	.70	1.00	.50
4	2.00	1.65	2.00	1.40
5	3.00	4.25	3.00	3.15
6	4.00	9.00	4.00	6.80
7	5.00	17.15	5.00	13.60
8	6.00	28.90	6.00	25.00
9	7.00	40.55	7.00	37.85
10	8.00	50.45	8.00	49.10
11	9.00	60.30	9.00	59.00
12	10.00	70.30	10.00	67.85
13	11.00	80.35	11.00	76.30
14	12.00	88.90	12.00	83.70
15	13.00	93.75	13.00	89.80
16	14.00	96.10	14.00	94.40
17	15.00	97.65	15.00	97.15
18	16.00	98.85	16.00	98.60
19	17.00	99.65	17.00	99.45
20	18.00	100.00	18.00	99.90

From this table, we can see that there are many percentile values for which there are no corresponding raw scores for either test form. How, then, do we determine the equated Form A score for an individual who obtained a Form B score of 6? A Form B score of 6 corresponds to a PR of 0.25, for which there is not a corresponding score on Form A. The most common approach to solving this problem is through interpolation (Livingston, 2004). In examining the table, we see that for Form A a score of 5 has a PR of 0.1715, and a score of 6 has a PR of 0.2890. Thus, given that the Form B percentile for the target score of 6 (0.25) is between the Form A percentile values of 0.1715 and 0.2890, the equated score on form A for a form B score of 6 should lie between 5 and 6. The interpolation equation in this case would be

$$5+\frac{0.25-0.1715}{0.289-0.1715}(6-5)=5+0.361(1)=5.361.$$

Livingston notes that while the interpolation solution to the problem of scores not all having corresponding PR values for the two forms is not perfect, it does provide useful and very accurate equated values.

With regard to equipercentile equating in the nonequivalent groups common items design, there are multiple approaches available. These differ in their relative complexity and in terms of the type of information that is required to use them. We have elected to focus on only one of these methods, known as chained equating, in large part because it is relatively straight forward to carry out, and is commonly used by professionals in the testing field (e.g., Livingston, 2004). However, we do recognize that there are other approaches available, and that while chained equating has been shown effective in many instances, it is not universally the optimal approach for this design. Nonetheless, we feel that the approach's very general utility, coupled with its relative ease of use make it a viable equating strategy for most instances in which the nonequivalent groups common items equating method is used.

In general, chained equipercentile equating is a relatively simple procedure. Let's assume that we want to take a score on Form B and equate it to a Form A score. With chained equating, this is attained through a three step process.

1. Use the equipercentile method described above to equate scores on Form B to scores on the common items scale.
2. Use the equipercentile method to equate scores on the common items scale to Form A.
3. Equate Form B to Form A by first converting Form B score to the common items scale, and then converting the common items scale to Form A.

To demonstrate the use of equipercentile chain equating, let's consider an example in which each of two nonequivalent groups of examinees (800 in Group 1 and 838 in Group 2) were administered separate math forms each comprised of 15 items. In addition, both groups were administered an additional 15 common items that were external to the main forms. We will use the chained equipercentile equating methodology to equate Form B scores to Form A. As noted above, this occurs in three distinct steps, each of which is carried out using the SPSS commands below. First, the data appears as:

	score	count1	count2	countcommon
1	.00	10.00	13.00	25.00
2	1.00	20.00	19.00	41.00
3	2.00	57.00	54.00	100.00
4	3.00	38.00	36.00	76.00
5	4.00	39.00	39.00	83.00
6	5.00	42.00	40.00	81.00
7	6.00	55.00	49.00	111.00
8	7.00	76.00	79.00	179.00
9	8.00	77.00	83.00	174.00
10	9.00	78.00	92.00	168.00
11	10.00	70.00	85.00	139.00
12	11.00	65.00	68.00	125.00
13	12.00	57.00	61.00	98.00
14	13.00	43.00	46.00	89.00
15	14.00	39.00	40.00	87.00
16	15.00	34.00	34.00	62.00

The count variables (count1, count2, and countcommon) provide the number of examinees in the sample with each score. In other words, there were 10 individuals in Group 1 who had a score of 0 on Form A, as compared to 13 in Group 2 who had a score of 0 on Form B. In addition, there were 25 individuals across the two samples who had a score of 0 on the common items.

To create the percentile ranks for each of the three scores (Form A, Form B, and the common form), we will need to use the weight function in SPSS. Let's consider the example of creating percentiles for Form A. To weight the scores by the number of individuals who were administered Form A that produced each, we use the menu sequence **Data ► Weight Cases**, and get the following window.

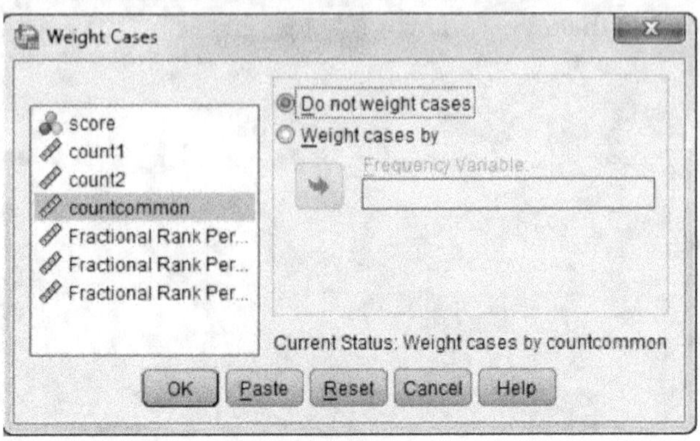

To weight cases by Form A performance, we click the radio button next to **Weight cases by**, and then move the variable count1 to the **Frequency Variable** box.

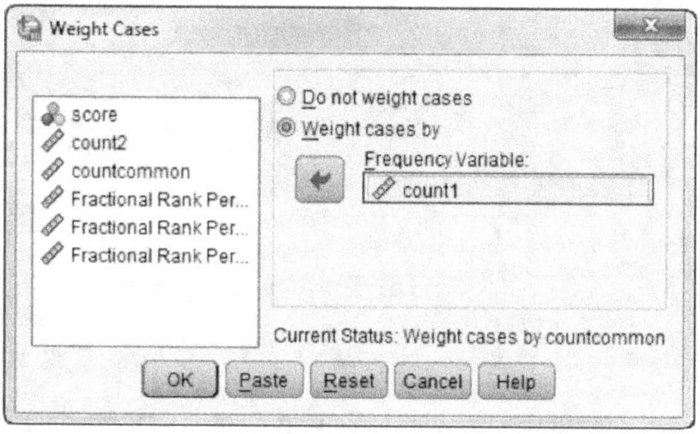

We click **OK**, and the weighting is turned on. We can now create the percentile scores for Form A just as we did in the examples above with the **Transform ► Rank Cases** menu commands.

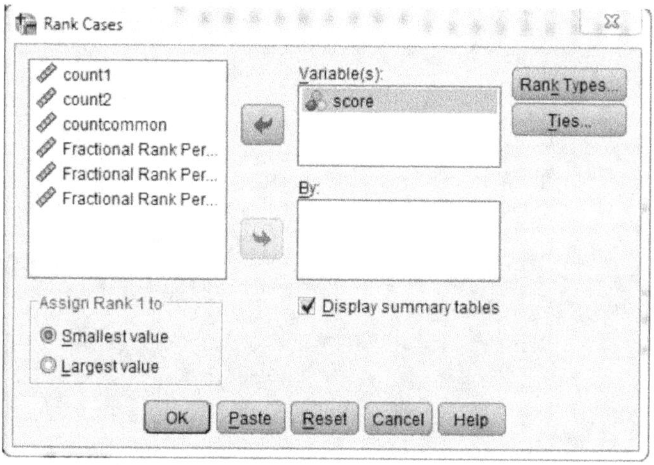

We would follow the same sequence of weighting cases by the appropriate form and creating the percentile scores for Form B and the common form. The resulting dataset will appear as:

	score	count1	count2	countcommon	Pscore1	Pscore2	Pscorecommon
1	.00	10.00	13.00	25.00	.69	.84	.79
2	1.00	20.00	19.00	41.00	2.56	2.74	2.81
3	2.00	57.00	54.00	100.00	7.38	7.10	7.11
4	3.00	38.00	36.00	76.00	13.31	12.47	12.48
5	4.00	39.00	39.00	83.00	18.13	16.95	17.34
6	5.00	42.00	40.00	81.00	23.19	21.66	22.34
7	6.00	55.00	49.00	111.00	29.25	26.97	28.21
8	7.00	76.00	79.00	179.00	37.44	34.61	37.06
9	8.00	77.00	83.00	174.00	47.00	44.27	47.83
10	9.00	78.00	92.00	168.00	56.69	54.71	58.27
11	10.00	70.00	85.00	139.00	65.94	65.27	67.64
12	11.00	65.00	68.00	125.00	74.38	74.40	75.70
13	12.00	57.00	61.00	98.00	82.00	82.10	82.51
14	13.00	43.00	46.00	89.00	88.25	88.48	88.22
15	14.00	39.00	40.00	87.00	93.38	93.62	93.59
16	15.00	34.00	34.00	62.00	97.94	98.03	98.14

Note that we changed the names of the percentiles to Pscore1, Pscore2, and Pscorecommon to make them easier for us to distinguish.

We can graph the results, much as we did in the previous percentile equating example, using the menu sequence **Graphs ▶ Legacy Dialogs ▶ Line**.

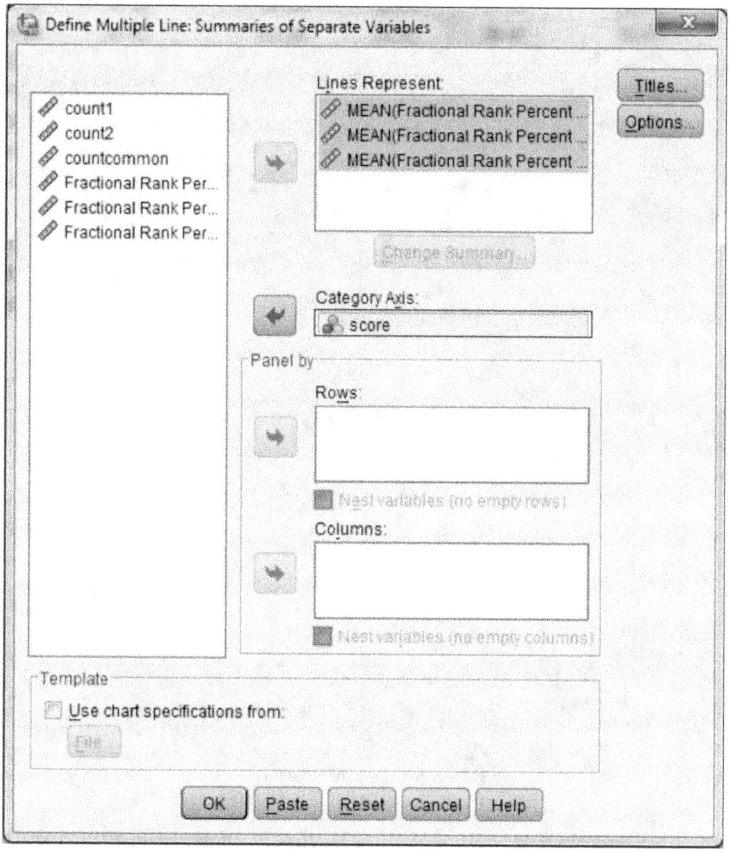
Define Multiple Line: Summaries of Separate Variables
count1
count2
countcommon
Fractional Rank Per...
Fractional Rank Per...
Fractional Rank Per...
Lines Represent:
MEAN(Fractional Rank Percent ...
MEAN(Fractional Rank Percent ...
MEAN(Fractional Rank Percent ...
Change Summary...
Category Axis:
score
Panel by
Rows:
Nest variables (no empty rows)
Columns:
Nest variables (no empty columns)
Titles...
Options...
Template
Use chart specifications from:
File...
OK
Paste
Reset
Cancel
Help

The resulting graph appears below.

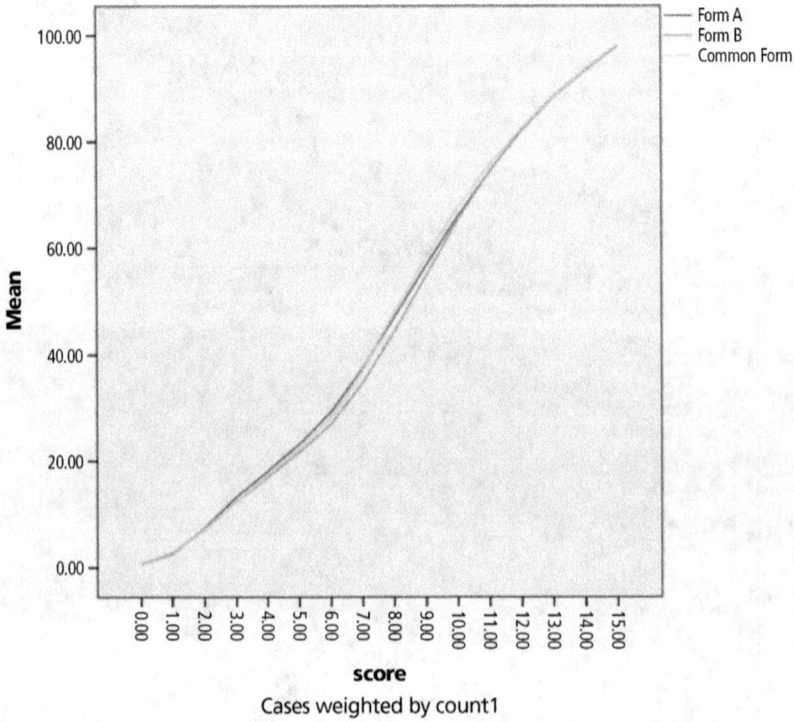

To demonstrate the actual practice of equipercentile chain equating, let's consider the table of percentile and score values. Assume that we would like to obtain the equated Form A score for a score of 3 on Form B. First, we must determine the percentile for the Form B score of 3, which is 0.125. We then must find the common items score corresponding to a percentile of 0.125, which in this case also happens to be 3. Finally, we must equate the common items score of 3 to Form A. The common items 3 score corresponds to the percentile value of 0.125, for which there is not a Form A score. Therefore, we will need to use interpolation, as demonstrated above. Note that in this example, the closest Form A score below a percentile of 0.125 is 2 at a percentile = 0.074, while the next highest score is 3, at percentile = 0.133. The interpolated Form A score would then be calculated as:

$$3+\frac{0.125-0.074}{0.133-0.074}(3-2)=2+0.864(1)=2.864.$$

Using chained equating, we see that a Form B score of 3 equates to a Form A score of 2.864.

With SPSS we can also create the scatterplot linking scores to percentiles. Thus, if we want to equate a Form B score of 6 to Form A graphically, we would simply find 6 on the *x*-axis, go directly vertical until we reach the line for Form C (common items score). We would then move directly horizontal until we again reach the line for Form B, and then move vertically down to the *x*-axis. This will take us to approximately 6.75. We would then move up vertically from this point until we reach the line for Form A, after which we move horizontally until we again reach the line for Form C, and then move down vertically to the *x*-axis. Although the lines are very close together in this example, we do move slightly down the *x*-axis to approximately 6.85, which is our equated Form A score for a Form B score of 6.

Chapter Summary

As provided in this chapter, there are a number of equating designs available to convert scores across multiple test forms assessing the same construct that differ slightly in difficulty. Each approach has distinct advantages and disadvantages. For example, mean equating is by far the simplest technique, but also provides the least flexibility. By assuming that any differences in form difficulty between the groups are constant across score levels, it offers the least in terms of flexibility. Linear equating relaxes the assumption of constant form difficulty difference through its inclusion of a measure of score variation. In this way, it may be a more accurate reflection of most realities in educational and psychological assessment. However, linear equating does assume that outside of variation, the shape of the score distributions is the same for the forms. In addition, using the linear methodology it is possible to obtain equated scores that are not in bounds of the actual data, as we have seen in our examples. The third alternative, equipercentile equating, solves both of these problems, even while bringing its own challenges to the table. Equipercentile equating typically does not produce scores outside of the possible range of values, nor does it force the skewness and kurtosis of the score distributions to be held constant. In these ways, it represents an advancement over linear equating. However, equipercentile equating presents its own set of challenges to equating research. As we have seen, this method tends to be more complex to use compared to either linear or mean equating. Often there are not scores for both forms at corresponding PR values, necessitating the use of interpolation. And, while interpolation typically provides very close approximations of the actual equated scores, it is not an exact method. In addition, the equipercentile approach is particularly sensitive to small sample size, and to imbalances in the score distributions. For scores that are uncommon, a small number of examinees can have an outsized impact on the equating results. In addition, if there are no individuals at a particular score, equating using the equipercentile approach is not possible. Finally, when applied to the nonequivalent groups common items design, equipercentile equating becomes particularly complex, whether with the chain equating approach demonstrated here, or some other method.

In the final analysis, recommendations from those heavily involved in equating seem to suggest that using multiple methods for the same problem may be a useful approach. This practice would allow the researcher to gain a deeper understanding of the variety of possible equated scores that might be obtained (Livingston, 2004). In addition, researchers are encouraged not to surrender blindly to the results of any statistical analysis, including equating. If the equated results for a particular method do not seem to agree with reality, the researcher is encouraged to reconsider the method and compare its results to those of other approaches with the same data. Results that do not make sense in the "real world" should be thought through very carefully, regardless of what the statistical analyses might conclude.

References

Agresti, A. (2002). *Categorical Data Analysis* (2nd Ed.). New York, NY: Wiley.

Akaike, H. (1987). Factor Analysis and AIC. *Psychometrika, 52,* 317–322.

Allen, M. J., & Yen, W. M. (1979). *Introduction to measurement theory.* Belmont, CA: Wadsworth.

Anastasi, A. (1986). Evolving Concepts of Test Validation. *Annual Review of Psychology, 37,* 1–16.

Bollen, K.A. (1989). *Structural Equations with Latent Variables.* New York, NY: John Wiley & Sons.

Bonett, D. G. (2002). Sample size requirements for testing and estimating coefficient alpha. *Journal of Educational and Behavioral Statistics, 27,* 335–340.

Brennan, R. L. (2001). *Generalizability theory.* New York, NY: Springer-Verlag.

Brown, T. A. (2015). *Confirmatory factor analysis for applied research (2nd ed.).* New York, NY: The Guilford Press.

Camilli, G., & Shepard, L. A. (1994). *Methods for identifying biased test items.* Thousand Oakes, CA: Sage.

Clauser, B. E., & Mazor, K. M. (1998). Using statistical procedures to identify differentially functioning test items. *Educational Measurement: Issues & Practice, 17,* 31–44.

Clauser, B., Mazor, K., & Hambleton, R. K. (1993). The effects of purification of the matching criterion on the identification of DIF using the Mantel-Haenszel procedure. *Applied Measurement in Education, 6,* 269–279.

Cohen, J. (1988). *Statistical power analysis for the behavioral sciences (2nd ed.).* New York, NY: Academy Press.

Cohen, J. (1992). A power primer. *Psychological Bulletin, 112,* 155–159.

Applied Psychometrics Using SPSS and AMOS, pages 273–277

Costello, A. B., & Osborne, J. W. (2005). Best practices in exploratory factor analysis: Four recommendations for getting the most from your analysis. *Practical Assessment, Research, & Evaluation, 10*(7), 179–185.

Crocker, L., & Algina, J. (1986). *Introduction to classical and modern test theory.* Orlando, FL: Harcourt Brace Jovanovich.

de Ayala, R. J. (2009). *The theory and practice of item response theory.* New York, NY: Guilford.

Donoghue, J. R., & Allen, N. L. (1993). Thin versus thick matching in the Mantel-Haenszel procedure for detecting DIF. *Journal of Educational Statistics, 18,* 131–154.

du Toit, M. (Ed.). (2003). *IRT from SSI.* Lincolnwood, IL: Scientific Software International, Inc.

Eason, S. (1991). Why generalizability theory yields better results than classical test theory: A primer with concrete examples. In B. Thompson (Ed.), *Advances in educational research: Substantive findings, methodological developments* (vol. 1, pp. 83–98). Greenwich, CT: JAI Press.

Ebel, R. L. (1965). *Measuring educational achievement.* Englewood Cliffs, NJ: Prentice-Hall.

Embretson, S. E., & Reise, S. P. (2000). *Item response theory for psychologists.* Mahwah, NJ: Lawrence Erlbaum

Feldt, L. S. (1965). The approximate sampling distribution of Kuder–Richardson reliability coefficient twenty. *Psychometrika, 30,* 357–370.

Feldt, L. S., & Brennan, R. L. (1989). Reliability. In R. L. Linn (Ed.), *Educational measurement* (3rd ed., pp. 105–146). New York, NY: American Council on Education and Macmillan.

Finch, W. H., & French, B. F. (2011). Estimation of MIMIC model parameters with multilevel data. *Structural Equation Modeling, 18,* 229–252.

Finney, S. J., & DiStefano, C. (2013). Nonnormal and categorical data in structural equation models. In G. R. Hancock & R. O. Mueller (Eds.), *A second course in structural equation modeling* (2nd ed., pp. 439–492). Charlotte, NC: Information Age.

Fisher, R. A. (1915). Frequency distribution of the values of the correlation coefficient in samples of an indefinitely large population. *Biometrika, 10,* 507–521.

French, B. F., & Maller, S. J. (2007). Iterative purification and effect size use with logistic regression for DIF detection. *Educational and Psychological Measurement, 67, 373–393.*

Gorsuch, R. L. (1983). *Factor Analysis.* Hillsdale, NJ: Lawrence Erlbaum Associates.

Haertel, E. H. (2006). Reliability. In R. L. Brennan (Ed.), *Educational measurement* (4th ed., pp. 65–110). Westport, CT: American Council on Education/ Praeger.

Hakstian, A. R., & Whalen, T. E. (1976). A *k*-sample significance test for independent alpha coefficients. *Psychometrika, 41,* 219–231.

Haladyna, T. M. (1999). *Developing and validating multiple-choice test items* (2nd ed). Mahwah, NJ: Lawrence Erlbaum.

Henson, R. K., & Roberts, J. K. (2006). Use of exploratory factor analysis in published research: Common errors and some comment on improved practice. *Educational and Psychological Measurement, 66,* 393–416.

Holland, P. W., & Thayer, D. T. (1988). Differential item performance and the Mantel-Haenszel procedure. In H. Holland & H. I. Braun (Eds.), *Test validity* (pp. 129–145). Hillsdale, NJ: Erlbaum.

Holland, P. W., & Wainer, H. (1993). *Differential item functioning.* Hillsdale, NJ: Lawrence Erlbaum Associates.

Horn, J. L. (1965). A Rationale and Test for the Number of Factors in Factor Analysis. *Psychometrika, 30,* 179–185.

Huberty, C. J., & Olejnik, S. (2006). *Applied MANOVA and Discriminant Analysis.* Hoboken, NJ: Wiley Interscience.

Iacobucci, D., & Duchachek, A. (2003). Advancing alpha: Measuring reliability with confidence. *Journal of Consumer Psychology, 13,* 478–487.

Jodoin, M. G., & Gierl, M. J. (2001). Evaluating type I error and power rates using an effect size measure with the logistic regression procedure for DIF detection. *Applied Measurement in Education, 14,* 329–349.

Kaiser, H. F. (1958). The varimax criterion for analytic rotation in factor analysis. *Psychometrika, 23*(3) 187–200.

Kaiser, H. F. (1962). Formulas for component scores. *Psychometrika, 27*(1), 83–87.

Kaiser, H. F. (1970). The second generation little jiffy. *Psychometrika, 35*(4), 401–415.

Kane, M. T. (2006). Current Concerns in Validity Theory. *Journal of Educational Measurement, 38(4),* 319–342.

Keeping, E. S. (1962), *Introduction to Statistical Inference.* New York, NY: D. Van Nostrand.

Kenny, D. A., Kaniskan, B., & McCoach, D. B. (2011). The performance of RMSEA in models with small degrees of freedom. Unpublished paper, University of Connecticut, Mansfield, CT.

Kline, R. B. (2016). *Principles and practice of structural equation modeling* (4th ed.). New York, NY: The Guildford Press.

Kolen, M. J., & Brennan, R. L. (2004). *Test equating, scaling, and linking: Methods and practices* (2nd ed.). New York, NY: Springer-Verlag.

Koning, A. J., & Franses, P. H. (2003, June). *Confidence intervals for Cronbach's Coefficient Alpha values.* ERIM Report Series Reference No. ERS-2003-041-MKT.

Linn, R. L. (2009). The concept of validity in the context of NCLB. In R. W. Lissitz (Ed.), *The concept of validity: Revisions, new directions, and applicatioins* (pp. 195–212). Maple Grove, MN: JAM Press.

Livingston, S. A. (2004). *Equating test scores (without IRT).* Princeton, NJ: ETS.

MacCallum, R. C., Browne, M. W., & Sugawara, H. M. (1996). Power analysis and determination of sample size for covariance structure modeling. *Psychological Methods, 1,* 130–149.

Mantel, N., & W. Haenszel (1959). Statistical aspects of the analysis of data from retrospective studies of disease. *Journal of the National Cancer Institute, 22,* 719–748.

Maydeu-Olivares, A., Coffman, D. L., & Hartmann, W. M. (2007). Asymptotically distribution-free (ADF) interval estimation of coefficient alpha. *Psychological Methods, 12,* 157–176.

Messick, S. (1989). Validity. In R. L. Linn (Ed.), *Educational Measurement* (3rd ed., pp. 13–104). New York, NY: Macmillan.

Michaelides, M. P. (2008). An illustration of a Mantel-Haenszel procedure to flag misbehaving common items in test equating. *Practical Assessment, Research, and Evaluation, 13(7),* Available online: http://pareonline.net/getvn.asp?v=13&n=7

Muraki, E. (1992). A generalized partial credit model: Application of an EM algorithm. *Applied Psychological Measurement, 16,* 159–176.

Mushquash, C., & O'Connor, B. P. (2006). SPSS, SAS, and MATLAB programs for generalizability theory analyses. *Behavior Research Methods, 38(3),* 542–547.

Narayanan, P., & Swaminathan, H. (1996). Identification of items that show nonuniform DIF. *Applied Psychological Measurement, 20,* 257–274.

Nunnally, J. C., & Bernstein, I. H. (1994). *Psychometric theory* (3rd ed.). New York, NY: McGraw-Hill.

O'Connor, B. P. (2000). SPSS and SAS programs for determining the number of components using parallel analysis and Velicer's MAP test. *Behavior Research Methods, Instruments, & Computers, 32,* 396–402.

Raju, N. S. (1988). The area between two item characteristic curves. *Psychometrika, 53,* 495–502. doi: 10.1007/BF02294403.

Raykov, T., & Marcoulides, G. A. (2011). *Introduction to Psychometric Theory.* New York, NY: Routledge.

Rogers, H. J., & Swaminathan, H. (1993). A comparison of logistic regression and Mantel-Haenszel procedures for detecting differential item functioning. *Applied Psychological Measurement, 17,* 105–116.

Roussos, L. A., & Stout, W. F. (1996). Simulation studies of the effects of small sample and studied item parameters on SIBTEST and Mantel-Haenszel type I error performance. *Journal of Educational Measurement, 33,* 215–230.

Samejima, F. (1969). Estimation of latent ability using a response pattern of graded scores. *Psychometrika Monograph Supplement, 17,* 1–68.

Schwarz, G. (1978). Estimating the Dimension of a Model. *Annals of Statistics, 6,* 461–464.

Shavelson, R. J., & Webb, N. M. (1991). *Generalizability Theory: A Primer.* Thousand Oaks, CA: Sage.

Swaminathan, H., & Rogers, H. J., (1990). Detecting differential item functioning using logistic regression procedures. *Journal of Educational Measurement, 27,* 361–370.

Tabachnick, B. G., & Fidell, L. S. (2007). *Using Multivariate Statistics.* Boston, MA: Pearson Education.

Thomas, D. R., & Zumbo, B. D. (1996). Using a measure of variable importance to investigate the standardization of discriminant coefficients. *Journal of Educational & Behavioral Statistics, 21,* 110–130.

Thompson, B. (2004). *Exploratory and Confirmatory Factor Analysis.* Washington, DC: American Psychological Association.

Thompson, B. (2003). A brief introduction to generalizability theory. In B. Thompson, (Ed.), *Score reliability* (pp. 43–58). Thousand Oaks, CA: Sage.

U.S. Department of Education, Office of Educational Research and Improvement, National Center for Education Statistics. *The NAEP 1998 Technical Report, NCES 2001-509,* by Allen, N. L., Donoghue, J. R., & Schoeps, T. L. (2001). Washington, DC: National Center for Education Statistics.

van der Linden, W., & Hambleton, R. K. (1997). Handbook of modern item response theory. New York, NY: Springer.

Weaver, B., & Koopman, R. (2014). An SPSS macro to compute confidence intervals for Pearson's correlation. *The Quantitative Methods for Psychology, 10*(1), 29–39.

Wilcox, R. R. (2009). Robust ANCOVA using a smoother with bootstrap bagging. *British Journal of Mathematical and Statistical Psychology, 62,* 427–437.

Wu. A. D., Li, Z., & Zumbo, B. D. (2007). Decoding the meaning of factorial invariance and updating the practice of multi-group confirmatory factor analysis: A demonstration with TIMSS data. *Practical Assessment, Research, and Evaluation, 12(3),* 1–26.

Yen, W. M., & Fitzpatrick, A. R. (2006). Item response theory. In R. L. Brennan (Ed.), *Educational measurement* (4th ed., pp. 111–154). Westport, CT: American Council on Education and Praeger.

Zumbo, B. D. (2007). Validity: Foundational issues and statistical methodology. In C. R. Rao & S. Sinharay (Eds.), *Handbook of statistics (vol. 26): Psychometrics* (pp. 45–79). Amsterdam, The Netherlands: Elsevier Science B.V.

Zumbo, B. D. (1999). *A handbook on the theory and methods for differential item functioning: Logistic regression modeling as a unitary framework for binary and likert-type (ordinal) item scores.* Ottawa, ON: Directorate of Human Resources Research and Evaluation, Department of National Defense.

Zumbo, B. D., & Thomas, D. R. (1997). *A measure of effect size for a model-based approach for studying DIF.* Working paper of the Edgeworth Laboratory for Quantitative Behavioral Sciences. Prince George, Canada: University of British Columbia.

Zwick, R. (2012). A review of ETS differential item functioning assessment procedures: Flagging rules, minimum sample size requirements, and criterion refinement. (ETA RR-12-08). Retrieved from http://www.ets.org/research/policy_research_reports/publications/report/2012/jevu

www.ingramcontent.com/pod-product-compliance
Lightning Source LLC
LaVergne TN
LVHW052258200926
848481LV00002B/405

9781681235264